The Song of Songs

A Feminist Companion to the Bible
(Second Series)

edited by Athalya Brenner and Carole R. Fontaine

'Go your Way: Women Rewrite the Scriptures
(Song of Songs 2.8-14)' © Klara Butting

Published by Sheffield Academic Press Ltd
Mansion House
19 Kingfield Road
Sheffield, S11 9AS
England

Printed on acid-free paper in Great Britain
by The Cromwell Press
Trowbridge, Wiltshire

British Library Cataloguing in Publication Data

A catalogue record for this book is available
from the British Library

ISBN 1-84127-0520

To the memory of

Fokkelien van Dijk-Hemmes

ת·נ·צ·ב·ה·

This page intentionally left blank

CONTENTS

ABBREVIATIONS

AnBib	Analecta biblica
BibInt	*Biblical Interpretation: A Journal of Contemporary Approaches*
BLit	*Bibel und Liturgie*
BZAW	Beihefte zur *ZAW*
HAR	*Hebrew Annual Review*
JBL	*Journal of Biblical Literature*
JPSV	*Jewish Publication Society Version*
JSOT	*Journal for the Study of the Old Testament*
JSOTSup	*Journal for the Study of the Old Testament*, Supplement Series
KJV	King James Version
OTG	Old Testament Guides
PL	J.-P. Migne (ed.), *Patrologia cursus completus…Series prima [latina]* (221 vols.; Paris: J.-P. Migne, 1844–65)
SBS	Stuttgarter Bibelstudien
SEÅ	*Svensk exegetisk årsbok*
SR	*Studies in Religion*
WTJ	*Westminster Theological Journal*
ZAW	*Zeitschrift für die alttestamentliche Wissenschaft*

This page intentionally left blank

LIST OF CONTRIBUTORS

Daphna Arbel, Department of Classical, Near Eastern and Religious Studies, The University of British Columbia, C265-1866 Main Mall, Vancouver, BC, Canada V6TT 1Z1

Jane Barr, Oxford, England and Claremont, CA 91711, USA

Jonneke Bekkenkamp, Department of Theology and Religious Studies, University of Amsterdam, OudeTurfmarkt 147, 1012 GC Amsterdam, The Netherlands

Fiona Black, Department of Comparative Literature, Religion and Film/ Media Studies, University of Alberta, 341 Old Arts Building, Edmonton, Alberta T6G 2EI, Canada

Athalya Brenner, Department of Theology and Religion Studies, University of Amsterdam, OudeTurfmarkt 147, 1012 GC Amsterdam, The Netherlands

Klara Butting, Luisenstr. 54, 29525 Uelzen, Germany

Cheryl Exum, Department of Biblical Studies, University of Sheffield, Arts Tower, Sheffield S10 2TN, England

Carole Fontaine, Andover Newton Theological School, 210 Herrick Road, Newton, MA 02459, USA

Maria Häusl, Universitat Würzburg, Sanderring 2, D-97070 Würzburg, Germany

Alicia Ostriker, 33 Philip Drive, Princeton, NJ 08540, USA

Ursula Silber, Casilla 138, Potosi, Bolivia

This page intentionally left blank

PREFACE

Carole R. Fontaine

'The Most Sublime Song', the 'Holy of Holies', 'SoS'—it is no accident that the very first volume of the first series, *A Feminist Companion to the Bible*, was on the Song of Songs. The Song has carried all these names throughout its history, long before feminist biblical scholars had ever arrived on the scene and appropriated this book as peculiarly their own. It happens so seldom that this particular community of scholars finds itself in agreement with mainstream/malestream scholarship that it is worth a bit of dancing, singing, banqueting and all around astonishment when we find our voices more or less at home in the chorus of praise for this earthy little book. So we say, 'We've done it again!' and allow ourselves the pleasures of reading as women on a topic that revels in sexuality (however dismal the literal realities may be), creation, and even boasts a female chorus as part of its cast of players.

It should not be thought that the present volume offers only praise and no critique, however. Like all the volumes of the Second Series of the FCB, this one seeks out new voices and perspectives, with articles especially commissioned for this collection, rather than reprints from the sometimes obscure venues in which early feminist biblical criticism was often first published. This volume takes up where the first left off, and provides a tangible measure of the progress and directions which feminist studies of Bible have taken since 1993 when the first volume appeared. Moving on from the early tasks of feminist literary criticism—the opening of the canon to the female gaze, the painstaking work of method-making to ask questions few had even framed before the 1970s, the recovery and reinterpretation of texts of concern to women readers—this volume more clearly engages questions of voice (*whose?*), the interplay (*what kind?*) between the resisting female reader and the received interpretations of Bible, and ventures into methodological territory which should be familiar to readers versed in current trends in biblical criticism.

You will encounter among these pages many whom you might not expect to find keeping company, often held together in audacious juxtapositions: from Rashi's reading to Carol Meyers'; Fray Luis de Léon and St Jerome tucked in among reminiscences of Haitian prostitutes and their songs of love. From allegory to archaeology and personal appropriation, the editors have sought to orchestrate a *babel* of variant readings in observance and response to the progress made in the focalization of female presence (whatever we may take that to mean) in the biblical text. Poets and professors alike have contributed, and you will even find a solemn warning or two, tucked in with reports of the Song used by women in—of all places!—the seminary and the church.

It was often the case in 'the early years' that women authorities, unused to having a public presence, would begin every public presentation with some sort of apology: not my area, not my best, not quite finished yet, not worthy of your time, but thank-you-o-so-much for coming to hear poor-little-me. No feminist scholar likes to be reminded of those times, I suspect, but we have all known them, and coped with our 'out-of-place'-ness in a variety of ways. The voices you will hear speaking to you from these pages make no apologies: like Dark Beauty, whose love is our text, we have solved our riddle with a Song, and learned to speak in harmony with the Shulamit's self-praise and desire. Proud and tall, terrible as an army with banners, coming out of the haunts of leopards and lions, we may dance for the onlookers, but the steps are our own.

Perhaps the newest methodological venture to be seen here is not some ultimate solution to questions of structure and original context, but the thoughtful passage into the territory of 'autobiographical criticism'. For some, this is as shocking an entry as feminist scholarship, at least in biblical studies, has ever broached. For centuries, women were considered the least rational of creatures, unused to orderly discourse, and given to 'subjective' judgments and preoccupations with the Contingent at the expense of the Eternal. Woman's experience was scarcely acceptable as a point of departure for scholarly work in the inception of our discipline, and no woman seeking to gain recognition or authority would have dreamed of showing her rootedness in a culture having anything to do with the female or her (putative) interests. We knew we were held as Other, and we took seriously our need to dress in grey ('manlette' style, so named by Claudia Camp), carry briefcases, sport shortened hair and hold down positions where we were expected to be twice as good as our male colleagues but with less than half of the support structure.[1] Like crying in public or admitting to 'female problems', we committed ourselves to fulfilling our purpose as 'pseudo-males', to use Heather McKay's term, in pursuit of a disinterested objectivity that trailed no petticoats.

Since those times, the world has gotten passing strange, and the postmodern revolution in literary criticism has touched us, too. At professional meetings, we are accustomed to lay aside our earlier assertions of *one* women's experience, since we are only too aware of how race, class, sexual orientation, age and a host of other factors work to structure the interpretations given to sexual difference that are encapsulated as 'gender' ideology. Still, it would be hard to find a feminist scholar who does not share, cross-culturally and cross-every other way, some of our collective delight in reading this book. After all, it's nice to have company for a change!

I suspect that this largely common appraisal of the Song of Songs is not just a function of the book itself, nor is it a simple reflection that many of us have been trained to read through the lens of shared methods. Rather, I think we celebrate the Song not because it is *so* good, but because the rest of the biblical tradition is *so bad*—at least for women who would like to embrace their own sense of worth, dignity and destiny on terms apart from those mandated by a religiously inscribed patriarchy. So, it makes perfect sense that the Dark Beauty of the Song should be taken as the 'type' for our own struggles: her search is bold and dangerous, her desire potent and unselfconscious, her voice the one for which we had been listening. We read and write on the Song because it is time to tend our own vineyards, and because we scorn so much what has been offered to us in the past in the name of Love. We hope that what we offer up here will be the fruit of that tending, but as always, Gentle Reader, it is for you to decide.

1. Ah, for a wife! Whose professional schedule would not immediately improve if we had one of those?

This page intentionally left blank

INTRODUCTION

Athalya Brenner

The essays in this collection are arranged in three groups. The first group—essays by Exum, Ostriker, Bekkenkamp, and Arbel—deals with broad issues that arise from and out of feminist readings of the SoS. Essays in the second group—by Black, Butting and Barr—are addressed to more closely defined texts, although the points raised might be of general significance as well. In the last three essays—by Brenner, Fontaine, and Häusl and Silber—the general approach is more personal than in the essays grouped under the first two headings.

1. *Feminist Appropriation of the SoS? In General*

The issues of feminist ownership, or eventual appropriation, of the SoS are far from resolved, as evidenced by the essays in this section. Interestingly, after about a decade of intense feminist preoccupation with this biblical book, and after it was virtually impounded by/for women, the pendulum has now begun to swing the other way or, at the very least, some hesitations remain.

Cheryl Exum agrees, in 'Ten Things Every Feminist Should Know about the Song of Songs', that 'At first glance, the Song of Songs seems to be a woman's text: it boldly celebrates female desire, and the behaviour of the woman or women (if the poems are unrelated) does not conform to the social norms we can construct from the rest of the Bible. A woman initiates sexual encounters; a woman roams the streets looking for her lover; a woman speaks openly about her desire; there is no indication that the couple or couples we meet in the Song are married...' Immediately thereafter, however, she proceeds to list a decalogue of uncertainties and risks awaiting for SoS feminist readers. And yet, she concludes, 'Feminist readers of this Best of Songs might do well to say to the ancient authors and traditionists who preserved it for us, 'thanks for your text, and I'll decide how to read it'.

Indeed. Not every feminist will look for the same voices in the SoS.

Alicia Ostriker is a poet and a scholar. Her 'A Holy of Holies: The Song of Songs as Countertext' is erudite poetry on the poetry of the SoS. Ostriker is also Jewish, and her interest in the SoS, beyond its aesthetic qualities, is a decidedly Jewish one—feminist, post-*Shoah* but anchored in Jewish practices of reading the SoS as holy and allegorical. Ostriker begins by reading 'love' in this biblical text as both and simultaneously sacred and profane, physical and spiritual. She then discusses the SoS as a radical countertext that contains an egalitarian image of mutual desire applicable to a non-divided reality, and raises the possibility of a non-hierarchical love relationship with God. Finally, Ostriker reads SoS 5.2-8 as a 'poem of spiritual yearning, our[1] exclusion by tradition and a plea for inclusion which appeals not only to desire but to justice'.

The usefulness of the SoS for a certain group of feminist readers is the starting point for Jonneke Bekkenkamp's 'Into another Scene of Choices: The Theological Value of the Song of Songs'. Bekkenkamp presents four models of reading for woman [Christian] theologians.[2] These models are not hierarchical and no value judgement is attached to either of them. In the author's own words, 'The first model fits feminist vicars; the second and third will suit university teachers who either want to integrate women's religious studies into theological curricula, or claim an autonomous status for such studies. The fourth model is meant for dialogic situations among equals.' Bekkenkamp's wish is to open up established literary and especially religious canons and to formulate alternative canons, suitable for women (theologians) and fresh dialogue. In her essay she demonstrates how different readings, and especially ones which use Adrienne Rich's *Twenty-One Love Poems* and a visual work by David Hockney as instructive intertexts, can illustrate new directions for reading the SoS (and other biblical and theological texts) as stepping stones for constructing identity.

One of the points Bekkenkamp makes is the reading of the SoS or parts thereof, at least according to one of the theoretical reading models she develops, as a woman's dream as told to a female audience ('daughters of Jerusalem'). Daphna Arbel, in 'My Vineyard, My Very Own, Is For Myself', rejects the 'dream' interpretation and reads

---

1.   Meaning Jewish women excluded by the Jewish Orthodox establishment, not only but also in Israel (editors' note).

2.   This is Bekkenkamp's milieu, against a west European (Dutch) backdrop, and she writes about it. On the other hand, her quest for new canons is certainly not limited to literature and intertexts of Christian provenance, as her essay (and the PhD thesis which the essay summarizes) amply illustrates.

the SoS as a continuous internal monologue delivered, and perhaps also composed, by a woman, who 'appears to describe a process in which she reflects upon her feelings of love and attraction towards her lover'. In her imagination, this constructed author/presenter assumes various personae and dramatic roles in various locations and moods. Such a process of dramatized and externalized female self-reflection would, according to Arbel, account for the variety of attitudes to love and desire in the SoS, while also referring to the issue of its possible female provenance.

2. *Specific Readings: Allegories and Feminist Readings*

Points 7 and 8 raised by Exum in her essay are, 'the female body is on display' and 'there is something wrong with the body'. In 'Unlikely Bedfellows: Allegorical and Feminist readings of the Song of Songs 7.1-10', Fiona Black discusses the exposed female body, or its absence, in the (perhaps) most revealing description of a female body in the SoS. Proceeding from the notion that feminist criticism may move in ways similar to the ways of allegory, Black juxtaposes a Jewish allegorical reading of SoS 7.1-10 (by Rashi) and a Christian one (by Nicholas de Lyra) on the one hand, and two feminist readings (by Brenner and Carol Meyers) on the other hand. Black asks whose interests, and what interests, the allegorical and feminist readings examined represent. In her opinion, the female body as read by all four interpreters is a *grotesque*, incongruous body. And this problematizes the option of feminist readings, especially when done by feminists.

Jane Barr, in 'Luis de León and the Song of Songs', examines another 'old' interpretation. Luis de León, a sixteenth-century Spanish friar and a professor of Bible at the University of Salamanca, translated the SoS from the Hebrew into his vernacular Spanish, with a commentary, at the request of a female cousin and as instruction for women. The translation was a daring and dangerous act. Barr shows how Luis focused on the 'literal' aspects of the text, claiming that the 'spiritual' (allegorical) aspects have been dealt with sufficiently by previous exegetes. She describes his translation and exposition methods as well as his attitudes to sexuality, women and women's social roles, as seen through his work. Delightfully, the life of this little-known scholar, much influenced by his views and work, is described as well.

Klara Butting begins her essay, 'Go Your Way: Women Rewrite the Scriptures (Song of Songs 2.8-14)', by stating that in allegorical readings of the SoS 'God's history and worldly love appear to be incompatible. Eroticism and love belong into the private sphere and have nothing to do with history or even God's history.' However, continues Butting, 'this construction of reality is contradicted in the Song of Songs'. Her approach, then, is similar to Ostriker's. However, it is differently constructed—denominationally and also textually. Whereas Ostriker reads the SoS (and especially ch. 5) with Jewish cultural history and existence as intertexts (in the larger sense), Butting reads her chosen passage (ch. 2) together with the Abraham–Sarah pericope of Genesis and with liberation theology, as applied to women's life situations and desires, and to gender mutuality. She concludes her reading by writing: 'When the liberation from suppression is celebrated... All spheres of life, eroticism included, have to be permeated by God's liberating power, so that the land can change to a land where women would like to live.' Fittingly, Butting quotes a poem by Joke Smit at the end of her essay. Thus, Butting's contribution is a companion piece to Ostriker's as well as an introduction to the more personal interpretations in the next section of this SoS collection.

3. *The Song of Songs, Personalized*

Clearly, feminists have embraced the SoS. Some of us in fact live with it; it features in our private and scholarly autobiography. Others would like to live with/by it. The first two essays in this section, written by the editors of this volume, exemplify the first condition; the third essay illustrates a concrete option of using the SoS to ameliorate women's lot today.

Brenner's '"My" Song of Songs' is a second rerun: the first version appeared in a previous volume she edited with Fontaine in this series, *A Feminist Companion to Reading the Bible* (1997). As a result of presenting it on various occasions in 1997 and 1998, it has changed considerably: not the basic autobiographical facts about growing up with the SoS in Israel, but their evaluation as a key for understanding scholarly views. Fontaine's 'The Voice of the Turtle: Now it's MY Song of Songs' charts her own journey with the SoS, from a child in the American South to a Bible scholar in the American North. We find that whereas our processes of appropriation differed—Brenner's was automatic, Fontaine's painfully acquired—the influence exerted by early experience does inform certain scholarly decisions for both of us. And to our delight, although our views may differ as much as our early experiences do, there is still sufficient common ground to warrant a theoretical discussion of autobiographical experience and its role in communal and personal scholarship.

A reproduction of a communal artwork Fontaine did with her students on the SoS (in Andover Newton, MA, USA) will also serve as a worthy introduction to Maria Häusl and Ursula Silber's report about a workshop they conducted several years ago (in Germany), entitled ' "You Are Beautiful, my Love": The Song of Songs of Women'. Häusl and Silber set out to organize a day of pleasure and spirituality, under the auspices of a local Diocese's Women's Spiritual Welfare program and within a framework of cooperation between the University and the community. The texts chosen were SoS 4.1-7 and 4.12–5.1. The participants were rural women, the aim to create a mood of self-awareness and self-esteem and to rediscover personal identity. The workshop, as befits the subject matter, included periods of physical activity as well as textual exploration, creativity as well as reflexivity, individual as well as group work, song and dance. Häusl and Silber write that the metaphor chosen to be central for the day's proceedings proved a fortunate one: the participating women were amazed at their own affiliations with and associations of this image. Thus, conclude the authors, the experience of having a day of pleasure and discovery, discovery of a little about the Bible and a little about the female self, was positive. To illustrate the point, two poems composed by participants in the workshop are given in an Appendix to their essay.

So what is the state of affairs with regard to SoS study by feminists, in my opinion as against Carole Fontaine's (see her Preface to this volume)? This volume is a lily-white one, a 'Western' bourgeois work. The participants in this volume hail from Canada, England, Germany, The Netherlands, Israel and the United States. Some are Christian. Others are Jewish. All, each after her own fashion, seem to be seduced by the SoS: even Exum, who warns us about this seductive power the SoS exerts over its feminist readers, does not seem exempt from it. Most—Black and Exum are the exception perhaps—would like to appropriate it as our own: be it through experience and re-experience, or creativity, or female spirituality, or attributing female voices to it. Certain re-visionary trends are much in evidence, and the renewed preoccupations with allegorical interpretations are one indication of these trends. Other approaches, being otherwise time- and place- and religion- and class- and ethnicity- bound, are of course possible. We are left with the wish for such other preoccupations with the SoS, of other hues, to come forward.

This page intentionally left blank

Part I

FEMINIST APPROPRIATION OF THE SONG OF SONGS?
IN GENERAL

TEN THINGS EVERY FEMINIST SHOULD KNOW
ABOUT THE SONG OF SONGS

J. Cheryl Exum

At first glance, the Song of Songs seems to be a woman's text: it boldly celebrates female desire, and the behaviour of the woman or women (if the poems are unrelated) does not conform to the social norms we can construct from the rest of the Bible. A woman initiates sexual encounters; a woman roams the streets looking for her lover; a woman speaks openly about her desire; there is no indication that the couple or couples we meet in the Song are married, yet they are clearly lovers, at least on the level of *double entendre*.

Feminist critics are virtually unanimous in their praise of the Song of Songs for its nonsexism, gender equality, and gynocentrism.

> In this setting, there is no male dominance, no female subordination, and no stereotyping of either sex.[1]

> The society depicted in the Bible is portrayed primarily from a male perspective, in terms of male accomplishments and in relation to a God for whom andromorphic imagery predominates. Yet in the Song, such characteristics disappear and in fact the opposite may be true; that is, a gynocentric mode predominates.[2]

> Remarkably, the Song seems to describe a nonsexist world, and thus it can act for us as an antidote to some of the themes of biblical patriarchy.[3]

> They [the women in the Song of Songs] come across as articulate, loud, clear, culturally and socially undeniably effective—even within the confines and inner circle of their patriarchal society.

1. Phyllis Trible, *God and the Rhetoric of Sexuality* (Philadelphia: Fortress Press, 1978), p. 161.
2. Carol Meyers, 'Gender Imagery in the Song of Songs', *HAR* 10 (1986), pp. 209-23 (218); reprinted in Athalya Brenner (ed.), *A Feminist Companion to the Song of Songs* (The Feminist Companion to the Bible, 1; Sheffield: Sheffield Academic Press, 1993), pp. 197-212.
3. Marcia Falk, 'The Song of Songs', in James L. Mays (ed.), *Harper's Bible Commentary* (San Francisco: Harper & Row, 1988), pp. 525-28 (528).

A role model to identify with?[4]

> The Song of Songs advocates balance in female and male relationships, urging mutuality not dominance, interdependence not enmity, sexual fulfillment not mere procreation, uninhibited love not bigoted emotions.[5]

And, finally, a glowing evaluation from one of the twentieth century's most influential critics outside the guild: 'The amorous Shulamite is the first woman to be sovereign before her loved one. Through such hymn to the love of the married couple, Judaism asserts itself as a first liberation of women.'[6]

1. So I come now to the first of my 'ten things every feminist should know about the Song of Songs':[7] *this text can be hazardous to your critical faculties.* Something about the Song turns even the most hardened of feminist critics into a bubbling romantic. Now there are some dissenting voices: Francis Landy draws attention to dissonance and countercoherence in his reading of the Song;[8] Ilana Pardes emphasizes the tension between female desire and patriarchal restraint;[9] Daphne Merkin sees the Song as a cautionary tale, 'a story about the risks of passion', whose moral is, 'Stay upstairs in the balcony [of the synagogue], Shulamite woman, for withheld consummation is the

---

4.   Athalya Brenner, 'An Afterword', in Brenner (ed.), *A Feminist Companion to the Song of Songs*, pp. 279-80 (280).

5.   Renita J. Weems, 'Song of Songs', in Carol A. Newsom and Sharon H. Ringe (eds.), *The Women's Bible Commentary* (Louisville, KY: Westminster/John Knox Press, 1992), pp. 156-60 (160). Gail Corrington Streete is also taken in, and cites Weems uncritically; *The Strange Woman: Power and Sex in the Bible* (Louisville, KY: John Knox Press, 1997), p. 72.

6.   Julia Kristeva, 'A Holy Madness: She and He', in her *Tales of Love* (trans. L.S. Roudiez; New York: Columbia University Press, 1987), pp. 83-100 (99).

7.   For the reader wondering why ten things, and not seven, or twelve, or more, the answer is the influence of the *Radio Times* (the UK's *TV Guide*) with its weekly section, 'Ten Things Every So-and-So's Fan Ought to Know' (ten things every Robert Redford Fan Ought to Know, etc.). But also because ten is the basis of our number system (we count by tens, on our fingers). There are ten commandments. In Umberto Eco's *Foucault's Pendulum*, one of the characters says, 'There have to be ten commandments because, if there were twelve, when the priest counts one, two, three, holding up his fingers, and comes to the last two, he'd have to borrow a hand from the sacristan'. There are ten plagues. A tithe is a tax of one tenth, etc.

8.   Francis Landy, *Paradoxes of Paradise: Identity and Difference in the Song of Songs* (Sheffield: Almond Press, 1983).

9.   Ilana Pardes, *Countertraditions in the Bible: A Feminist Approach* (Cambridge, MA: Harvard University Press, 1992), pp. 118-43.

best kind';[10] and Fiona Black looks at the darker side of desire and the body as grotesque.[11] But I wonder if it is simply an accident that, with the exception of Merkin and Black, the strongest critique of sexual relations in the Song (that I know of) comes from men—David Clines (in his book *Interested Parties*) and Donald Polaski (in an article in *Biblical Interpretation*).[12]

On the whole, the Song seems to have weathered feminist critique rather well. As the citations above indicate, it appears to be our final refuge. Why should that be? Is it that we are romantics at heart? We want to believe that erotic love transcends gender interests, and so that is what we find in the Song. The Song arouses our desire—by which I mean a woman's desire to have an ancient book that celebrates woman's sexuality and whose protagonist is an active, desiring, autonomous subject. Women have a stake in this text. Do we identify too closely with the woman[13] because she has an ahistorical or transhistorical quality about her? The fact that names are not provided for the lovers of the Song is, I think, a poetic way of identifying them with all lovers, facilitating our identification with this strong-willed woman.[14]

I will return to this point because it and my other nine points are interconnected. In speaking of 'ten things every feminist should know about the Song of Songs', I am not offering axioms, but rather seeking

10. Daphne Merkin, 'The Women in the Balcony: On Rereading the Song of Songs', in Christina Buchmann and Celina Spiegel (eds.), *Out of the Garden: Women Writers on the Bible* (New York: Fawcett Columbine, 1994), pp. 238-51 (249, 250).

11. Fiona C. Black, 'The Grotesque Body in the Song of Songs' (PhD dissertation, University of Sheffield, 1999). See also her essay in this volume.

12. David J. A. Clines, 'Why Is There a Song of Songs, and What Does It Do to You If You Read It?', in his *Interested Parties: The Ideology of Writers and Readers of the Hebrew Bible* (JSOTSup, 205; Gender, Culture, Theory, 1; Sheffield: Sheffield Academic Press, 1995), pp. 94-121; Donald C. Polaski, ' "What Will Ye See in the Shulammite?" Women, Power and Panopticism in the Song of Songs', *BibInt* 5 (1997), pp. 64-81.

13. Or women, if the Song is a collection. I use the singular for convenience.

14. Convinced by Mieke Bal that providing names for unnamed biblical women is a way of restoring them to a subject position denied them by the text, I earlier experimented with calling the woman (or women) protagonist of the Song 'Shulamit' (J. Cheryl Exum, 'Developing Strategies of Feminist Criticism/ Developing Strategies for Commentating the Song of Songs', in David J.A. Clines and Stephen D. Moore [eds.], *Auguries: The Jubilee Volume of the Sheffield Department of Biblical Studies* [JSOTSup, 269; Sheffield: Sheffield Academic Press, 1998], pp. 206-49); I now prefer to follow the Song's practice in an attempt to reflect this feature of the Song's poetic artistry.

to problematize certain interpretive issues.

2. *The immediacy of the Song is an illusion*—an illusion that Renita Weems, among others, is taken in by. In her commentary on the Song of Songs in *The New Interpreter's Bible*, she writes, ' ... the protagonist's voice in Song of Songs is the only unmediated female voice in all of Scripture. Elsewhere, women's perspectives are rehearsed through the voice of narrators, presumably male ... '[15] But just because a narrator doesn't intrude doesn't mean there is no narrator. Every text has a narrator; it's just that in the Song there is no narrative description. Unlike other biblical texts, Canticles consists entirely of speeches. We seem to hear the lovers in the act of addressing each other, using imperatives that underscore the sense of immediacy: 'let him kiss me', 'draw me after you', 'let us run', 'tell me', 'come', 'be like'. Coupled with imperatives, vocatives strengthen the impression of the lovers' presence at the moment of utterance: 'you whom I love', 'my sister, bride', 'O, fairest of women'. Voices that seem to reach us unmediated lend the illusion of immediacy to what is actually reported speech, a written text whose author and narrator are brilliantly effaced.[16] Which takes us to my next point.

3. *There are no real women in this text.* The Song is not a transcript of a lovers' tryst. It is not a record of the words real women spoke to or about their lovers. It is a text, an artistic creation, and the man and woman/men and women are literary personae, literary constructs. We know from our reading experience that a person who speaks in a text is not the same as the author, but, when it comes to the Song, commentators tend to forget it, as, for example, when Marcia Falk hears 'women speaking out of their own experiences and their own imaginations' and men's speech 'authentically self-expressive'.[17] Michael Fox is an important exception; he recognizes that: '[I]f the speakers are personae we must ask not only what the lovers are like, but also

15. Renita J. Weems, 'Song of Songs', *The New Interpreter's Bible* (Nashville: Abingdon Press, 1997), p. 364; similarly, Weems, 'Song of Songs', *Women's Bible Commentary*, pp. 156, 157.

16. See J. Cheryl Exum, 'How Does the Song of Songs Mean? On Reading the Poetry of Desire', *SEÅ* 64 (1999), pp. 47-63.

17. Marcia Falk, *The Song of Songs: A New Translation and Interpretation* (illustrated by Barry Moser; San Francisco: HarperSanFrancisco, 1990), pp. 117, 118. I am not sure what Roland Murphy means when he says, 'the author may have been a woman; and surely she was, at least in part'; Roland E. Murphy, *The Song of Songs: A Commentary on the Book of Canticles or the Song of Songs* (Hermeneia; Minneapolis: Fortress Press, 1990), p. 70.

how the poets view them and present them to us'.[18] It follows, then, that we cannot use the Song as evidence of 'what [ancient Israelites] in love commonly did and felt'. To quote Fox again: '... we learn how particular writers have perceived love and defined its potentialities, but their view of love need not conform to the picture of social realities we get from other sources... A poet may choose to reject the common attitudes of society, to push them into the background, or simply to ignore them'.[19]

4. *The woman, or women, in this text may be the creations of male authors.* Anyone who reads fiction knows that writers can assume other people's identities and voices.[20] The woman of the Song, then, might well be the creation of an androcentric narrator, as I have argued about other women characters in biblical narrative.[21] But perhaps I need to adjust my view. The woman is the focalizer. She is the fantasizer; she quotes the man, but he does not quote her. Do we have in the Song a female voice, or an 'F voice', to use Athalya Brenner and Fokkelien van Dijk-Hemmes's term for gendering the text, not the author?[22] Or do we have, as David Clines proposes, a male fantasy in which a male author has created his ideal dream woman?[23] We could perhaps turn this around and think of 'double consciousness' on the part of women: is the Song a *woman*'s fantasy, one that reflects women's status as members of the dominant culture and as a sub-group within it even as it challenges that status?[24] Does

18. Michael V. Fox, *The Song of Songs and the Ancient Egyptian Love Songs* (Madison: University of Wisconsin Press, 1985), p. 253.

19. Fox, *Song of Songs*, p. 297.

20. See, e.g., Richard Bauckham, 'The Book of Ruth and the Possibility of a Feminist Canonical Hermeneutic', *BibInt* 5 (1997), pp. 29-45.

21. Especially in J. Cheryl Exum, *Fragmented Women: Feminist (Sub)versions of Biblical Narratives* (JSOTSup, 163; Sheffield: JSOT Press, 1993; Valley Forge, PA: Trinity Press International, 1993) and Exum, *Was sagt das Richterbuch den Frauen?* (SBS, 169; Stuttgart: Katholisches Bibelwerk, 1997).

22. Athalya Brenner and Fokkelien van Dijk-Hemmes, *On Gendering Texts: Female and Male Voices in the Hebrew Bible* (Leiden: E.J. Brill, 1993). See also S.D. Goitein, 'Women as Creators of Biblical Genres', *Prooftexts* 8 (1988), pp. 1-33; Goitein, 'The Song of Songs: A Female Composition', in Brenner (ed.), *A Feminist Companion to the Song of Songs*, pp. 58-66; Jonneke Bekkenkamp and Fokkelien van Dijk, 'The Canon of the Old Testament and Women's Cultural Traditions', in Brenner (ed.), *A Feminist Companion to the Song of Songs*, pp. 67-85; Ria Lemaire, 'Vrouwen in de volksliteratuur', in Ria Lemaire (ed.), *Ik zing mijn lied voor al wie met mij gaat: Vrouwen in de volksliteratuur* (Utrecht: HES, 1986), pp. 11-42.

23. Clines, *Interested Parties*, pp. 102-106.

24. See John J. Winkler, 'Double Consciousness in Sappho's Lyrics', in Winkler

the situation—love, a one to one relationship—allow a certain free-dom from social constraints? Does the genre, love poetry, or the social setting, private rather than public life,[25] account for the seemingly different portrayal of gender relations we find here?[26]

It makes a difference for interpretation along gender lines whether one sees the Song as a collection of unrelated love poems, featuring different protagonists and exhibiting different attitudes toward love, or as a unity in which the protagonists, their attitudes, and their love for each other remain the same throughout. If the Song is a collection, we might well expect to find a male voice reflected in some of the units and a female voice in others; we might also find very different attitudes to love, sex, and the body.[27] The Song, however, *works* as a unity, so well, in fact, that distinguishing different voices and atti-tudes is not easy and nothing approaching a consensus is in sight. Even commentators who see the Song as an anthology tend to read it as though its attitude toward love is uniform and the protagonists are the same two people throughout.[28]

A promising approach, though it remains to be tested, is suggested by Athalya Brenner: 'each lyric can be read twice: as if it were the product of male authorship or, conversely, of female authorship'.[29]

The Constraints of Desire: The Anthropology of Sex and Gender in Ancient Greece (New York: Routledge, 1990), pp. 162-87.

25. Meyers, 'Gender Imagery', pp. 210-12.

26. See the caveats about reading gender in relation to genre in Alice Bach, *Women, Seduction, and Betrayal in Biblical Narrative* (Cambridge: Cambridge University Press, 1997), pp. 82-88.

27. More than anyone, Brenner has convinced me of the need to consider the Song as composed of unrelated poems; see esp., Athalya Brenner, ' "My" Song of Songs', in Athalya Brenner and Carole Fontaine (eds.), *A Feminist Companion to Reading the Bible: Approaches, Methods and Strategies* (Sheffield: Sheffield Academic Press, 1997), pp. 567-79. But I cannot agree with Brenner when she says, 'At the end of the Song, love and desire are in exactly the place they were at the begin-ning' ('To See Is to Assume: Whose Love Is Celebrated in the Song of Songs?', *BibInt* 3 [1993], pp. 268-69 [267]). She is referring to the fact that the first and the last poem in the Song present a similar situation, 'a female voice calling for an absent male lover'. But it isn't the same for the readers, since we have read every-thing in between (unless we haven't and have skipped from ch. 1 to ch. 8) and what precedes it inevitably influences the way we hear the 'last' poem; see Exum, 'How Does the Song of Songs Mean?', pp. 59-63.

28. For example, Weems identifies 'thirteen shifts in speakers, in some instances, and moods of speeches (in other instances)', but says that the Song 'chronicles one woman's journey to find fulfilling love' ('Song of Songs', *New Inter-preter's Bible*, pp. 371, 373).

29. Athalya Brenner, 'On Feminist Criticism of the Song of Songs', in Brenner

5. *There is no gender equality.* Why is the man such an elusive lover? He's always off bounding over the hills somewhere, while her fondest wish is to get him inside, to seize him and bring him to her mother's house. Does his freedom of movement reflect a social reality that she has interiorized, since this is how she thinks of him? Not only does he appear to enjoy an autonomy she lacks, he also has a sexual freedom she does not share, for his chastity, unlike hers, is not an issue.[30]

There may not be gender equality, but there is gender bending. Erotic coding in the Song crosses conventional gender lines, as both Landy and Meyers have shown.[31] Similar imagery, such as the deer and the dove, is applied to both female and male lovers. The female body is masculinized and the male body is feminized in terms of the canons of femininity and masculinity that operate in the rest of the Bible. Architectural and military images are used to describe the woman (a neck like a tower of David upon which warriors' shields are displayed [4.4], a defensive wall with breasts like towers [8.10]), whereas the man is described as having arms of gold set with jewels, a belly of ivory adorned with sapphires, and golden and alabaster legs (which leads Daphne Merkin to conclude that 'Any putatively male love object described with such a decided lack of virility and such a decidedly female sense of adornment presents ripe territory for study').[32] One could argue on the basis of such gender symbolism that the Song destabilizes conventional biblical gender stereotypes. But this is not the same thing as saying the Song of Songs affirms the equality of the sexes.

6. Another thing feminists should know about the Song of Songs is that *bad things happen to sexually active, forward women.* For example, her mother's sons are angry at her: 'they made me keeper of the vineyards, but my own vineyard I did not keep'. We know, moreover, that foxes, little foxes, threaten to spoil vineyards (2.15). In speaking to the daughters of Jerusalem about her appearance, the woman exhibits a dread of the gaze ('Do not look at me', 1.6). And then there's the

(ed.), *A Feminist Companion to the Song of Songs*, pp. 28-37 (29); cf. Brenner and van Dijk-Hemmes, *On Gendering Texts*, p. 9: 'F readers will listen to F voices emanating from those texts; M readers will hear themselves echoed in them. This is to say that, in many cases, two parallel readings are possible. In such cases, we feel, a presentation of both parallel readings is preferable to privileging any one of the two more than the other.'

30. As Pardes points out (*Countertraditions*, p. 128), this distinction reflects patriarchal assumptions.

31. Landy, *Paradoxes of Paradise*, pp. 73-112; Meyers, 'Gender Imagery'.

32. Merkin, 'The Women in the Balcony', p. 242.

pressure of convention (if only he were her brother, she could love him openly, 8.1). The worst thing that happens to an autonomous woman is her beating at the hands of the watchmen, who encounter her in the streets at night looking for her lover.

> The watchmen found me
> > those who go about in the city.
> They beat me; they wounded me.
> They lifted up my mantle from upon me,
> > those watchmen of the walls (5.7).

This disturbing encounter, in particular, unsettles both the idyllic picture of romance and the romanticized picture of female autonomy so many readers applaud. The beating scene is so problematic that it is usually ignored by commentators, or explained away. Is it 'only a dream'? This raises the question, How much of the text is wishing (as opposed to acting)? Take kissing, for example. The two occurrences of נשׁק in the Song are both expressions of the desire for kissing but not actual kissing: in 1.2, the woman longs for her lover's kisses—'let him kiss me'; in 8.1, she wishes he were a brother so that she could kiss him openly without reproach—'If only you were my brother...' There is a good deal of dreaming, or fantasizing, in the Song. Yet it seems the woman has internalized social constraints, as the point about being able to kiss him openly without reproach if he were her brother indicates. If the beating by the watchmen is a dream or fantasy—and we need to keep in mind that this is a poem, not a police report; that is, it is constructed by a poet—if this is a dream or fantasy, why the need for punishment? Why does a woman face such a threat?

Female eroticism in the Song is paradoxically celebrated and controlled, but it does not ever seem to be successfully controlled, either by the woman's angry brothers ('my own vineyard I did not keep'), or by the watchmen who beat her (she continues her search and eventually finds her lover), or by the unidentified speakers of 8.8-9, whose view of her as sexually immature she challenges in v. 10.[33] Brenner raises the 'possibility that in love poetry, perhaps also in premarital love relations in general, ancient Near Eastern women were allowed a freedom denied to them in other life situations'.[34] Such freedom is difficult to reconcile with the circumscribed social position of women

---

33. Many commentators understand the woman's brothers of 1.6 to be the speakers of 8.8-9, but I think they could well be the daughters of Jerusalem, the only other speakers otherwise in the Song besides the lovers.

34. Brenner, 'To See Is to Assume', p. 274.

that we find in the rest of the Bible, but, as Fox observes, there is
much we simply do not know.

> [I]t is surprising to find such a society [with strong religious and social
> strictures on unmarried sexual activity] producing a poem that accepts
> premarital sexuality so naturally that is does not even try to draw
> attention to its own liberality. But of vast areas of Israelite life, society,
> and attitudes we know nothing, for the overwhelming majority of the
> documents we have were preserved because they served religious and
> ideological purposes of various groups within that society. (In the case
> of Canticles, it was not the book itself but an interpretation of it that
> served religious purposes.)

He continues, however, to make the important point that poetic fancy
need not correspond to social reality and may offer an escape from
social constraints.[35]

7. *The female body is on display.* (So is the male body—but is it the
same thing?) Who is looking at whose body, and what motivates the
intimate, detailed (even if sometimes obscure) descriptions? To take
one example, does the so-called 'dream-sequence' of 5.2-8 invite us to
become voyeurs by doubly suggesting the woman's nakedness, first
in her bedroom ('I had put off my garment, how could I put it on?'),
and then when she is stripped by the watchmen?[36] The question of the
ownership of the gaze is crystallized in the *wasfs* describing the female
body, where the gaze is male,[37] and female and male readers are
asked to adopt a male gaze at the body of the 'fairest among women'.
But if the text places us in the position of voyeurs, are the descriptions
of the woman's body provided only so that we can look? Or do they
invite our participation by offering us poetic access to the pleasure of
looking at, and knowing, the body? I would prefer to distinguish
between the voyeuristic gaze, looking that intrudes upon that which

---

35. Fox, *Song of Songs*, pp. 313-15, 297; the citation is from p. 315.

36. Polaski, ' "What Will Ye See?" ', p. 78; the male lover is also a voyeur, a
Peeping Tom, as Polaski calls him, in Song 2.8-9, where she visualizes him looking
in the windows and through the lattice. Pardes, *Countertraditions*, suggests an
answer that has to do with the logic of patriarchal control of female sexuality: 'A
woman who does not maintain her nakedness under cover exposes herself to the
danger of being undressed in public' (p. 135).

37. See E. Anne Kaplan, 'Is the Gaze Male?' in Kaplan, *Women and Film: Both
Sides of the Camera* (London: Routledge, 1983), pp. 23-35. The question raised by
feminist film critics, Why are we so attracted to the films of the 40s and 50s and
60s?, provides a useful analogy to the question I raised earlier, Why are feminist
biblical scholars so attracted to the Song of Songs?

is seen,[38] and the erotic gaze, looking that participates in that which is seen.[39]

Only the woman is concerned with self-description (1.5-6; 8.10), and perhaps she is looking at herself through her lover's eyes. Has she internalized the male gaze? Whereas she clearly 'glories in the status which the male gaze appears to give her', as Polaski says,[40] does it necessarily follow that looking can only be objectifying and controlling, and not turned by lovers—and readers—into something else? The double authorial voice complicates focalization. Is a man imagining his lover enjoying his visual pleasure? Is a woman enjoying the visual pleasure she gives to her lover?

In Song 5.10-16, we have a description of the male lover's body, which some commentators find more static, less imaginative, and less sensuous than the descriptions of the woman.[41] Whether or not the male body is subject to a female gaze, the male lover of the Song never offers himself to the woman's gaze in the same way that she offers herself to his, for in the *waṣfs* he addresses her as 'you', whereas she speaks of him as 'he', describing him to the daughters of Jerusalem rather than addressing him directly.[42] Both, however, are looked at by more viewers than just their lover. She invites other women to share her gaze at him in 5.10-16, where she describes him somewhat intimately, much as the gaze at her in 7.1 [ET 6.13] is a group affair: 'Turn, turn, Shulamit, turn, turn, that we may look upon you', which is followed by a detailed intimate description of her.

8. *There is something wrong with the body.* The woman of Canticles is not a complete woman, but a collocation of body parts: a tower-like neck, a belly like a heap of wheat, breasts like two fawns, eyes like pools, a tower-like nose. My point, however, is not simply that other

38. As, for example, when King David spies on the bathing Bathsheba; see J. Cheryl Exum, 'Bathsheba Plotted, Shot, and Painted', in my *Plotted, Shot, and Painted: Cultural Representations of Biblical Women* (JSOTSup, 215; Gender, Culture, Theory, 3; Sheffield: Sheffield Academic Press, 1996), pp. 19-53.

39. Even if we accept this distinction, however, we need to distinguish different subject positions for the characters in the text and readers of the text.

40. Polaski, ' "What Will Ye See?" ', p. 74.

41. E.g. Richard N. Soulen ('The *waṣf* of the Song of Songs and Hermeneutic', *JBL* 86 [1967], pp. 183-90), who attributes the differences to 'the limited subject matter' in 5.10-16, and possibly even 'the difference in erotic imagination between poet and poetess' (p. 216 n. 1). I find it questionable to assume a female gaze in 5.10-16 and then to draw conclusions about differences between a male and female gaze on such scant evidence.

42. Polaski (' "What Will Ye See?" ', pp. 74-76) argues that the male successfully avoids the gaze.

parts are missing but that *the body is absent*. I do not mean, as Clines argues, that such a woman as described in the Song does not exist and has to be invented,[43] but rather that the Song is a poetic attempt to construct the body and endow it with meaning by means of signifiers that both denote and seek to overcome the absence of the signified, the body. 'Representation of the body in signs endeavours to make the body present', writes Peter Brooks, 'but always within the context of its absence, since use of the linguistic sign implies the absence of the thing for which it stands'.[44] In the Song, speech embodies desire by calling bodies into being and playing with their disappearance in a kind of infinite deferral of presence. Unlike real bodies, bodies in the Song of Songs are not vehicles of mortality. They cannot fade, but also, like Keats's figures on a Grecian urn, they cannot attain their bliss.[45]

9. *The poetry of the Song is seductive.* One reason that criticism of the Song, feminist or otherwise, has been so respectful is that its commentators are emotionally and intellectually captivated by the language of this 'masterpiece of pure poetry'.[46] But we might ask, What claims does this text make upon the female reader? What subject position does it invite us to take? This is a complex matter, as Stephen Moore's work on que(e)rying the Song of Songs indicates, and in the long history of allegorical interpretation, female and male readers have adopted the woman's subject position with revealing results.[47] The female protagonist of the Song does have a point of view, even if one constructed for her by the poet. Unlike prophetic pornography, where women are clearly asked to read against our interests, by identifying with the divine point of view against the woman,[48] the Song offers the

43. Clines, *Interested Parties*, p. 106.

44. Peter Brooks, *Body Work: Objects of Desire in Modern Narrative* (Cambridge, MA: Harvard University Press, 1993), pp. 7-8.

45. In Keats's poem, she cannot fade while he cannot attain his bliss; the Song reverses these gender positions.

46. Denis Buzy, 'Un chef-d'œuvre de poésie pure: le Cantique des Cantiques', in *Mémorial Lagrange* (Paris: J. Gabalda, 1940), pp. 147-62; I include myself but I am also thinking of other lovers of the Song, such as Brenner, Landy and Falk.

47. See Stephen D. Moore, 'The Song of Songs in the History of Sexuality', *Church History* (forthcoming).

48. The literature, and the debate, on prophetic pornography is growing; see, *inter alia*, Brenner and van Dijk-Hemmes, *On Gendering Texts*, pp. 167-95; Exum, *Plotted, Shot, and Painted*, pp. 101-28; Robert P. Carroll, 'Desire under the Terebinths: On Pornographic Representation in the Prophets—A Response', in Athalya Brenner (ed.), *A Feminist Companion to the Latter Prophets* (The Feminist Companion to the Bible, 8; Sheffield: Sheffield Academic Press, 1995), pp. 275-307; Athalya

female reader a wider choice. Women are invited to identify with an object of desire, but also with a desiring subject. It is here, with readers, that I come to the tenth thing every feminist should know about the Song of Songs.

10. *Feminists don't have to deny ourselves the pleasure of the text.* All we need to do is misread it (I mean misreading in a positive, Bloomian sense).[49] Readers know this on a fundamental level, for readers have always appropriated their cultural heritage as they see fit.[50] Not to do so would leave us culturally impoverished. Why should an ancient author's intention matter? Let us assume for the sake of argument that Clines and Polaski are right, that the subject position the Song constructs for women is one in which the woman is to see herself as the man sees her; in other words, that the text subtly encourages women to adopt a male vision of woman. It does not follow that I have to read it that way. Our protagonist is assertive, determined, and, not least important, vulnerable.[51] This combination makes her an irresistible subject for further feminist investigation. Feminist readers of this Best of Songs might do well to say to the ancient authors and traditionists who preserved it for us, 'thanks for your text, and I'll decide how to read it'.[52]

Brenner, 'Pornoprophetics Revisited: Some Additional Reflections', *JSOT* 70 (1996), pp. 63-86; Athalya Brenner, *The Intercourse of Knowledge: On Gendering Desire and 'Sexuality' in the Hebrew Bible* (Leiden: E.J. Brill, 1997), pp. 153-74; and the articles in *BibInt* 8 (2000).

49. Harold Bloom, *A Map of Misreading* (New York: Oxford University Press, 1975).

50. For an application of this principle to the book of Ruth, see Exum, *Plotted, Shot, and Painted*, pp. 129-74.

51. Landy, *Paradoxes of Paradise*, p. 69. In addition to the woman's vulnerability, which makes her a true lover, other areas for consideration include the absence of any notion of pollution in the Song, of anxiety about bodily fluids, and not just the absence of an emphasis on procreation but a lack of concern about the possibility of pregnancy.

52. I cite the memorable words of Mieke Bal from a lecture I once heard her give on the rape of Lucretia. Deciding how to read it seems to me to be, in one sense, what Brenner is doing when she reads the *wasf* of ch. 7 in a way that, for her, gives the woman a voice by making the *wasf* a parody. To some extent it may be what the scholars I cited at the beginning of this essay are doing, but by 'misreading' I mean something different from reading.

A HOLY OF HOLIES:
THE SONG OF SONGS AS COUNTERTEXT

Alicia Ostriker

'Let him kiss me with the kisses of his mouth; For thy love is better than wine' is the famous opening of the Song of Songs.[1] With this pronoun-blurring sentence we are plunged into a breathlessly seductive and ultimately mysterious love scene. The remainder of the Song is essentially an erotic dialogue between two lovers who alternately yearn for, recall, invite and celebrate each other's caresses in language laden with metaphors that are at once explicit and cryptic, and have thus produced endless scholarly debates over their meaning.

I first sat down to read the Song of Songs as a teenager, for a high school English class. I had no trouble understanding it. The unutterably sweet words seemed to come not from outside but from within myself, as if my most intimate truth were projected onto the screen of the page. For lo, the winter is past, the rain is over and gone. A garden shut up, a fountain sealed, is my sister, my spouse. I am my beloved's, and his desire is toward me. I was sixteen, in love with a boy two years older whose eyes and laugh and body were so lovely to me that they appeared to contain and enclose the stars, and the spaces between the stars. He stood with the grace of trees. He came leaping upon the mountains. Our kisses were sweet, playful, intense, almost unbearable, just right. Whatever phrases in the poem eluded me did not matter. I understood the tone. Meeting and parting, parting and meeting—in love and playing at love, in a state of entire confidence. I had no doubt that this experience, in the poem and in my life, was the most holy thing I knew.

In my rapt innocence I assumed that my reading of the poem was the only one possible. It is not. How is it, contemporary readers tend to ask, that the Song of Songs came to be included in the Bible? What is this most erotic sequence of poems doing in a sacred book? The question is an ancient one, and it raises the larger question of what we

---

1. Except where specified, I use the translation in *The Holy Scriptures According to the Masoretic Text* (Philadelphia: Jewish Publication Society of America, 1973).

mean—or might mean—by 'sacredness' and by 'the erotic'. In this paper I wish to make three suggestions to the feminist reader, female or male, of the Song of Songs. First, the love celebrated in the Song may be understood as simultaneously natural and spiritual. It is no accident that every mystical tradition on earth speaks of God as the beloved, and that everyone in love sees the beloved's face and form as holy. If elsewhere we must divide the 'sacred' from the 'secular', that division is annihilated in the Song. Here, for once, it becomes mean-ingless. Secondly, the Song is the most startling countertext in the Bible both in its sexual content and for formal reasons. Not only does it offer an extraordinarily egalitarian image of mutual love and desire; its poetic structure and language imply alternatives to normative modes of perceiving and categorizing reality, including spiritual reality. Reading the Song as an image of human passion leads us to the possibility of a mutually delighting love-relationship with God, which is not contingent on obedience or subordination. Thirdly, I want to suggest that 5.2-8, a uniquely painful episode in the Song, may be read as a poem of women's spiritual yearning, our exclusion by tradition and a plea for inclusion which appeals not only to desire but to justice.

1. *Torah: What's Love Got to Do with it?*

How did the Song of Songs come to be included in the Bible? To this question we have only speculative answers.[2] We know that a debate

2.   The canonization process remains shrouded in the mists of antiquity for all the books of the Jewish Bible, not only for the Song. But cf. Robert Alter, 'General Introduction', in Robert Alter and Frank Kermode (eds.), *The Literary Guide to the Bible* (Cambridge, MA: Harvard University Press, 1987), pp. 12-13, who speculates, with the Song, Job and Ecclesiastes in mind, that 'the selection was at least some-times impelled by a desire to preserve the best of ancient Hebrew literature rather than to gather the consistent normative statements of a monotheistic party line'. Athalya Brenner, *The Song of Songs* (OTG; Sheffield: Sheffield Academic Press, 1989), pp. 13-14, lists as the probable reasons for its canonization the attribution to Solomon; its popularity among the people; and, most important, the endorsement of its allegorical interpretation as the 'officially valid exegesis'. Ilana Pardes, *Coun-tertraditions in the Bible: A Feminist Approach* (Cambridge, MA: Harvard University Press, 1992), suggests further that the Song 'had the potential of filling a religious need' within monotheistic incorporeality for a sense of God's more intimate pres-ence, and as a counterweight to 'the misogynist prophetic degradation of the nation [and of women]', pp. 124-127. See also Marvin H. Pope, *The Songs of Songs: A New Translation with Introduction and Commentary* (AB; Garden City, NY: Doubleday, 1977), pp. 18-19, and Roland E. Murphy, *The Song of Songs: A Commen-tary* (Hermeneia; Minneapolis: Fortress Press, 1990), pp. 5-6.

occurred over the Song's canonical status, for we have two famous quotations from Rabbi Akiba on the topic. 'No man in Israel', he is supposed to have exclaimed over the heads of a dubious rabbinical committee, 'ever disputed the status of the Song of Songs... The whole world is not worth the day on which the Song of Songs was given to Israel, for all the writings are holy, but the Song of Songs is the Holy of Holies.' To Akiba also, however, is attributed the following warning: 'He who trills his voice in chanting the Song of Songs in the banquet house, treating it as an ordinary song, has no part in the world to come'.[3] Thus in the same epoch as the Song was declared sacred, it was declared off limits for a secular interpretation. For the next two thousand years, rabbinic commentary would interpret it as an allegory of the love between God and Israel, or as a coded narrative of covenantal history, or as a symbolic evocation of the soul's yearning. So too, throughout the complicated history of Christian exegesis, the Song has been understood as allegorizing the love of Christ for the Church, or for the individual Christian soul, or the mystical marriage of God and the Virgin Mary. Both Jewish and Christian mystical writings have been deeply indebted to its representations of longing and ecstasy, but commonly at the cost of denying the banqueting house of the flesh. For the great Christian rhapsodies of the high Middle Ages, such as Teresa of Avila, St John of the Cross or Bernard of Clairvaux, whose language overflows with the metaphors of the Song, sacred ecstasy was contingent upon bodily celibacy. Only in the last century has the Song of Songs been widely read as a secular love poem.

We may wonder, however, whether the official allegorical whiteout has ever quite blotted the Song's portrait of fleshly passion from the thoughts of its human singers and readers. Akiba's admonition informs us that the Song must indeed have been sung in taverns, with or without theological approval; and every rabbinical protest that the Song is not to be understood in its 'simple' sense seems to confirm that it inevitably was so understood. Late in the first century CE, the Mishnah recounts that on the fifteenth of Av and the Day of Atonement, unmarried girls of Jerusalem would dress in white and go out to the vineyards to dance and sing for prospective husbands, chanting verses from the Book of Proverbs and the Song of Songs.[4] This suggests that Jews in the early rabbinic era were less inclined to

3.   Pope, *Song of Songs*, p. 19.
4.   Ariel Bloch and Chana Bloch, *The Song of Songs: A New Translation with Introduction and Commentary* (New York: Random House, 1995), p. 30.

differentiate between spiritual and bodily love than we are. Perhaps it suggests that they regarded Israel's survival—dependent in the post-exilic era on bodily love, which alone could guarantee posterity—as itself sacred.

'A poem about erotic love would seem out of place in Holy Scripture', Chana and Ariel Bloch remark in the Introduction to their recent translation of the Song, 'if one's point of reference is the antipathy to sexuality in the New Testament. But sex is no sin in the Old Testament.'[5] On the contrary, the Hebrew Bible tends to support the joining of man and woman as one flesh along with other bodily satisfactions, and indeed to see all bodily functions as potentially sacramental, in ways that remain influential throughout the future course of Judaism. Daniel Boyarin persuasively claims, on the basis of talmudic endorsements of marriage and sexuality, that the encrusted body-spirit dualism of Western thought derives from Hellenistic rather than Judaic culture.[6] Within Jewish mysticism, sexual symbolism is not occasional but pervasive; just as the wedded state is the human ideal, so the Oneness of God is ultimately androgynous. 'When is a man called complete in his resemblance to the Supernal?' asks the Zohar. 'When he couples with his spouse in oneness, joy and pleasure'.[7] Conversely, it is only through embodiment that spiritual love becomes effective:

> But if kisses are from there, what need have we of Jacob here? Do not the kisses proceed from Him? The matter is thus. 'Let Him kiss me'— the One who is hidden above. But how? Through that plane in which all the colors are reflected and joined together, and that is Jacob.[8]

Raphael Patai reminds us that Lurianic Kabbalists welcomed the Sabbath bride with words from the Song of Songs, and believed it a *mitzvah* (commandment) to embrace their wives on sabbath eve. 'On Friday after midnight a man should make love with his wife, saying "I fulfill the commandment of copulation for the unification of the Holy one, blessed be He, and the *Shekhinah*" '. As Patai somewhat coyly notes, 'the scriptural libretto for those proceedings in which earthlings emulated and stimulated the divine bride and groom ...

5.   Bloch and Bloch, *Song of Songs*, p. 11.

6.   Daniel Boyarin, *Carnal Israel: Reading Sex in Talmudic Culture* (The New Historicism: Studies in Cultural Politics, 25; Berkeley: University of California Press, 1993).

7.   Pope, *Song of Songs*, p. 165.

8.   *Zohar* 2.146b, cited by Arthur Green, 'Bride, Spouse, Daughter: Images of the Feminine in Classical Jewish Sources', in Susannah Heschel (ed.), *On Being a Jewish Feminist* (New York: Schocken Books, 1983), pp. 248-60 (258).

was, and continues to be, most appropriately, the Sublime Song of
Love ascribed to Solomon, who is renowned for his zeal and devotion
in this way of worship'.[9] A charming corollary is the story of the
student who hid under his rabbi's bed and heard him chatting and
laughing while making love with his wife. However exceptional the
tale, there is something quintessentially Jewish in its mix of comedy,
spirituality and the erotic: when his master discovered his presence
and tried to chase him away, the disciple replied, 'It is Torah and I
must learn it'.[10]

The origin and authorship of the Song remain as mysterious as its
biblical canonization, but here again, there is reason to suppose that it
stems initially from cultures in which physicality and spirituality
were not sharply divided. Conventionally attributed to King
Solomon, commentators have dated it anywhere between the tenth
and the second century BCE. It may have been written in part or
altogether by a woman or women, if, as Athalya Brenner claims, 'the
composition and public recitation of poetry were largely practised by
professional women' in the Ancient Near East.[11] Marvin H. Pope,
surveying theories of the Song's origin, considers the possibility that it
may be a set of popular wedding songs, may derive from fertility
rituals (despite the fact that the lovers are evidently unmarried and
that their joy in each other's embraces has to do with pleasure, not
progeny), and may stem from as far back as Sumerian poems celebrating the sacred marriage of the Sumerian goddess Innanna, 'queen of
the universe', and her consort Dumuzi, or from the cult of Ishtar–
Tammuz; he also summarizes the evidence that strong parallels to the
Song exist in Tamil love poetry and in the Gita-Govinda as well as
Ancient Near Eastern poetry.[12] In all these traditions love between
gods is a model for ideal love between men and women.

But what of modern and contemporary readings? Roland Murphy,
recounting the history of the Song's interpretation, observes that a
few critics in the seventeenth century began to read the Song as an
epithalamion; that readings of it as secular love poetry became more
frequent in the eighteenth century beginning with Herder; and that
this has become 'the prevailing view'.[13] A number of writers have

9.   Raphael Patai, *The Hebrew Goddess* (New York: Avon, 1978), pp. 267, 325
n. 60.
10.   Boyarin, *Carnal Israel*, p. 59.
11.   Brenner, *Song of Songs*, p. 33; see also pp. 65, 89-90.
12.   See Pope, *Song of Songs*, pp. 54-89, 145-153.
13.   Murphy, *Song of Songs*, p. 39.

gone on record insisting that the Song should not be understood religiously at all. Yet interpreters who claim that the Song is purely spiritual and not secular, and those who claim it is purely secular and not spiritual, resemble the investigators of the elephant who think it is either only a trunk or only a tail. Bearing in mind that the body-spirit division foundational to religion and philosophy in the Western world is the same division that subordinates women to men by the convenient gesture of identifying 'body' with femaleness, it should be as important to the feminist reader to question purely secular readings of the Song as it is to question purely spiritual ones.[14] As Grace Schulman suggests, 'it seems a pity to miss the Song's wider implications by regarding it as being either religious or secular, without entertaining simultaneously sacred and erotic interpretations ... many deeply religious works are to be read with the whole of our sensibility, including physical love, and great love poems call for a spiritual reading as well'.[15] A religion in which the deity's declaration 'I will be your God, and you shall be my people' (Lev. 26.12) parallels a bridegroom's wedding vow, and in which we are asked to love God with all our hearts, souls and minds, can make room for the twining of flesh and spirit in the Song of Songs. For Murphy, Scripture expresses 'the recognition that human love and divine love mirror each other ... What links the literal sense of the Song to the expository visions of synagogue and church is an exquisite insight: the love that forms human partnership and community, and that sustains the whole of creation, is a gift of God's own self'.[16] As above, so below. Let me add the view of a student, which offers yet another perspective:

> One way to make sense of the seeming problem is to say that the god-like status of the lovers is the result of the spiritually elevating, divine power of human love. God in this poem is present in the interaction

14. Judith Plaskow, *Standing Again at Sinai* (San Francisco: Harper & Row, 1990), p. 199, discusses the Song's representation of a 'love without dominion that is also the love of God' in the context of defining the need for 'a new theology of Sexuality' in Judaism. See also Phyllis Trible, *God and the Rhetoric of Sexuality* (Philadelphia: Fortress Press, 1978), chapter 5; Arthur Waskow, *Godwrestling* (New York: Schocken Books, 1978), chspter 6.

15. Grace Schulman, 'The Song of Songs: Love is Strong as Death', in David Rosenberg (ed.), *Congregation: Contemporary Writers Read the Jewish Bible* (New York: Harcourt Brace Javonovich, 1987), pp. 346-59 (358-59).

16. Murphy, *Song of Songs*, pp. 104-105. See also Sallie McFague, *Models of God: Theology for an Ecological, Nuclear Age* (Philadelphia: Fortress Press, 1987), chapter 5, 'God as Lover', which speaks of God's erotic need as well as ours.

between two of God's creatures recognizing, honoring and celebrating the divine in one another. This is not the same as saying, as the neighbors of the Israelites did... that sex itself is divine, or that reproduction is, but that through the love for another person, humans are sanctified and uplifted. With this reading, it is not necessary to force the love poem into an idealized allegory.[17]

2. *Countertext: Content and Form*

What do we find when we read the Song without attempting to press it into some supposed consistency with biblical tradition? What does it tell us, what does it whisper to us, if we permit ourselves to hear it as the combined voices of lover and beloved outside of law, outside of constraint, leaping upon the mountains and feeding among the lilies in apparent neglect of every rule of property governing human and divine relationships elsewhere in the Bible?

That the Hebrew Bible is a set of widely various texts composed over a period of centuries if not millennia, and redacted for several centuries more, is assumed by all current biblical scholarship. While fundamentalists and literalists continue to treat Scripture as a monolithic book with a single message, contemporary literary commentary on the Bible emphasizes its heterogeneity and probes its fractures. Robert Alter remarks in the 'Introduction' to his and Frank Kermode's volume, *The Literary Guide to the Bible*, that Scripture incorporates radically diverse conceptions 'of history, ethics, psychology... of priesthood and laity, Israel and the nations, even of God'.[18] Harold Bloom points out in *The Book of J* that the narrative voice in much of Genesis is far from pious.[19] Anson Layton's *Arguing With God* examines numerous biblical passages from Genesis to Job which challenge or reject the assumption of God's goodness.[20] Numerous feminist scholars, from Phyllis Trible in *God and the Rhetoric of Sexuality* to Ilana Pardes in *Countertraditions in the Bible*, while deploring biblical androcentrism and misogyny, discuss gynocentric passages in the Bible ranging in length from a phrase to a book. Biblical literature, according

17. Julie M. Goldberg, unpublished seminar paper. Quoted by permission of the author.

18. Alter and Kermode (eds.), *The Literary Guide*, p. 12.

19. Harold Bloom, *The Book of J* (trans. by David Rosenberg; interpreted by Harold Bloom; New York: Grove Weidenfeld, 1990).

20. Anson Layton, *Arguing With God: A Jewish Tradition* (Northvale, NJ: J. Aronson, 1990).

to each of these accounts, is woven of surprisingly diverse sorts of yarn.

All such studies are explorations of countertexts, a term which I derive from Pardes and employ to denote any biblical text, brief or extended, which in some sense resists dominant structures of authority, divine and legal, as defined by the Bible as a whole and by the history of its interpretation. Major instances of countertexts would include anti-doctrinal books like Job and Ecclesiastes, and gynocentric books like Ruth, Esther and the Song of Songs. All the Writings, in fact, stand at diverse odd angles to the Law and the Prophets. But countertexts also include brief episodes such as Abraham's bargaining with God at Mamre (Gen. 18), Rebecca's and Rachel's roles as tricksters (Gen. 27 and 31), the wrestling of Jacob (Gen. 32), Tamar's gamble (Gen. 38), the midwives' civil disobedience (Exod. 1) and the conspiracy of women following it (Exod. 2), Moses' exclamation 'Would that all the Lord's people were prophets' (Num. 11.29), Jeremiah's question of questions, 'Why do sinners' ways prosper?' (Jer. 12.1), and the God of Isa. 45.7 who asserts 'I form the light and create darkness; I make peace and create evil; I am the Lord, that doeth all these things'.

In one sense, then, the apparent anomaly of the Song of Songs is not anomalous at all. Still, by any measure, the Song constitutes the most remarkable countertext in an otherwise firmly patriarchal Hebrew canon. Whether we interpret it as a residue of pre-patriarchal poetry inserted into the patriarchal context, or whether we see it as a late formation, the Song is, in effect, the quintessence of the non-patriarchal. It contains no mention of God or any other superior being; neither does it mention law, ritual, the nation of Israel, the history of its people or the genealogies of its men. It includes no representation of hierarchy or rule, no relationship of dominance and submission, and (almost) no violence. Where the Bible concerns itself overwhelmingly with obedience, the Song inscribes an alternative story of voluntary love and pleasure.

Unlike the bulk of biblical narrative, which begins by granting humankind sovereignty over nature and pays little attention to the environment in which humans act thereafter (except to deal with issues of ownership), the Song is abundantly and tenderly descriptive. Its primary setting is a pastoral world of fertile nature, of flocks and birds, fruit trees and vineyards, gardens and oases, mountains and their wild creatures. Moreover, the lovers are not 'sovereign' over their environment, but virtually interchangeable with it. 'I am a rose of Sharon, A lily of the valleys', says the woman. 'As a lily among thorns, so is my love among the daughters', the man replies (2.1-2).

'My beloved is mine and I am his. He feedeth among the lilies', says the woman. 'Be like a gazelle, a young hart on the mountains of spices', she tells him (2.16-17). 'A garden shut up is my sister, my bride; a spring shut up, a fountain sealed. Thy shoots are a park of pomegranates, with precious fruits', he says to her (4.12-13). The refrain which asks the daughters of Jerusalem 'by the gazelles, and by the hinds of the field, that ye awaken not, nor stir up love until it please' (2.7; 3.5; 8.4), implies acceptance and reverence for men and women's own creaturely nature. Descriptions such as these alternate with the sumptuous fantasied setting of a noble or royal court, valued for its beauty rather than its political power, and interchangeable with the male form. 'His body is as polished ivory overlaid with sapphires. His legs are as pillars of marble set upon sockets of fine gold' (5.14-15). In this world of nature, and of occasional artifact, the male lover sometimes seems a shepherd, sometimes King Solomon—or so the woman imagines him, just as he imagines her at times to be a princess, at times a landscape, at times 'my myrrh with my spice...my wine with my milk' (5.1). Place names in the Song are associated not with politics, war and conquest, as elsewhere, but with pleasure and fantasy. The rose of Sharon, the mountains of Bether, the flock of goats from Mt Gilead, the fishpools of Heshbon, and so on, are part and parcel of the lovers' play.

Rooted in wedding songs or not, the Song depicts the joys of love unconnected with marriage or procreation. This is in sharp contrast to the normative models of sexuality in the Bible, in which women are property and wives are essentially breeders. Here the lovers mutually seek, mutually praise, mutually enjoy one another. For both, love is eating and drinking; kisses and embraces are like wine; the lover is a tree 'whose fruit was sweet to my taste' (2.3); the woman is a garden in which the lover browses, eating the honeycomb with the honey. Both lovers are associated with doves, deer, gazelles. At times they mirror and echo each other's phrases, their speeches gliding into each other without the obstruction of 'he said', 'she said':

> I am a rose of Sharon,
> A lily of the valleys.
> As a lily among thorns,
> So is my love among the daughters.
>
> As an apple tree among the trees of the wood,
> So is my beloved among the sons (2.1-3).

> Let my beloved come into his garden
> And eat his precious fruits.
> I am come into my garden, my sister, my bride,
> I have gathered my myrrh with my spice (4.16–5.1).

The drama of the poem rests not on any story of inaccessibility but on the dialectic fluctuations of presence and absence, pleasure anticipated and recollected, pleasure in the moment: 'My beloved ... feedeth among the lilies' (2.16). 'I have gathered my myrrh with my spice' (5.1). 'My beloved is gone down to his garden, to the beds of spices, to feed in the gardens, and to gather lilies' (6.2).[21]

Where the curse of Eve in Genesis declares that a woman's desire shall be toward her husband, and he shall rule over her, the woman in the Song proudly announces 'I am my beloved's, and his desire is toward me' (7.11). The woman speaks more lines of the dialogue, including the opening and final ones. She is, as well, more aggressive, more introspective, and more philosophical than her lover. Hers is the quest for the beloved in the city streets (3.2-4; 5.7), hers the adjuration to the daughters of Jerusalem not to awaken love until it is ripe (2.7, 3.5, 8.4), hers the fantasy that her lover might be like her brother, suckling from the same mother's breasts (8.1), hers the pronouncement that love is fierce as death and that the attempt to purchase it should be despised (8.6-7). Elsewhere in the Bible we are admonished to fear God. But in this text it is the woman who is awesome, even terrifying, her eyeglance dazzling to the lover, her presence 'terrible as an army with banners' in the KJV and JPSV versions (6.10; cosmic as sun, moon, and stars in their courses, according to Ariel and Chana

21. I here disagree with Julia Kristeva, who argues in 'A Holy Madness: She and He', in Kristeva, *Tales of Love* (trans. Leon S. Roudiez; New York: Columbia University Press, 1987), that the lovers are actually in love with each other's absence, that 'the presence of the loved one is fleeting ... no more than an expectation ... an unceasing rush' (p. 113), and that sexual satisfaction does not in fact take place between them. Similarly, Daphne Merkin, 'The Women in the Balcony: On Rereading the Song of Songs', in Christina Buchmann and Celina Spiegel (eds.), *Out of the Garden: Women Writers on the Bible* (New York: Random House, 1994), pp. 238-51, calls the Song 'this infamously titillating text' but also claims that 'the two amorphously defined lovers ... never come close to consummating their relationship' (pp. 247, 250). The text indicates otherwise. Among the passages which represent lovemaking as either taking place at present or being happily remembered, are 2.3-6, 16; 5.1; 6.2-3, 11-12 (cf. the Blochs' commentary on this passage, and their argument that 'the sexual relationship between the two lovers is not just yearned for—-as has often been assumed—but actually consummated' [Bloch and Bloch, *The Song of Songs*, pp. 3-4]).

Bloch's translation of this obscure passage).[22] Again, where Israelite social structure in the Bible is represented almost exclusively by men—the Book of Ruth is a partial exception—the Song does not mention fathers or the father's house, but twice mentions the mother's house as a place to bring the lover (3.4; 8.2). Perhaps these passages suggest a residue of matrifocal marriage; surely they suggest something mysteriously gratifying about the scene of maternal conception (3.4) and mother–daughter instruction (8.2).[23] In one of these episodes we may be uncannily reminded of Jacob's wrestling and embrace of a divine antagonist, but Jacob's 'I will not let thee go except thou bless me' (Gen. 32.26) becomes the woman's triumph:

> By night on my bed I sought him
> Whom my soul loveth:
> I sought him but I found him not.
> The watchmen that go about the city found me.
> Saw ye him whom my soul loveth?
> Scarce had I passed from them,
> When I found him whom my soul loveth.
> I held him and I would not let him go
> Until I had brought him into my mother's house,
> And into the chamber of her that conceived me (3.2-4).

In 8.2, where the mother's house is a place of maternal instruction, the ensuing fantasy of having the lover drink 'spiced wine from the juice of my pomegranate', then lying with his left hand under her head and his right hand embracing her, suggests that mother may have taught daughter the rites of lovemaking. Yet both these episodes close with the woman's direction to 'the daughters of Jerusalem' not to awaken love until it please, which suggests an idea of love clearly separable from parental dictate or the dominance of either lover over the other. Elsewhere she speaks antiphonally with the chorus of women (5.8-16),

22. Bloch and Bloch, *Song of Songs*, p. 191, discusses this interpretation.

23. Carol Meyers, 'Returning Home: Ruth 1.8 and the Gendering of the Book of Ruth', in Athalya Brenner (ed.), *A Feminist Companion to Ruth* (Sheffield: Sheffield Academic Press, 1993), pp. 85-114, argues that the phrase 'mother's house', wherever it is found in Biblical texts (including Gen. 24.28 and the Song of Songs) instead of the more conventional 'father's house', may register the historical reality of an 'internal gender balance rather than gender hierarchy' within normal Israelite households, which 'occasionally … can be glimpsed even in the male-oriented canon' (p. 99), and may also indicate a woman-authored text. Meyers notes that some ancient versions of Ruth substitute 'father's house' for 'mother's house' (p. 92), and that numerous ancient and modern translations delete or alter 'she instructs me', making the teacher male or reverting to the image of maternal conception and birth (p. 105).

in a way which suggests a women's community independent of male control.

Two brief moments imply possible limits to the woman's freedom of erotic choice. In 1.6 she elliptically recalls her brothers' anger: 'My mothers' sons were incensed against me, they made me keeper of the vineyards; but mine own vineyard I have not kept'. The tone might be equally regretful and apologetic, or mocking and defiant. In 5.7, when she seeks her lover through the nocturnal city streets—we do not know if this episode is a dream or a 'real' event—in contrast to the episode just quoted, the watchmen find her and beat her. A verse later, however, she seems unharmed as she engages in boastful dialogue with the daughters of Jerusalem over the beauties of her lover. In sharp distinction to her role everywhere else in Scripture, nothing in the Song suggests that woman is the second sex. Yet one does not, in reading the Song, think of the female as dominant over the male, thanks to the aura of pleasure enveloping both. Indeed, so much do the lovers mirror each other, and so little does the poem seem to stress sexual difference as such, that it makes itself available to same-sex lovers in much the same metaphorical way as it makes itself available to lovers of God.

As countertextual as its content is the poem's form. The poetry of the Song of Songs distinguishes itself from the two modes of discourse—narrative and law—which dominate the Hebrew Bible, and it differs as well from other biblical poetry. Technically, the Song is designed in numerous ways to defy our normal sense of divisions and categories. The Masoretic version takes the form of prose, cadenced but without line divisions, and part of the Song's erotic charm consists precisely in its dreamlike blurring of distinctions, as the speech of one lover glides into and is mirrored by the other's, and as one episode slips into the next without apparent boundaries. Numerous commentators have mentioned that it is sometimes difficult to tell who is speaking. The lines between sleeping, waking and fantasy experience are also at times unclear. In contrast to linear narrative, the lyrics of the Song occur in a continuing present, with the reassuring occurrence of refrains, but no particular order. Notwithstanding the efforts of generations of commentators to impose a coherent narrative plot on the Song, it goes nowhere and ends without closure. Ambiguity and riddling are part of its fabric. What is the meaning of the pronoun slide in the poem's opening line? Does the Shulamite say she is 'black *but* comely', or 'black *and* comely' (1.5)? The Hebrew *w^e* makes possible the woman's finely ambiguous tone; possibly she is defensive (if racial difference or agricultural work has darkened her skin), but possibly she is boasting. Are the lovers courtiers playing shepherds, or shepherds playing courtiers? Who are the 'foxes' (2.15)? Who is the 'little sister' (8.8)?

'One might be tempted to call the Song subversive, were it not the least polemical of books', remark the Blochs.[24] One might argue to the contrary that the very absence of polemics renders the Song infinitely subversive because infinitely defiant of institutional religion's need to impose fixed order, meaning and definition upon experience, to subdue reality to categories. In this respect it differs radically from Ecclesiastes and Job, those other extraordinary texts. It is not a protest poem, it is not anti-patriarchal; rather, it lives in an alternative dimension, as if patriarchy did not exist.

Among its many literary qualities, the most pervasively counter-textual is the Song's overwhelmingly rich use of metaphor. For metaphoric language is the opposite of legal language, and legal pronouncement, along with narrative, is a mode of biblical discourse upon which much of what we take to be 'Jewish' rests. Where the Law concentrates on establishing and maintaining distinctions—Israel versus the nations, man versus woman, clean versus unclean—metaphor requires that we apprehend likeness and difference simultaneously and instantaneously. Law strives for maximum precision, metaphor pulls away from precision and toward fluidity. Antithetical to logic, resting on absurdity, it proposes that A and non-A are one. Eluding fixity, it produces not definitions but indefinite ripples of meaning, dependent for their existence on the audience's capacity to participate in their creation.

Metaphorically, a name can be ointment, lovemaking can be like (but better than) wine, hair can be a flock of goats, a young woman (or her body or some part of her body) can be a garden, a fountain, a mare, a dove; a man can be a bundle of myrrh, an apple tree, a roe or a young hart, a pillar of smoke—but always and only if the reader's mind can grasp what qualities may be shared between the terms, and register at that same moment the distance between them. Metaphor's root meaning has to do with connection, as the Greek *metapherein* means to transport or transfer. It is in essence an amatory figure of speech both in its treatment of terms as fused-yet-separate, and in its engagement of the audience, which must enter into its game. (In the Gospels, the equivalently powerful literary device is the parable, which also demands a leap of participation from the reader, and which also retains a core of mystery.) Due to the extraordinarily rich

24. Bloch and Bloch, *Song of Songs*, p. 14.

layering of metaphor in the Song, we are prevented from thinking of humanity as dominant over animals and plants, or the beauties of artifact and architecture as altogether distinct from those of taste and smell, or eating and drinking as distinguishable from sex. As Robert Alter has astutely noted, 'in the poetics of intertwinement manifested in the imagery of the poem, these seemingly opposed semantic fields actually overlap, run into each other'.[25]

At structural and linguistic levels, then, the Song replicates the absence of dominance and hierarchy, the blurring of boundaries and distinctions, which we see in the relationship of the lovers. As a secular text these characteristics render it exceptional enough. For those who experience the Song as erasing the border between sacred and secular, it offers a sense of the holy at odds with what is usually understood as religious.

What then are the spiritual implications of the Song's portrait of mutual desire and joy? What happens when, having read the 'simple' sense in some such way as I have done here, we consider what that sense signifies for our relationship with God? Despite certain readers, who have asserted that desire is always deferred in the Song of Songs, we should more properly think of it as having been always already satisfied, and hence anticipated with confidence rather than anxiety. Theologically, this would be equivalent to the conviction, the knowledge, that we are loved with an absolute love, by a being who has been present to us and will be present again. The happiness of the Song of Songs helps us, or can help us, to feel, to know, that this is indeed the case. And that that same love is extended to the world of which we are a portion. Again, where readers assert that the erotic/spiritual experience toward which the Song gestures has something to do with 'sovereignty', 'mastery', 'authority', one being subduing another—which is indeed what we find in most 'religious' texts in the Western world—we may instead conclude that the power relationships which dominate both religion and sex in our world (with each system of dominance reinforcing the other) have tragically blinded such readers even to the possibility of an alternative.[26] What is extra-

25. Robert Alter, 'Afterword', in Bloch and Bloch, *Song of Songs*, p. 125.

26. For Kristeva the lover is 'the one who subdues [the subject]—the Master', *Tales of Love*, p. 94; erotic passion is subdued by his 'regal authority', p. 96; the love of the Song is conjugal and is kept 'under the husband's rule', p. 99; the Shulamite's utterance is 'to submit to him', p. 99. These palpable misreadings of the text seem to me dependent not only on Kristeva's view of the lover as 'king, husband, or God', but on her assumption that an amatory relationship is necessarily a submissive one. Merkin, 'The Woman in the Balcony', seems disconcerted

ordinary in the Song is precisely the absence of structural and systemic hierarchy, sovereignty, authority, control, superiority, submission, in the relation of the lovers and in their relation to nature; the same holds for the relation of classes, since the shepherd may play the part of a king as well as the reverse, just as humans played the part of gods in celebrating sacred marriages in the pagan rituals from which these songs may be derived.

In the boundary-blurring tradition of the Song, I turn now to my own memories and my own subjectivity. It seems to me that relationship in the Song of Songs, like every glimpse I have had of holiness from the age of sixteen to the present, is defined by a sense of powerful connection which is not subordination. I do not submit to the other, neither does the other submit to me. Light passes through us, and we see the light welling up in the world. And this is quintessentially true of my relation with any beloved, any friend, when the connection feels blessed. Feels heavenly. In those moments I do not need to know whether the through-flow of spirit was made in heaven, or whether we create heaven as a projection of our love. I do know, in those moments, that a spiritual world exists, and that I belong to it. Not that this state of awareness is normal. But am I wrong to name it as my ideal desire? Am I wrong to fantasize, to dream, to imagine, to suppose, that God's love of us, and ours of God, might ideally be as tenderly ardent and as free of power-play as the love enacted in this Song? Feminist theology today asks us to 're-imagine the unimaginable':[27] to learn to see God not merely as the traditional God–He who is father, warrior, judge, and not merely as disembodied *ein-sof*, but also as the God–She who is *Shekhinah*, wisdom, the God who is friend, companion, co-creator, the God who is both place and abyss, transcendent and immanent. Surely God is all these things; 'diverse images of God are not the names of multiple divinities but guises of the One that manifests itself in and through the changing forms of the many'.[28] But what of God as lover? What of God as a being who yearns toward us, as we yearn back, unconditionally? The Song stares us in the face—unique among texts, a Holy of Holies. If we are to take

by the 'remarkably diffuse boundaries', the 'emotional lability' and the absence of gender-stereotyped behavior in the poem (pp. 239-42). Plaskow, *Standing Again at Sinai*, p.119, makes the point that 'since different forms of hierarchy and oppression intersect with and reinforce one another, none finally will be abolished until all have fallen'.

27. Plaskow, *Standing Again at Sinai*, chapter 4.

28. Judith Plaskow, 'Spirituality and Politics: Lessons from B'not Esh', *Tikkun* 10.3 (May–June 1995), pp. 31-32, 35.

the Song in its spiritual sense, does it not invite us to affirm this wildest dream?

3. *The Song and the Real World*

What I have just written will seem absurd, I assume, to most readers. It seems absurd to me as well. God as lover? God as the lover who is equal to the self? Our spiritual quest as one in which God wants to meet us halfway? God's desire for us outside the Law? Impossible. And very much more impossible if we are women.[29]

Curiously enough, the Song itself offers a description and analysis of that seeming impossibility. When I teach the Song of Songs and describe it as differing from the dominant depictions of gender relations in the Bible—when I point out how Eden-like its world is, how non-oppressive, how non-violent—students sometimes correct me by pointing to 5.6-7. In this passage, which at first seems to parallel the successful quest-episode of 3.1-4, the woman leaves her house to seek her beloved in the street.

> I sought him but I could not find him;
> I called him but he gave me no answer.
> The watchmen that go about the city smote me;
> The keepers of the walls took away my mantle from me.

What about that, my students ask indignantly. The minute the woman does not know her place, the minute she dares to go public, she gets beaten up and treated like a whore. By the cops. They probably rape her. They probably say she was asking for it.

---

29. We are accustomed to the generalization that the woman in the Song of Songs stands for Israel; however, 'Israel' signifies a male community perceiving itself as God's lover. Howard Eilberg-Schwartz, in his provocative and brilliant study *God's Phallus: And Other Problems for Men and Monotheism* (Boston: Beacon Press, 1994), chapter 4, discusses the marriage metaphor in Hosea, Jeremiah and Ezekiel, pointing out that 'The images of a female Israel ... were addressed primarily to men and conceptualized their male relationship to God. Men were encouraged to imagine themselves as married to and hence in a loving relationship with God.' What did this imply for their masculinity? Ch. 7 discusses in detail rabbinic readings of the Song of Songs which feminize the figures of the patriarchs, Moses and Aaron, David, and indeed all observant Jewish males in relation to God as lover. Women, according to Eilberg-Schwartz, pose a threat not merely to male authority insofar as it emulates God's authority, but also to the male–male love relationship between men and God. If men 'do not take their proper role as God's wives, then the human women are always ready to assume that role' (p. 160). If men are metaphoric women in relation to God, then actual women must be excluded altogether from the circle of immediate spiritual relationship.

When I reply that this scene is just a minor episode, a brief evocation of loss and pain that is quickly over and seems to be in the poem
almost for the sake of contrast, to heighten our sense of the pleasure
and safety that otherwise abound, these students shake their heads.
They are not having any. They know better. For them, this scene and
this scene alone is a portrait of the real world. In a sense, I have come
to admit, they are right. Within the larger structure of the Bible, the
Song is like a loophole through which we peek into an alternative
existence. Within the Song, this episode is like a loophole through
which we peer back at existence as we know it.

As has often been observed, it is impossible to ascertain whether
5.2-8 is a 'real' event or a dream. Perhaps it is in some sense both.
'History is a nightmare from which I am trying to awake', remarks
Stephen Dedalus in Ulysses; and perhaps the exclusion of women
from central spiritual roles in Judaism should also be seen as a bad
dream. A dream of several thousand years. 'Open to me', says the
lover, but women understandably hesitate to do so. 'I have put off my
coat, How shall I put it on?' (5.2-3). Better to stay safely in one's place,
not make waves. For what happens—according to respected Jewish
tradition—to a woman who goes public with her spiritual need,
whose yearning is larger than a kitchen? What happens to the woman
who does not hide behind a *m^eḥîṣāh*, the curtain separating men's and
women's sections in an Orthodox synagogue, designed to protect men
at prayer from the distraction of women's voices? What becomes of
the learned Beruria, the one woman whose opinions are in fact cited
in the Talmud? According to legend, her devoted husband Rabbi Meir
instigates one of his disciples to seduce her in order to prove that
women are flighty. When the disciple finally overcomes her resistance, she kills herself for shame, but nobody seems to think Rabbi
Meir should be ashamed.[30] What happens to Yentl? What happens to
the women at the Wall?[31] We are not speaking of allegory here, but of

30. See Leonard Swidler, 'Beruriah: Her Word Became Law', *Lilith* 1.3 (Spring–
Summer 1977), pp. 9-12; and Rachel Adler, 'The Virgin in the Brothel and Other
Anomalies: Character and Context in the Legend of Beruriah', *Tikkun* 3.6 (1992),
pp. 28-32, 115-21.
31. In 1988 a group of women following a feminist conference in Jerusalem
assembled to pray at the Western or 'Wailing' Wall in Jerusalem, in defiance of the
prohibition against public prayer by women. They were attacked for this breach of
custom. The Women at the Wall movement has subsequently brought women to
monthly prayer at the Wall; the issue continues to be contested in the Israeli
Supreme Court. See Susan Schnur and Sarah Blustain, 'Paradoxes and Mysteries of
Sacred Space: Sacred Wall?', *Lilith* (Spring-Summer) 1996), p. 14.

real life. Women who dare to pray aloud with Torah in hand at the *Kotel* (the Western or 'Wailing' Wall in Jerusalem) have been spat on, cursed, called whore. They have had chairs thrown at them, they have been beaten up and hospitalized, and they—they, not their assailants—have been arrested. Although nothing in *halakhah* (rabbinic law) actually forbids these women's activity, the Supreme Court of Israel pronounces that 'custom' should be observed. As of this date, women are permitted to gather as a group at the *Kotel* but not to pray aloud, or carry Torahs, or wear *tefillin* (phylacteries) or prayer shawls. As it is uncannily written, 'The keepers of the walls took away my mantle from me' (5.7).

The text of 5.8 requires particular attention. The KJV reads, 'I charge you, O daughters of Jerusalem, if ye find my beloved, that ye tell him, that I am sick of love'. In the JPSV, 'I adjure you, O daughters of Jerusalem, if ye find my beloved, what will ye tell him? that I am lovesick.' The Bloch version has: 'Swear to me, daughters of Jerusalem!' What is interesting here is the legal language, earlier (2.7; 3.5) used apparently playfully—I charge you, or adjure you, or ask you to swear, that you will not waken love until it is ready—and here in earnest. Or perhaps both usages are more earnest than we imagine. In a society in which marriages are arranged by the parents of the bride and groom, it is revolutionary to argue for love-marriage. In a society whose Law divides a woman's prayer from a man's prayer, which forbids women to testify in a court of law, in which—to use Rachel Adler's phrase—a woman is 'the Jew who wasn't there',[32] what is being perpetuated is injustice. When the Shulamite appeals to the daughters of Jerusalem with the solemnity of an oath, she should awaken our longing for justice. *Justice, justice shalt thou seek.* When she cries that she is sick with love—sick because of frustrated love (5.8)— she should remind us of our own condition within the Jewish world. She begs us to be her allies. We ought to answer her call.

But, in the first place, we ought to respond to the call of the Holy One. קוֹל דּוֹדִי קוֹלִי! דּוֹדִי דוֹפֵק, 'The voice of my beloved. My beloved knocking'. פִּתְחִי לִי!, 'Open to me, says the lover'. And why? Though the language is somewhat obscure, the translations converge on something like 'For my head is filled with dew, my locks with the drops of the night' (5.2). Which is to say that the Holy One, בָּרוּךְ הַשֵּׁם ('the blessed name'), our lover, is out there in night and fog. The night and

---

32. Rachel Adler, 'The Jew who Wasn't There: Halakhah and the Jewish Woman' is the opening essay in S. Heschel (ed.), *On being a Jewish Feminist*, pp. 12-18.

fog that is not only the World War II of Resnais' melancholy Holocaust film, but all of human history. The night and fog (and it ought to
break our hearts to think this) that is all of Jewish history too.

In her pathbreaking essay 'Notes Toward Finding the Right Question', Cynthia Ozick argues that 'it is not the upsurge of secular feminism that has caused the upsurge of Jewish feminism' but, rather, that
'in the wake of the cataclysm' which was the destruction of European
Jewry, all Jews find themselves receiving 'a share in its famously
inescapable message: that after the Holocaust every Jew will be more
a Jew than ever before—and not just superficially and generally, but
in every path, taken or untaken, deliberate or haphazard, looked-for
or come upon'. Pursuing the image of incalculable loss, Ozick points
out that the exclusion of Jewish women from the ongoing creative and
intellectual life of the Jewish people is 'a loss numerically greater than
a hundred pogroms... A loss culturally and intellectually more debili-
tating than a century of autos-da-fé; than a thousand evil bonfires of
holy books...yet Jewish literature and history report not one wail, not
one tear'.[33] I want to agree with and extend Ozick's lament. Not only
has the Jewish mind denied itself half its potential. So has Jewish
spirituality. The Song speaks to all these losses. קוֹל דּוֹדִי. In night and
fog—from who knows how far back, from the time of the Kingdom,
from the time of exile, the time of Akiba, throughout the diaspora to
this very moment—the lover knocks at our womanly door, saying
'Open to me'. And we want to open, but we are afraid, and when we
go to the door it is too late, and we regret our hesitation. נַפְשִׁי יָצְאָה
בְדַבְּרוֹ, my soul failed at his speech. But the Song is timeless, the Song
is still there, the beloved still knocks. How long will it take us to
answer fearlessly?

33. Cynthia Ozick, 'Notes Toward Finding the Right Question', in Heschel
(ed.), *On Being a Jewish Feminist*, pp. 133-38. The essay originally appeared in *Lilith*
6 (1979), pp. 19-29.

INTO ANOTHER SCENE OF CHOICES:
THE THEOLOGICAL VALUE OF THE SONG OF SONGS

Jonneke Bekkenkamp

Introduction

With whom do you believe your lot is cast?
From where does your strength come?

I think somehow, somewhere
every poem of mine must repeat those questions

which are not the same. There is a whom, a where
that is not chosen that is given and sometimes falsely given

in the beginning we grasp whatever we can to survive[1]

For me, pondering the theological value of the Song of Songs is considering in what sense the Song might help in answering the questions Adrienne Rich articulates in the poem cited above: 'With whom do you believe your lot is cast?/ From where does your strength come?'. Is it a strengthening song or just a text I grasped in the beginning to survive as a feminist theologian? Clergymen questioning the theological value of the SoS usually did so out of disapproval of its erotic undertones. But the erotic mode of the SoS is exactly what I appreciate so much: the being with, the looking at, the caressing of, the wrapping up in the beloved, in which the boundaries we are used to set up between corporeality, spiritual contact, religious feelings and nature-experiences fall off.

This description is taken from Ria Lemaire's study of the Portuguese *cantigas de amigo*, early medieval women's love poetry, which in Europe, like the German *Frauen-* or *Mädchenlieder*, the English 'Woman's lament', the Spanish *jarchas* and the French 'refrains' preceded the far better known courtly poetry of men.[2] The apparent similarities between these songs and the SoS brought me to the suggestion that the SoS might be a women's song as well, a refined

---

1. Adrienne Rich, *Sources* (California: The Heyeck Press, 1983), p. 12.

2. Ria Lemaire, 'Vroegmiddeleeuwse vrouwenlyriek en hoofse mannen-poëzie', in *Sprekend: Teksten Lezingencyclus 'Vrouwen en Letteren'* (Nijmegen: de Feeks, 1981), pp. 125-56.

product of women's oral traditions.[3] But is my personal appreciation of the SoS, and its historical value as one of the few possible remnants of women's cultures, an indication of its theological value? Which texts are of theological value and why?

Referring to the study of literature, Barbara Herrnstein Smith speaks of an exile of evaluation.[4] Within theology, especially within the Protestant tradition I am raised in, this is notably true with regard to the Bible. The value of the Bible's texts is beyond dispute, its function as a prime source of theology established. But again, why? The Bible as a given source of theology for women often turned out to be falsely given. Already a hundred years ago Elizabeth Cady Stanton made this point in her introduction to the *Woman's Bible Commentary*. She concluded: 'We have made a fetish of the Bible long enough. The time has come to read it as we do all other books, accepting the good and rejecting the evil it teaches.'[5]

Remarkable in Stanton's position is that she does not, out of feminist frustration with civil and clerical authorities that used the divine authority of the Bible against women, reject the Bible as a whole. She does not get trapped into the false dilemma of biblical *or* other books. I agree on this, as I agree with Carol P. Christ and other feminist scholars that we should search for alternative texts and traditions.[6] But how to choose among the millions of books written, or rather, how to communicate and take responsibility for our choices? If the Bible is no longer the norm, if the SoS becomes a love song among many others, what then are the possible criteria for deciding on theological value or relevance?

3.   Jonneke Bekkenkamp, *Want ziek van liefde ben ik* (Amsterdam: University of Amsterdam Press, 1984); 'Het Hooglied: Een vrouwenlied in een mannentraditie', in Ria Lemaire (ed.), *Ik zing mijn lied voor al wie met mij gaat: vrouwen in de volksliteratuur* (Utrecht: HES, 1986) and J. Bekkenkamp and Fokkelien van Dijk-Hemmes, 'The Canon of the Old Testament and Women's Cultural Tradition', in M. Meijer and J. Schaap (eds.), *Historiography of Women's Cultural Traditions* (Dordrecht: Forest Publications, 1987), pp. 91-108. For an overview of the current debate on a possible female 'authorship' of the SoS, see A. Brenner and F. van Dijk-Hemmes, *On Gendering Texts: Female and Male Voices in the Hebrew Bible* (Leiden: E.J. Brill, 1993), pp. 71-83.

4.   Barbara Herrnstein Smith, 'Contingencies of Value', in Robert von Hallberg (ed.), *Canons* (Chicago: University of Chicago Press, 1983), pp. 5-40.

5.   Elizabeth Cady Stanton, *The Woman's Bible*, II (New York, 1895–1898; repr.; Edinburgh: Polygon Books, 1985), p. 8.

6.   Carol P. Christ, 'Feminist Studies in Religion and Literature: A Methodological Reflection', in Rita M. Gross (ed.), *Beyond Androcentrism: New Essays on Women and Religion* (Missoula, MT: Scholars Press, 1977), pp. 35-51 (35-36).

In *Canons and Choices: The Song of Songs and Adrienne Rich's Twenty-One Love Poems as Sources of Theology*, I dealt with these questions.[7] In outlining four models of reading as a feminist theologian, I attempted to chart feminist efforts to open up the theological canon. By presenting visible moments of choice, by exposing the often implicit criteria that dominate what and how to read, I aimed to facilitate discussions about the value of biblical and other texts as sources of theology. The experimental fourth model aimed at showing that feminist critiques of androcentric canons need not lead to the formation of new, founded by feminists but equally exclusive, canons. However, by clarifying the ways in which each form of feminist reading nevertheless depends on the formation of a female canon, I highlighted the issue of canonicity as a hermeneutic issue.

I tried out the models in intertextual readings of the SoS and Adrienne Rich's *Twenty-One Love Poems*. Some results regarding the interpretation of the SoS and the ways it can be valued as theologically relevant will be presented here. As the evaluation of the SoS as a source of theology depends on what counts or should count as theology, I start with the question of how to read as a feminist and a theologian.

Reading as a Theologian (M/F)

Looking for possibilities for reading as a theologian, one has to confront the question of what counts as theology. Within academic theology answers to this question can be derived from numerous statements about what is *not* theological. Only debates in which academic theology itself is in a defensive position offer more direct definitions. For that reason I made a case study of the actual debate on the scientific status of the discipline in Dutch State Universities. Definitions of theology resulting from this debate are: theology as 'science of God' and theology as 'science of "God"'. Both definitions have their own internal problems. In defining theology as the 'science of God', the status of claims for truth is problematic. In defining theology as the 'science of "God"', the science of God as brought to speech by people, one avoids this problem by turning theology from metaphysics into a cultural science. However, the problem of the confinement of the object of theology remains, not only because the

---

7. J. Bekkenkamp, *Canon en Keuze: Het bijbelse Hooglied en de Twenty-One Love Poems van Adrienne Rich als bronnen van theologie* (Kampen: Kok Agora, 1993). This [Dutch] book is the published version of my PhD dissertation, supervised by Professor Dr Mieke Bal and Professor J. Th. Witvliet.

word 'God' occurs in the most diverse contexts and meanings, but
also because experiences or opinions some people express in god-talk
might be articulated in goddess or godless talk as well. This problem
is recognized and taken into account. However, studies of goddess- or
godless-talk, just like studies of non-Christian god-talk, become
labelled as thealogy, a/theology or religious studies, not as theology.[8]
This points to the limits of etymological definitions of theology: such
definitions do not explain actual exclusions, the exclusive focus on
male, institutional Christianity.

The fact that close readings of the SoS—a text in which God does
not occur—are easily accepted as theological, whereas similar readings
of canonical scriptures of non-Christian groups, religious or secular,
are likely to be disregarded as such unless conventional theological
themes are highlighted, can only be explained by approaching theology as a discourse, as a practice of reading and writing, organized and
controlled by procedures of exclusion, internal rules and procedures
of selection.[9] In establishing the internal and external reference sys-
tems of a discourse, canons play an important role. Within theological
discourse, especially within Protestant variations of this discourse, the
texts collected in the Bible form the central canon.

Canons stabilize the value of the texts they contain. The stabiliza-
tion of the value of biblical texts has its repercussions on practices of
reading. Let me illustrate this point by a simple scheme, Figure A
below. It depicts the relation between the value, meaning and function of a text.

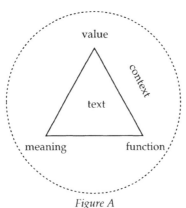

Figure A

8.   The distinction between theology and religious studies is confusing because
it is based on two interacting differences: differences in object (official Christianity
versus all other official or unofficial religions), and differences in method.

9.   Cf. Michel Foucault, *L'ordre du discours* (Paris: Editions Gallimard, 1971).

The meaning of a text is context-bound: new contexts, new meanings. Hence new contexts provoke a change either in the function or in the value of a given text. The function of a theology source-text can be described as giving shape, value and direction to human existence. If one does not change this function—for example by using biblical texts as fodder for a collective psychoanalysis—one has to re-evaluate and reshape the biblical canon as the central theological canon with the passage of time. Refusing to do so causes shifts in the interpretation of biblical texts that go beyond what Umberto Eco called the limits of interpretation. In that respect, the history of SoS interpretation is revealing. In the course of history the most divergent meanings have been given to this text—from stories of an unequal covenant between a loving God and an adulterous nation, to a defence of the so-called sexual revolution.

Feminist theologians who claim for women (and other 'others') the right not only to read given canonical texts from a feminist perspective, but also to select alternative texts and traditions as sources of theology, have to challenge the boundaries of theological discourse. The discourse character of theology makes it difficult to reconsider the value of biblical texts and to consider the value of other texts on criteria other than criteria of tradition. Let us listen to Annette Kolodny: '... we read well, and with pleasure, what we already know how to read; and what we know how to read is to a large extent dependent upon what we have already read'.[10] However, the discourse character of theology also opens up the possibility of applying the insights of feminist theory on reading, to reading and writing as a theologian.

In *On Deconstruction* Jonathan Culler discerns three moments or modes of feminist criticism. In the first mode of feminist criticism, women's experience is treated as a firm ground for interpretation. In the second, the complexity of this appeal to experience is accounted for. The third mode of feminist criticism focuses on the method of criticism, its procedures, presuppositions and goals, and how these secure male authority.[11] By analogy to these moments or modes of 'reading as a woman', it is possible to discern a similar development within feminist readings 'as a theologian': a first moment, in which

10. Annette Kolodny, 'Dancing Through the Minefield: Some Observations on the Theory, Practice and Politics of a Feminist Literary Criticism', in Elaine Showalter (ed.), *The New Feminist Criticism: Essays on Women, Literature and Theory* (London: Virago, 1985), pp. 144-67 (154).
11. Jonathan Culler, *On Deconstruction: Theory and Criticism after Structuralism* (London: Melbourne & Henley, 1983), pp. 43-64.

theological identity is not or hardly questioned; a second moment, in which notions about what one wants animate critical practice; and a third moment, in which the framework of choice, theological concepts and categories and the connections between them, is questioned. The third moments/modes of criticism are of interest with regard to issues such as the need to label readings as theological or feminist. The discussion does not yield alternative models of reading, but criticizes current criticism. Combining the first and second moments of reading as a theologian and as a woman creates four options for relating simultaneously to feminist and theological discourse.

Rosemary Radford Ruether, in *Womanguides: Readings toward a Feminist Theology*,[12] Judith Plaskow in *Sex, Sin and Grace: Woman's Experience and the Theology of Reinhold Nieubuhr and Paul Tillich*,[13] and Carol Christ in *Diving Deep and Surfacing: Women Writers on Spiritual Quest*,[14] in a way realized three of these options. I have used these books for delineating basic models of selecting texts and reading them. Radford Ruether tries to settle the conflict between feminist and theological discourse (model 1), while Plaskow questions what it means to read as a woman (model 2), just as Christ questions what it means to read as a theologian (model 3). In the absence of feminist theological readings in which *both* readerly identities (feminist and theologian) are put into play, I have designed a fourth model. The design of this model (model 4) is inspired by David Hockney's philosophy of photography.[15] The theological valuation of the SoS differs from model to model.

Criteria for Qualifying Texts

Explicating current and possible criteria within the differing models clarifies the differences between them, while at the same time refining them. About text criteria in general it should be noted that a text, any text, can be evaluated on different levels. According to the different relations in which a text can be viewed, it is possible to discern six types of criteria:

12. Rosemary Radford Ruether, *Womanguides: Readings Toward a Feminist Theology* (Boston: Beacon Press, 1985).

13. Judith Plaskow, *Sex, Sin and Grace: Woman's Experiernce and the Theology of Reinhold Niebuhr and Paul Tillich* (Lanham, MD: University Press of America, 1980).

14. Carol Christ, *Diving Deep and Surfacing: Women Writers on Spiritual Quest* (Boston: Beacon Press, 1986).

15. Paul Joyce, *Hockney on Photography: Conversations with Paul Joyce* (London: Jonathan Cape, 1988).

- reality-related criteria;
- criteria of emotivity, relating a text to its effects on the reader;
- criteria of opinion, relating the text to the established opinions of the reader;
- text-inherent criteria, depending on the internal relations between text-components;
- criteria of tradition, relating a text to a tradition of texts;
- author-related criteria.

In my opinion this classification of criteria, borrowed (and slightly modified) from Jan van Luxemburg, Mieke Bal and Willem Weststeijn in their (Dutch) *Introduction to Literary Studies*, is helpful in discussing the (theological) value of texts, if only because it prevents the playing off of aesthetic criteria against moral ones. One can appreciate the composition, the rhythm and the alliterations of a given text, while at the same time taking a stand against its sexism, racism or whatever else is against one's established opinions. Differentiating levels of evaluation invites us to reflect on our judgements: why is it that I put a text aside, or on the contrary, recommend it to others? Besides, this differentiation helps to disentangle the complex concept of a 'woman's text'. On every level of text-evaluation it is possible to discern female or feminist factors: the reality represented might be a reality especially women have to deal with. For example, a text containing a rape scene might have specific effects on female readers; or a text can be explicitly feminist; or the I-figure may be a woman; or a text might fit in within a tradition of women's literature and may have been written by a female author. We identify a text as a 'woman's text', then, when the F factor is dominant.[16]

Returning to the models of reading as a theologian: common to all four models is the consideration of theology's claim to fulfil a function. The functional component of theology may be stressed by defining theology as a 'hermeneutics of existence by means of the Christian tradition'; or by radically redefining theology as a discipline of questioning. In either case, this functional approach facilitates the development of criteria for qualifying texts as theologically (ir)relevant. The valuation of a literary work, as the valuation of whatsoever, depends on the *function* we assign to it. Different functions result in

16. Brenner and van Dijk-Hemmes introduce the concepts of F-texts and voices, in which F stands for female/feminine. They define these concepts on the level of the text itself (*On Gendering Texts*, p. 7). However, in actual usage, the concept 'F text' shares the complexity of the concept of 'woman's text'.

other criteria, or in another hierarchy of the applied criteria.[17] The function theology claims to fulfil—giving shape, value and direction to 'our' existence—calls forth specific criteria. The demand to shape our experiences establishes reality-related criteria. The demand to value our existence establishes criteria of emotivity. The demand to give direction to life's flow establishes criteria of opinion. Worked out in different ways, in all models of reading as a feminist theologian these types of criteria are highlighted. However, despite the apparent appeal on the function theology claims to fulfil, in the first three models criteria of tradition and author-related criteria restrict choices.

Before I turn to an elaboration of these models, and the way the SoS might come into the picture in each of them, two final remarks about criteria for qualifying texts. The first is about criteria of emotivity, expressing the effect of a given text on a given reader. Following the authors of the *Introduction*, I allowed those criteria a separate status, but it is important to note that the effect of a text on a reader can only be explained in terms of criteria of other types. In order to communicate a choice, such criteria must be explained. Just saying that a text is 'shocking' or, on the contrary, 'touching', is using the valuation of a text as a way of escaping from reading it. My second remark is about the playing off of valuation against reading. Notwithstanding what I just said about the [mis]use of criteria of emotivity, and all that could be said about a similar singling out of criteria of other types, an articulation of criteria on all levels of a text stimulates close readings while, at the same time, structuring them. Explicating criteria for selecting texts is at the same time explicating a way of reading, insofar as the motifs for selecting a text are the same as the motifs that guide the selection of text-elements within a given text. Moreover, the motivation which underlies the process of reading lends the selected texts their functionality.

The Daughters of Jerusalem

How to read the SoS as a feminist theologian? Should a feminist read the SoS as a theologian, projecting onto it the expectation that it might shape, value and give direction to the flow of (women's) life? Within the first model of reading as a feminist theologian, the second question is hardly a question. As the Model 1 reader neither questions her identity as a theologian, nor her identity as a woman, she has to inte-

17. Jan van Luxemburg, Mieke Bal and Willem Weststeijn, *Inleiding in de literatuurwetenschap* (Muiderberg: Coutinho, 1982), p. 82.

grate feminist and theological discourses. Given the dominance of theological discourse, she will be tempted to integrate feminist discourse into theological discourse rather than the other way around. The SoS, as a biblical text normative within theological discourse, looks like a feminist text *avant la lettre*, and in her efforts to transform theological discourse she can use it as a 'canon within the canon'. This option is visualized in the model below (f = function, m = meaning, v = value, as in Figure A above)

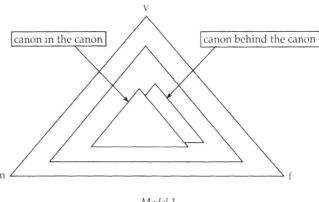

Model 1

This is a model of growth: through the selection of texts, a new canon arises as a transformation and transgression of the old canon. First, the old canon is opened up by discerning a 'canon within the canon'. Secondly, a search is launched by looking behind the canon for texts excluded in the process of its formation. Finally new texts, in which inspiring biblical core themes are actualized in non-patriarchal settings, are proposed for inclusion.

Possible criteria for text selection within this model are:

1. Enriching Christian tradition (criterion of tradition).
2. Feminist (criterion of opinion).
3. Consciousness raising (criterion of emotivity).
4. Offering knowledge of the past (reality-related criterion).
5. Relation to the intentions of Bible authors (author-related criterion).
6. Composing a whole (text-inherent criterion).

What might a reading of the SoS, guided by these criteria, look like? As a Model 1 reader, I would look back at the history of interpretation and lay bare the prejudices that guided it.[18] I might glean from the

18. In *Canon and Choices* (in Dutch, *Canon en keuze*, pp. 120-29) I showed evi-

text a refreshing view of the social reality of Hebrew women in the
time of its origin. To facilitate the inclusion of my favourite feminist
modern poetry in the theological canon I would, as most critics do,
present my personal version of feminist interpretation on the SoS as
the intention of its author(s), and the modern poetry of my choice as
an actualization of this intention. I would, again as most critics do,
delineate text-structures that underscore my interpretation.[19] Most of
all, I would stress the role of the daughters of Jerusalem. As I will
argue below, it is their 'hearing to speak' function which renders the
SoS its gynocentric character, and it is this gynocentricity, together
with the eroticism of the SoS, that might enrich or even reorient
Christian tradition.

Especially since the publication of Phyllis Trible's *God and the Rhetoric
of Sexuality*, many authors have stressed the non-sexist character of
the SoS. Marcia Falk, for instance, speaks of 'a thoroughly non-sexist
view of heterosexual love'.[20] If we define sexism as the making of
differences, based on sex, in which the one sex (normally the female)
is regarded as inferior with regard to the other sex (normally the
male), then indeed the SoS is not sexist. Compared to the other

dence of role conflicts in male readings of the gynocentric SoS, as an indirect way
of illustrating the conflicts a female reader faces when reading androcentric texts.

19.   Delineating textual structures is a matter of interpretation, not a procedure
that precedes interpretive strategies. In my interpretations of the SoS I take over
elements of the differing visions of Francis Landy, Marcia Falk and Phyllis Trible
on the SoS (lack of) unity and structure. I subscribe to Landy's description of the
unity of the text—thematic coherence, erotic mode, the reappearance of the same
elements in diverse contexts (Landy, *Paradoxes of Paradise: Identity and Difference in
the Song of Songs* [Sheffield: Almond Press, 1983], p. 56)—but as a description of the
unity of the *text*, not as a signal of an original unity or unity of authorship. I share
with Falk the consideration of the likely possibility that the SoS was originally oral
literature, that is, orally composed and transmitted (Falk, *Love Lyrics from the
Hebrew Bible: A Translation and Literary Study of the Song of Songs* [Sheffield: Almond
Press, 1982], p. 65). However, where Falk views the SoS as a skilful edited collection of 31 short poems, I work with the hypothesis that the skilful compilation of
what indeed might have been several separately circulating songs, is the result of
an ongoing oral tradition. Only this hypothesis can explain the musical, audible,
unity of the SoS. From Trible I take over her consideration of the repeated inure-
ment of the female 'I' figure in the address of the daughters of Jerusalem as the
refrain and, as such, as the most important structuring element (Trible, *God and the
Rhetoric of Sexuality* [Philadelphia: Fortress Press, 1978], p. 146). When listening to a
song, it is the refrain that keeps playing in the head of the audience, and if we
assume that the SoS is the product of an oral tradition, the structure that presents
itself at first hearing is of utmost importance.

20.   Falk, *Love Lyrics from the Hebrew Bible*, p. 86.

biblical texts, the absence of sexism in the SoS is significant. But if we read the SoS independently of other biblical texts, granting it a theological status of its own, the characterization of 'non-sexist' loses its sense. It then becomes more meaningful to speak about a female-oriented view of heterosexual love.[21]

The SoS text is female-oriented in the sense that the female I-figure sings her love for the one she loves in and for herself, in the presence of the daughters of Jerusalem, sometimes explicitly addressing them. Contra Falk, I would argue that these daughters, and not the male lover, are the overall implied audience of the SoS.[22] In the dream-sequence of SoS 5.2-8 she tells *them*, and not the one she loves, the story of her dream. In this dream-story she records the voice of her lover, as Falk rightly states, as a monologue within a monologue:

Song of Songs 5.2-3:

אני ישנה ולבי ער קול דודי דופק פתחי לי אחתי רעיתי יונתי תמתי שראשי נמלא
טל קוצותי רסיסי לילה:
פשטתי את כתנתי איככה אלבשנה רחצתי את רגלי איככה אטנפם:
דודי שלח ידו מן החר ומעי המו עליו:
קמתי אני לפתח לדודי ודי נטפו מור ואצבעתי מור עבר על כפות המנעול:
ודודי חמק עבר נפשי יצאה בדברו בקשתיהו ולא מצאתיהו קראתיו ולא ענני:
פתחתי אני לדודי
מצאני השמרים הסבבים בעיר הכוני פצעוני נשאו את רדידי מעלי שמרי החמות:
השבעתי אתכם בנות ירושלם אם תמצאו את דודי מה תגידו לו שחולת אהבה אני:

(I slept, but my heart was awake. Listen! my beloved is knocking. 'Open to me, my sister, my love, my dove, my perfect one; for my head is wet with dew, my locks with the drops of the night' I had put off my garment, how could I put it on? I had bathed my feet, how could I soil them? [NRSV].)

The woman tells other women about her dream, in which she hears her lover. This structure appears throughout the SoS: in addition to speaking more than anyone else, the woman's words frame her lover's

21. Reading the SoS as a text that primarily defines its own contexts of significance prevents the female element's dominance throughout the text from being perceived as the attribute of the SoS, a shortcoming noticeable elsewhere in the Bible too. This tendency even appears in feminist interpretations. Trible writes (*God and the Rhetoric of Sexuality*, p. 145): 'By this structural emphasis her equality and mutuality with the man is illuminated'.

22. Falk (*Love Lyrics from the Hebrew Bible*, p. 73) explains her use of the term 'implicit audience' as follows: 'Even when the beloved is not directly addressed, however, we might say that s/he remains the *implicit* audience because s/he is the real focus of a speaker's feelings'. By addressing the focus of a speaker's *feelings*, rather than the focus of her/his *words*, she notes her unorthodox use of the term.

statements. Her lover is not the implicit audience in the dream.
Instead he is the object, as subjectivized in v. 2 (and 3?). The woman
dreams of him and about him. He appears in her dream: she hears his
knock on the door, his voice, she feels his hand pushing through the
[key]hole (v. 4). Even in her dream, he is more absent than present:
she calls him, but he does not answer, she searches for him in vain
(v. 6). She and these daughters refer to her lover exclusively in the
third person. Anybody who reads the SoS as a male–female dialogue
or as the expression of an I–Thou relationship (as Falk does) overlooks
the remarkable fact that, both in this dream scene and throughout the
SoS, the woman speaks more *about her lover* than *to him*.[23] The
woman tends to be more 'I' than 'thou' and more 'thou' than 'she'.
Conversely, the man is more 'he' than 'thou' and more 'thou' than 'I'.
He generally speaks to the woman directly.[24] These direct forms of
address may be viewed as taking place within her memory or
imagination.[25]

In her dream the woman hears the man telling her: 'Open to me'
(פתחי לי...). These words are not an official invitation, as Falk asserts
on the basis of tradition, but a request for admittance. Reading v. 3
makes the request even more enticing:

פשטתי את־כתנתי איככה אלבשנה רחצתי את־רגלי איככה אטנפם

(I had put off my garment; how could I put it on again? I had bathed my
feet; how could I soil them?' [NRSV].)

The absence of any indication of a change in speakers and the impli-
cation of the male sex by the word 'feet' suggest that the man is
responsible for this verse.[26]

---

23. The song in which she sings about his handsomeness is, unlike the passages in which he extols her beauty, in indirect speech. The few sentences where
she addresses him directly may be understood as secret desires (1.4, 7; 7.11; 8.1)
and as affection expressed in thoughts (1.2, 16; 8.14). These forms of address occur
only at the beginning and the end of the SoS.

24. Only three times throughout the SoS does the man refer to the woman in
the third person (2.2; 4.12; 6.9). To whom might the man be speaking about his
loved one? Unlike the female figure, the male figure does not have an explicit
audience in the SoS. 4.12 and 6.9 should probably be interpreted as theme indica-
tors. I will consider 4.12 as the motto of the sequence 4.12-15 in my reading of this
pericope, within Model 3. Like in the dream sequence beginning in 5.2, 2.2 contains
a monologue within a monologue.

25. Cf. Chaim Rabin, 'The Song of Songs and Tamil Poetry', in *Studies in
Religion* (1973), pp. 205-19 (219): 'A case could be made out of the theory that
everything the lover says is imagined by her, even if this is not expressly stated'.

26. Cf. Exod. 4.25; Isa. 6.2; 7.20; 36.12 and Ruth 3.4, 8. This reference comes

In the many verses written in the I-persona, the woman expresses her self-awareness and formulates her feelings about her lover. She describes the impact of her love on her experiences with the outside world. She consistently indicates her desires and longings. She repeatedly implores the daughters of Jerusalem not to arouse love until she considers the time right. Trible interprets this refrain as an appeal to the daughters of Jerusalem 'to let love happen according to its own rhythm'.[27] Falk offers an interpretation of the oath that differs from the standard versions:

> Literally, the last two lines of the oath are, 'Do not waken, do not arouse love until it desires, OR is satisfied' ... But why, in the context of these poems, should a female speaker warn the city women not to arouse their own, or their lovers', passion? ... I read this line to mean, 'Do not waken, do not rouse us (the lovers) until we are satisfied'; that is 'Do not rouse us from our lovemaking until we are ready to be disturbed.' Hence my translation' 'Not to wake or rouse us/ Till we fulfill our love.'[28]

Both Trible and Falk view the SoS as a romantic, erotic song of praise for heterosexual love focusing on unification, sexual unity and a man–woman intimacy that will eventually exclude the daughters of Jerusalem. In that context, the woman's effort to restrain the daughters of Jerusalem from stirring up her own love or that of her lover's appears strange. The verse closing the book (8.14),

ברח דודי ודמה־לך לצבי או לעפר האילים על הרי בשמים

is decidedly disconcerting. Falk's interpretation tones down the closing verse ('it is actually a veiled invitation to return later') and corrects the oath's translation; Trible adjusts the translation of the closing verse ('make haste, my lover') and submits a neutralizing interpretation of the entreaties. When we dismiss all the prejudicial approaches to the love poems since the rise of the romantic love ideal, an entirely different interpretation of these sections is made possible. The key to such an interpretation lies in the dream sequence cited above. If we read SoS 5.8 as 'I adjure you, O daughters of Jerusalem, if you find my beloved, tell him this: I am faint with love', it is not a variation on the incantation of 2.7 and 3.5 but, rather, her explana-

---

from Mimi Deckers-Dijs, *Begeerte in bijbels liefdespoëzie: Een semiotische analyse van het Hooglied* (Kampen: Kok, 1991), p. 208. These cases do not generally use 'feet' as euphemisms for 'sex organs', but refer specifically to the male genitals.

27. Trible, *God and the Rhetoric of Sexuality*, p. 146.
28. Falk, *Love Lyrics from the Hebrew Bible*, p. 116.

tion.[29] The situation is essentially the same.[30] I propose an interpretation in which the entreaty not to arouse love concerns the love of the
daughters very little or not at all. Rather, her own love is involved.
The presence of the daughters stimulates the woman to express her
desire. The daughters satisfy a 'hearing to speech' function for the
woman.[31] They create an opportunity to compose poetry, to dream
and to complete dreams through poetry. The language that is sought
and found expresses emotions of infatuation as independent feelings.
Such language does not trivialize eroticism. Instead, trivial aspects of
daily life acquire erotic connotations. The woman uses this language
to project her desire; to raise the erotic tension until she can stand it
no longer: 'Sustain me with raisins, refresh me with apples; for I am
faint with love' (2.5). This takes us back to the entreaties. At points
where the woman reaches her personal limits—entreaties continually
follow the passages eulogizing togetherness—she beseeches the
daughters who have heard her speech to let her love be for the
moment.

In 8.4, the entreaty is formulated as a question: 'I adjure you, O
daughters of Jerusalem, what will you stir up and awaken (מהתעירו
ומהתעוררו) love until it is ready'. Here, the daughters have driven the
woman beyond her limits, either deliberately or by accident. To
understand what happened, let us return to SoS 5.2-8. After she has
finished recounting her dream, the woman places her fate in the
hands of the daughters by imploring 'I adjure you, O daughters of
Jerusalem, if you find my beloved, tell him this: I am faint with love'.
They provoke her by asking how her lover is better than other lovers.
This question is inviting rather than sceptical and achieves the desired
effect. The woman crosses the line. The daughters use the woman's
question to help her cling to her dream—from which she had awakened
by the intrusion of a different, cruel reality. She describes her lover in
a torrent of images (5.10-16). Again, the daughters help her onward
(6.1-3):

> Where has your beloved gone, O fairest among women?
> Which way has your beloved turned, that we may seek him with you?
> My beloved has gone down to his garden, to the beds of spices,
> to pasture his flock in the gardens, and to gather lilies.
> I am my beloved's and my beloved is mine;
> he pastures his flock among the lilies.

---

29. Trible, *God and the Rhetoric of Sexuality*, p. 148.
30. Cf. SoS 2.5.
31. Nelle Morton, *The Journey is Home* (Boston: Beacon Press, 1985), pp. 202-209.

Falk interprets the answer in vv. 2 and 3 as an exclusion of the daughters: '...the woman reaffirms the I–Thou relationship and excludes her explicit audience, the city-women, from participation in it'. She likens the daughters of Jerusalem to the guards, as both are outsiders hostile to the lovers: 'Like the city guards, the city women seem to be a foil against which the intimate world-of-two emerges as an ideal'.[32] Perhaps it is not the text from the SoS that excludes the daughters of Jerusalem but, rather, the ideal of an 'intimate world-of-two'?

Analysis of the language of the speech acts suggests that the SoS text is not an 'I–Thou' monologue or a 'he–she' dialogue. The text reads like the erotic dream of a female I-persona, a dream she elaborates while talking with the daughters of Jerusalem. I attribute the text's theological significance to this dream; or, rather, to the power the woman derives from this dream: a concept of eroticism that assigns value and a sense of purpose to life. The SoS erotic language mobilizes the senses and mobilizes the woman. Upon sensing the strength the woman derives from desire, the daughters use the woman's question about the lover to encourage her not to exhaust her erotic energies by becoming ill from love, but to use them to stretch her limits. This desire is hers, that energy is hers. It could be used in a hundred ways, and going to search for her lover could be one of them.[33] Like a fleeting object of desire, her lover drives her to unknown heights.[34]

Within us and against us, against us and within us
Model 1 enables the reader to bridge the gap between church-and-theology on the one hand, and women's movement and feminism on

---

32. *Love Lyrics from the Hebrew Bible*, pp. 78, 91. Falk is not alone in her negative assessment of the daughters. SoS 1.5-6 is generally believed to substantiate this assessment. Falk characterizes the daughters as a 'hostile audience'. I believe the woman feels so safe with the daughters (who address her in 6.1 and possibly also in 1.8 as היפה בנשים, 'the most beautiful of women') that she has the courage to question her own body and ideal of beauty.

33. Loosely based on the poem 'Reforming the Chrystal', in Adrienne Rich, *Poems: Selected and New 1950–1974* (New York: W.W. Norton, 1975), p. 227.

34. In SoS 6.12 the word 'soul' appears for the seventh and last time:

לא ידעתי נפשי שמתני מרכבות עמי־נדיב

Falk considers this verse so incomprehensible that she has omitted it from her translation. While the meaning is unclear, the woman obviously no longer remembers (לא ידעתי). Her soul takes her to the unknown, to a place she can only describe, so to speak.

the other. However, in connecting biblical tradition to the feminist movement, the reader is in danger of producing readings that are both manipulative and wishful. In the second model, in combining the first mode of reading as a theologian with the second form of reading as a woman, the reader purposefully creates a tension between theological and feminist discourse.

As in the first reading model, in Model 2 theology is perceived as the hermeneutics of human existence, with the help of a specific religious tradition (in this case, Christianity). Unlike in model 1, this tradition is viewed here (Model 2) not as an unfulfilled past but as a dominant present. The tradition that appears as a living memory is confronted with women's experiences, and vice versa.

This second option for reading as a woman and as a theologian is visualized in the figure below. The small triangle on the right represents the biblical canon, and the larger triangles represent actual manifestations of Christian tradition. The triangle on the left presents a motivated selection of women's literature.

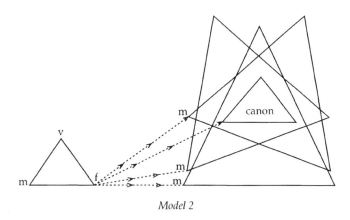

Model 2

This second model is a model of confrontation. The canon is opened up from an outside position that is not assumed to be the same for all women. From a point of view created through reading women's literature, the reader verifies whether canonical theological texts fit their function in a specific context. The criteria for text selection have to be described in two interdependent sequences. Criteria for guiding the selection of texts from the biblical and theological canons might be:

1. The text is authorized within Christian tradition (criterion of tradition).
2. It evokes ambivalent emotions (criterion of emotivity).
3. It is written by a prominent author (author-related criterion).

4. It illuminates, possibly in spite of the author, situations regarded as relevant (criterion of opinion).
5. It offers typical representations of reality (reality-related criterion).
6. The structure of the text is androcentric[35] (text-inherent criterion).

Possible criteria for the selection of texts from which to deduce a hypothetical woman-reader are:

1. Telling truths about women's experience (reality-related criterion).
2. An authentic female author (author-related criterion).
3. Evoking discontinuous reading experiences (criterion of emotivity).
4. Providing a feminist perspective on canonical texts (criterion of tradition).
5. Contributing to the development of feminist theory (criterion of opinion).
6. Being gynocentric (text-inherent criterion).[36]

In my reading of the SoS, which is motivated by the above mentioned criteria, I focus on the by far most cited verse of the song, SoS 8.6:

שִׂימֵנִי כַחוֹתָם עַל־לִבֶּךָ כַּחוֹתָם עַל זְרוֹעֶךָ
כִּי עַזָּה כַמָּוֶת אַהֲבָה קָשָׁה כִשְׁאוֹל קִנְאָה
רְשָׁפֶיהָ רִשְׁפֵּי אֵשׁ שַׁלְהֶבֶתְיָה

(Set me as a seal upon your heart, as a seal upon your arm; for love is strong as death, passion fierce as the grave. Its flashes are flashes of fire, a raging flame [NRSV].)

As a woman, I find this verse a source of ambivalence. While attributing such massive significance to love is beautiful, who will absorb this weight? The emerging relationships—which appeal to the biblical authority—between Eros and Agape, between love and death, between uniqueness and possession, determine the relevance of rereading from a feminist perspective in the second reading model.

As this model concerns the current text, I will cover both the text and its method of reflection in authoritative commentaries. I will focus on *Paradoxes of Paradise*, Francis Landy's literary theological commentary. In considering the SoS and Landy's reading of it from a woman's perspective, I will not use my own intuition as in the first

35. Androcentric in the sense described by Culler, *On Deconstruction*, p. 166. The androcentric texts are chosen to indicate the internal divisions within these texts.

36. Gynocentric texts in this context are not androcentric texts in which the sex roles have been reversed but texts in which sex plays a different, non-exclusionary role. However, both androcentricity and gynocentricity refer to primary subject-positions in a text.

model. Instead, I will use Adrienne Rich's *Twenty-One Love Poems*.[37] I will use these poems to learn to read as a woman. Like Plaskow, who has used Lessing's series of novels *Children of Violence* to elaborate a sex-specific perspective of 'sin and grace', I search for a feminine perspective of love in *Twenty-One Love Poems*.

While reviewing her work, Rich notes that her former inner conflict between womanly, maternal, altruistic love and egotism was a false dilemma: 'We know now that the alternatives are false ones—that the word "love" is itself in need of re-vision'.[38] She supplies a re-vision in *Twenty-One Love Poems*. The word 'love' occurs sporadically in this cycle: six times it appears as a verb (in poems II, V and VIII and three times in poem XVII); once in 'lovers' ('we were two lovers of one gender', poem XII); once in 'love-making' (The Floating Poem), and only once as a noun (Poem XVII). All in all, 'love' occurs nine times in the cycle, including four times in the seventeenth poem, which is explicitly polemical and provocative.

> No one's fated or doomed to love anyone.
> The accidents happen, we're not heroines,
> they happen in our lives like car crashes,
> books that change us, neighborhoods
> we move into and come to love.
> *Tristan und Isolde* is scarcely the story,
> women at least should know the difference
> between love and death. No poison cup,
> no penance. Merely a notion that the tape-recorder
> should have caught some ghost of us: that tape-recorder
> not merely played but should have listened to us,
> and could instruct those after us:
> this we were, this is how we tried to love,
> and these are the forces they had ranged against us,
> and these are the forces we had ranged within us,
> within us and against us, against us and within us.

'Tristan and Isolde is scarcely the story,/ women at least should know the difference/ between love and death'. Does that mean that the very least women should know about love diametrically opposes the ultimate authority of the SoS? Landy's reading strongly suggests such a situation. Before elaborating on Rich's view of love and its con-

---

37. Adrienne Rich, *Twenty-One Love Poems* (California: Effie's Press, 1976). This poetry cycle appears in Adrienne Rich, *The Dream of a Common Language: Poems 1974–1977* (New York: W.W. Norton, 1978). Permission sought.

38. Adrienne Rich, 'When We Dead Awaken: Writing as Re-Vision', in *idem*, *On Lies, Secrets, and Silence: Selected Prose 1966–1978* (New York: W.W. Norton, 1978), p. 47.

trast with Landy's interpretation of SoS 8.6-7, I will briefly present Landy's perspective, and wherever possible in his own words.

Landy considers SoS 8.6-7 the climax and the credo of the whole SoS. The preceding verses condense different motives from chs. 2 and 3. The climax of vv. 6 and 7a might, however, transcend the world of the lovers. As Landy rightly notes, these verses lack any corollary elsewhere in the poem:

> Scarcely one word of this passage occurs elsewhere in the Song; the new forces—death, Sheol, fire, God—give the Song a different dimension. This is compounded by the dropping of conventions—for the first time the Song seems to speak through its own voice and not through its personae. This is its message to the world, affirmed directly, and not through riddles, the enigmatic jigsaw of the Song. As Rosenzweig... says, for the first time the 'I' falls silent. Yet the apparently clear statement is full of difficulties.[39]

Landy identifies problems concerning verbal and contextual ambiguities. When the woman speaks, he questions the objectivity of the assertion that love is as powerful as death.[40] He considers the significance of the imperative שִׂימֵנִי, 'set me', as ambiguous, along the lines of the ambiguous connotation of חוֹתָם, 'seal'. In his opinion, the imperative שִׂימֵנִי is both demanding and insecure: as a seal, she longs to be his instrument. Landy feels here the pain of autonomy, the desire for unity, and its insurmountability. Similarly, the tone appears uncertain to him. The woman's lover must cherish his memory of her: underlying the insistence is anxiety that he will forget her. Yet the image apparently suggests the opposite: indissolubility, fusion. A seal is a sign of identity, according to Landy. She is thus impressed on his heart, that is, his feelings and thoughts, as his identity; she governs his relations with the world. Landy mentions a third meaning of the word 'seal', namely the seal as a sign of completeness, of a covenant between the lovers. The Lover's seal (*sic*) binds their relationship.[41]

According to Landy, the repetition in 8.6 emphasizes the urgency of the request and is, at the same time, a wilful anticlimax, bathos that in fact distracts attention from the vital centre.[42] He regards the imperative שִׂימֵנִי (which forms the sentence's main clause) as an introduction to the subordinate credo 'love is...' The ambiguous conjunction כִּי

39. Landy, *Paradoxes of Paradise*, p. 121.

40. 'It is the Beloved speaking; the grand statement is in her mouth. To what extent then is it objective, and not an expression of her personal experience?', Landy, *Paradoxes of Paradise*, p. 121.

41. Landy, *Paradoxes of Paradise*, p. 122.

42. Landy, *Paradoxes of Paradise*, p. 123.

('for/that'), which can be relative as well as explanatory, links the credo with the introduction. Thus, the credo's verbal contents may be both (1) the text of the seal's inscription and (2) the explanation of the imperative. Landy considers the second option the most likely.[43] This view raises the question about the logical connection between the credo and the woman's plea to set her as a seal on the man's heart. I will return to this point shortly.

Landy summarizes the credo in the sentence, God is love:

> The conclusion that God is Love supposes a duality—that all the nega-
> tive forces, Death, Sheol, and Chaos, are excluded. But it is a provisional
> and ambiguous duality, for the opposites are interdependent, creativity
> implies destruction. Love seeks to integrate Death, as Death swallows
> life.[44]

Landy's view of love, based on SoS 8.6-7, extends beyond juxtapos-ing love against death to a comparison of the two states. Love and Death are represented as resembling enemies. Both are creative and destructive. They resemble each other, moreover, in that both offer fusion, final integration. For the ego, then, they are equally threaten-ing: 'Love threatens dissolution in the other—who represents all others—Death is the dissolution of consciousness'.[45]

The preceding paragraphs represent Landy's views. The differences between the experiences submitted by Landy for understanding SoS 8.6 as a climax, and the experiences that Rich conceptualizes in the *Twenty-One Love Poems*, are striking. With one citation from Poem XVII—'women at least should know the difference/between love and death'—a confrontation has begun. I shall now execute this con-frontation.

Landy considers the difference between love and death as relative. They are adversaries. In the sense that love threatens the ego, how-ever, it resembles death. The *Twenty-One Love Poems* lack any trace of this death quality in love. Any instances of death or dying are con-trasted with living: death as a natural boundary of life, as a threat to life, and as a symbol of a life without passion or a life that has lost its lustre. As an experience, love is not described as a subconscious state but as a heightened state of awareness.[46] Insight into the limits intensifies love. Instead of creating a fear of death, love leads to a

43. Landy, *Paradoxes of Paradise*, p. 124.
44. Landy, *Paradoxes of Paradise*, p. 132.
45. Landy, *Paradoxes of Paradise*, p. 123.
46. See for example the third poem. Rich, *The Dream of a Common Language*, p. 26.

modified view of living and dying. Death is not the ultimate enemy to be slain. Instead, it is an obstacle that people can help one another overcome.

Rich's cycle does not relate a desire to overcome or to exclude death, which is the longing that Landy considers fulfilled in the credo of the SoS.[47] He explains the fear of love, presumed by readers, as a fear to be dissolved in the other who represents all others. The fear of the other, and his or her difference, embodies a fear of change (a threat to the ego). In Landy's story of reading, the lovers therefore do not emerge changed. Instead, they are renewed (self-renewal) and reborn by their relationship of love. I consider this difference the most significant distinction between the experience that Landy submits for understanding SoS 8.6 and a reading based on *Twenty-One Love Poems* from a woman's perspective. The mythical image evoked by Landy's SoS interpretation of love (and death) as instinctive forces is diametrically opposed to the opening line of Poem XVII, cited above: 'No one is fated or doomed to love anyone'. As I have already noted, 'love' primarily figures in the cycle as a verb, thus substantiating the view of love as a process. In 'Women and Honor: Some Notes on Lying', Rich offers the following definition of love: 'An honorable human relationship—that is, one in which two people have the right to use the word "love"—is a process, delicate, violent, often terrifying to both persons involved, a process of refining the truths they can tell each other'.[48] In the constant quest to expand the possibilities of truth and the possibilities of life between one another, changes may seem frightening but certainly not destructive. The word 'change', which figures prominently both in Rich's poetry and in her interpretation of poetry, appears only in the seventeenth poem in *Twenty-One Love Poems* ('books that change us'). It is one of the verbs ('happen', 'change', 'move', 'come') that change the concept of a fatal love into an understanding of love as a bold venture: 'this is how we tried to love'. The

47. In Landy's story of reading, love (as in the experience of sexual unification) does not exclusively resemble death and is not merely as powerful as death: love is *more* powerful than death. The transition from 'as powerful as death' to 'more powerful than death' seems to be based on the substitution of the mother as an 'archetype of love' (*Paradoxes of Paradise*, pp. 65-66) by God (the Father, p. 127). He uses his faith in a paternal God symbolic of love to overcome the aspects of motherly love that he considers negative and frightening. Surprisingly, Landy—notwithstanding his appreciation of the ambivalent qualities in the words of SoS 8.6—unilaterally uses the female suffix designation *-āh* as an abbreviation for the name of God.

48. In Rich, *On Lies, Secrets and Silences*, p. 188.

'forces' in the concluding line are not the primal forces of love and death but include the ideology that love, suffering and death are a series of related concepts. Reading from a woman's perspective, we are warned to notice if love, as in Landy's interpretation of the SoS, appears as a universal, instinctive force in the battlefield of Love and Death, of Sheol and Chaos, which is controlled by God.

The fact that the woman speaks in SoS 8.6 is less likely to lead those readers educated to read as a woman by the *Twenty-One Love Poems* to question the validity of these great words; rather, it would cause them to ponder who will bear the burden of such love. My question targets the connection between the imperative 'set me as a seal' and the statement that love has the same power as death. The conflicting duality within Landy's interpretation is significant. The experience underlying the so-called credo appears to be the fear of losing the self in love. Conversely, Landy interprets the imperative as a sign of insecurity, pain of autonomy and desire for unity. The logical connection between the ultimate truth of the 'credo' and 'the Beloved's plea'—as formulated by Landy—is missing. Landy suggests that we should seek the logical connection in the threat of estrangement that adds a note of urgency to the woman's request. Still, some questions remain unanswered. Why would the woman wish to be placed on his heart like a seal if she feared estrangement? This explanation is illogical from the subject's perspective (i.e. the woman). Landy's perception of the credo's truth—love as the only resource against destruction—thereby ceases to hold true for the woman. Rather than protect her from estrangement, such an act might alienate her from herself. The imperative is not a plea but a proposition: take love, take me into your heart so that you will find strength against death. The price of the credo's transcendental truth is the forfeiture of feminine subjectivity. Reading Landy's interpretation as a woman, this verse is a tragic nadir in the song rather than a climax. The song's theological value as a whole is thus very open to challenge.

Can we justify the theological value of a song that culminates in a verse like SoS 8.6? The model 2 reader has three options for answering this question: she can dismiss 8.6 as an editorial addition, she can read the verse as a parody, or she can offer an explanation for the text's ambiguities that is unilaterally positive (for women).[49] Trying to

---

49. In *Canon en keuze* I extend my analysis beyond 8.6 to Landy's interpretation of SoS 8.5-14. My argument, on the basis of 8.6, applies in a comparable manner to all verses following 8.4.

provide a positive explanation for the text's ambiguities resembles an interpretation that follows Model 1. The difference, which relates to the questioning of what reading as a woman means, is the proposal that reading is relativized according to a specific context. Other interpretations are not ignored or dismissed but regarded as possible readings and evaluated on the basis of their harmful effects on women.

Can we interpret 8.6 not only as not harmful but, perhaps, also even as an inspiration to women? I consider such an interpretation impossible. Unequivocally viewing the 'seal' as a symbol of identity is the only possible positive perspective. Anchoring my interpretation as a woman once again in Rich, I conclude that such a view is not a viable alternative but a confused image of love as false power: 'Powerless, women have been seduced into confusing love with false power—the "power" of mother-love, the "power" of gentle influence, the 'power' of nonviolence, the "power" of the meek who are to inherit the earth'.[50]

Dismissing the verse as a subsequent addition seems to be a more obvious approach. The text contains strong arguments for substantiating this option. As Landy notes, vv. 6 and 7 lack any corollary elsewhere in the SoS. Landy hears in these words an ultimate truth that transcends the world of the lovers, but they could have reflected a male editor's perspective as well. The SoS seems to come to a natural end in 8.4—in a final repetition of the incantation, here transformed from reluctant to expectant. Repeating assorted elements of the SoS in 8.5 could be the editor's deliberate strategy for imposing his own postscript on the SoS as a whole.

Interpreting the text as a parody might reflect the *illogical* relationship between 'set me as a seal on your heart, as a seal on your arm' and the statement 'for love...' The headstrong anticlimax 'as a seal on your arm' may be regarded as an act of withdrawal; the anagrammatic link between the 'seal' on his arm and his mother's labour pains (in the immediately preceding verse, 8.5) as ridiculing the male quest for a second, subordinate—and therefore no longer threatening—mother. Such an interpretation allows readers to appreciate these verses as an ideological critique and thus indirectly relevant to theological concerns. Model 2, by virtue of its relative outsider position, prevents readers from articulating any positive theological value in the SoS.

50.   Rich, *On Lies, Secrets and Silences*, p. 254.

A Locked Wave

Model 2 enables the reader to see her own reading in perspective. Other readings are taken into account as possible readings, and scrutinized for their potentially damaging effects on a female reader. The Model 2 reader justifies her selection of women's literature not only on the basis of her womanhood but also on the basis of the womanhood she longs to achieve. However, she does *not* apply the women's literature that appeals to her as the primary text. In the third reading model, this is the next step taken. In this model, the role of women's literature shifts: from a script for reading canonic sources of theology to a new, authentic and autonomous source of theology.

Let me now present this third option for reading, Model 3. As can be seen from the figure below, a new canon is proposed. Such a canon, containing the holy texts of the women's movement, would fulfil the same function for women as the Koran for Moslems, the Bible for Christians and Homer for the ancient Greeks.

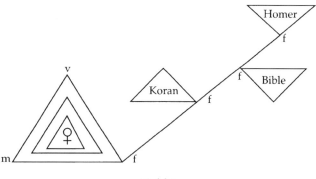

Model 3

The concept of religion, and hence the definition of theology, is radically functionalized here. Regardless of any given content, religion is understood as a function open to differing fulfilments. This functional approach implies a focusing on literature (or any other matter) that actually fulfils a religious function for a group, in this case, women. What women have in common is seen as more important than how they differ. Theology (thealogy) becomes a hermeneutics of existence by means of a tradition of women's culture, yet to be reconstructed. Tradition is regarded as gerundial, as what (as yet) has to be transmitted. Here the criteria for text selection might be described as:

1. Written by a woman writer, expressing an authentic female religious outlook (author-oriented criterion).
2. Gynocentric and coherent (text-inherent criterion).
3. Constitutive of a tradition of women's culture (criterion of tradition).
4. Transformative (emotivity criterion).
5. Stripping away the facade of conventional reality (reality-related criterion).
6. Realistic–imaginative (criterion of opinion).[51]

For the Model 3 reader to read or not to read the SoS is an open question. Priority will be given to modern literature that directly appeals to a feminist reader.[52] However, the Song might be read as a text recounting how women in another time and place attempted to love. The Song might be constitutive of a tradition of women's culture, and hence of theological value.[53]

Read from the presuppositions of patriarchal culture, the images of the SoS poem seem stereotypical; but what if we read it from a tradition of women's culture? What would such a reading of, for instance, 4.12–5.1 reveal?

גן נעול אחותי כלה גל נעול מעין חתום
שלחיך פרדס רמונים עם פרי מגדים כפרים עם־נרדים
נרד וכרכם קנה וקנמון עם כל־עצי לבונה מר ואהלות עם כל־ראשי בשמים
מעין גנים באר מים חיים ונזלים מן־לבנון
עורי צפון ובואי תימן הפיחי גני יזלו בשמיו
יבא דודי לגנו ויאכל פרי מגדיו:
באתי לגני אחתי כלה אריתי מורי עם־בשמי אכלתי יערי עם־דבשי שתיתי ייני עם־חלבי
אכלו רעים שתו ושכרו דודים

(A garden locked is my sister, my bride, a garden locked, a fountain sealed.
Your channel is an orchard of pomegranates with all choicest fruits, henna with nard,

51. Christ, 'Feminist Studies in Religion and Literature', p. 39.
52. In *Canon en Keuze* I paid a lot of attention here to the poetry of Adrienne Rich, because, as Margaret Atwood writes on the back cover of *The Dream of a Common Language*: 'Rich's poems do not demand the willing suspension of disbelief. They demand belief, and it is a measure of her success as a poet that most of the time they get it.'
53. The possibility of proving that the SoS is a product of women's culture is questionable, as well as the affinity of the song's text to such culture. As I have argued elsewhere (Bekkenkamp, *Want ziek van liefde ben ik*; 'Het Hooglied: Een vrouwenlied in een mannentraditie'; and Bekkenkamp and van Dijk-Hemmes, 'The Canon of the Old Testament and Women's Cultural Tradition'), however, it is plausible to work with the hypothesis (or fiction) of a female author.

nard and saffron, calamus and cinnamon, with all trees of frankincense, myrrh and aloes, with all chief spices—
a garden fountain, a well of living water, and flowing streams from Lebanon.
Awake, O north wind, and come, O south wind! Blow upon my garden that its fragrance may be wafted abroad. Let my beloved come to his garden, and eat its choicest fruits.
I come to my garden, my sister, my bride; I gather my myrrh with my spice, I eat my honeycomb with my honey, I drink my wine with my milk. Eat, friends, drink, and be drunk with love [NRSV].)

Interpreting this poem according to model 1, I would primarily try to identify a feminist text here. I would emphasize 4.16a, indicating that the repeated male I-persona in 5.1 is more conspicuous in the translations than in the Hebrew. On the transition from 'my garden' to 'his garden' , I would suggest that *her* garden is *his* garden only as long as she loves him. Reading this poem as prescribed by Model 2, I would highlight rather than erase the tension between feminist and patriarchal text elements. In a patriarchal culture, comparing a woman with a locked garden (domesticated nature) is loaded with connotations. The same applies to the transition from 'my garden' to 'his garden'. Landy's reading here illustrates this point: 'It is not clear that the garden is any less hers for being his... Moreover, the garden may always have been "his"; it was for his sake that the fruit ripened and the spices grew redolent'.[54] But what if we expect here neither to find a feminist text nor a text provocative for feminists?

Model 3 nurtures the reader's feminism with contemporary texts enabling her to reread an old text as the Song of Songs. For example, Rich's self-confidence in recapturing women's traditional images of nature in the *Twenty-One Love Poems* averts initial impediments to my understanding of 4.12–5.1. Using her poetry as a hermeneutic key, it is possible to trace in the SoS poem a displacement of connotations, a relation between sexuality and spirituality and a language of the female body.

Let me begin with the poetic strategy of the transformation: comparing the woman to a locked garden might symbolize a quotation from the patriarchal culture that appears with modified significance in the SoS. The word 'garden', גן, occurs 32 times in biblical scriptures, including 21 times in the Garden of Eden, or of the Lord, and eight times as the 'royal' garden (among others as Naboth's vineyard that Ahab wishes to use as a royal garden). In this context, the word's primary associations are property and wealth. If we perceive the

54. Landy, *Paradoxes of Paradise*, p. 106.

analogy of a woman as a locked garden as a quotation from the patri-archal culture, the garden's locked condition reinforces the association with private property: the woman is the man's private property, 'for his sake' the fruit ripens in her garden amid fragrant delicacies. A formal argument for interpreting v. 12a as a quotation is that in the preceding and subsequent sections of the text an unspecified audience replaces the woman as the party directly addressed. This interruption may be caused by the women who personify an ideal male lover and are serenading a cherished woman friend while inserting a statement from a normal man to his friends in the song of praise. Including the quotation in its own context changes the meaning.

In Hebrew the words גַּן ('garden') and גַּל ('wave') differ by one letter only. Nevertheless, imagining a locked garden is as easy as imagining a locked wave is difficult. A wave is an overpowering force of nature. The word מַעְיָן, which I translate as 'well', means: water spurting out of the ground or the place where this process occurs. The patriarchal representation of sexuality as a dangerous male passion aroused and embodied by women (who should therefore remain locked behind the doors of their keepers) appears transformed into a depiction of sexuality as the female body's life-giving expression. A locked wave and a closed fountain convey a social reality and its untenability. The untenability harbours a promise that is fulfilled in v. 13:

שְׁלָחַיִךְ פַּרְדֵּס רִמּוֹנִים עִם פְּרִי מְגָדִים כְּפָרִים עִם־נְרָדִים

The word שְׁלָחַיִךְ is derived from the root שׁלח, meaning 'let go', 'extend', 'send'. The seal seems to burst off like the skin of a ripe pomegranate, the bolt is released from inside.[55] In addition to land-scapes, bodies of water are traditionally associated with women. Here, where the image of the locked garden has been transformed, these images reinforce one another. Gardens generally need to be watered by their owner or their owner's servants. In Deut. 11.10 the promised land, flowing with milk and honey, a land of mountains and valleys that drink water from the rain from heaven, is compared with Egypt, a vegetable patch (גַּן הַיָּרָק) in need of irrigation. The garden's dependence on someone to sprinkle the ground figures, in its role as a metaphor, in Isaiah and Jeremiah.[56] Attributing the qual-ities of both a garden and a well to the woman makes her the subject of her own sexuality (the garden). Moreover, she can partake in her

55. Cf. SoS 5.5-6, where the woman opens the bolt/lock of her door for her lover.

56. Aside from SoS 4.16; 5.1 and probably 6.2, the 'garden' as a metaphor appears only in Isa. 58.11 and Jer. 31.12.

sexual identity, like a fountain of the gardens (plural) and a well of
living waters. The water images, 'a locked wave, a closed well', modify the connotation of 'garden' as property while reinforcing the connotation of 'garden' as wealth. Verses 13 and 14 elaborate on the garden's wealth by listing its opulence. Rather than serve as a complete
metaphor, the image is disruptive.[57] The garden is particularized by a
coordinated arrangement of trees and plants, fruits and delicacies. Its
erotic attraction is not a single tree from which only the owner may
pluck fruit. Rather, all its elements allow the garden to stretch beyond
its borders. The garden's abundance, symbolized by its members
united through the non-hierarchical conjunction ו ('and') and the four
occurrences of the word עם ('alongside, with'), is a source of intense
delight in 5.1:

אריתי מורי עם בשמי
אכלתי יערי עם דבשי
שתיתי ייני עם חלבי

(I gather[ed] my myrrh with my spice, I eat [ate] my honeycomb with
my honey, I drink [drank] my wine with my milk.)

Understanding 5.1 as an extension of the above interpretation suggests not 'a song of greedy exploitation, of masculine triumph,
expressive of satiety'[58] but, rather, the male persona's extreme pleasure in the aura exuded (4.10-14) by the woman. The situation does
not involve a unifying sexuality. Instead, it pursues an interactive
eroticism. I agree with Falk that the concluding line,

אכלו רעים שתו ושכרו דודים

('Eat, O friends, and drink: drink deeply, O lovers', NRSV; or, alternatively, 'Eat, friends, drink, and become inebriated with affection'),
addresses both lovers. Not because 'to read the line as an invitation to
other friends by one of the lovers violates grotesquely the metaphor of
the garden as an enclosed and private world-of-two',[59] but because
the woman in the SoS is addressed as רעיתי ('my woman friend'); and
because, although only she is compared with a garden, she too experiences the man's love as eating and drinking and becoming inebriated with affection.[60] I also question whether the invitation to eat and
drink is primarily and exclusively directed at both lovers. The view of

57. Contra Falk, *Love Lyrics from the Bible*, p. 122. Only in v. 16 does the garden
figure as a metaphor.
58. Landy, *Paradoxes of Paradise*, p. 108.
59. Falk, *Love Lyrics from the Bible*, p. 123.
60. 1.2; 2.3; 3.6; 5.2, 13, 16.

ideal love may be less exclusive in the SoS than in the Western perspective.[61] Picturing the garden as an 'enclosed and private world-of-two' conflicts with vv. 15 and 16. The wind blows where it pleases, scents waft in all directions, currents are difficult to block.

Addressing the woman as רעיתי evokes the image of an erotic self-expression that extends further than a woman's relationship with her lover and runs deeper than passionate infatuation. The female persona's erotic energy appears inextricably linked with her zest for life. Any relationship between sexuality and spirituality in this text remains a source of speculation at this time. Parallels with Hebrew literature contained in the Hebrew Bible appear sporadically. Parts of the Bible, such as Prov. 7.17-18 and Ps. 80.13, shed light on the erotic–sexual significance of words like 'myrrh', 'aloe', and 'cinnamon', as well as 'plucking' and 'drinking', which we have already noticed in SoS 4.12–5.1. Because those excerpts appear in a context in which female sexuality is criminalized or not considered in its own right, the erotic–spiritual significance remains hidden. The context for understanding the spiritual dimension of the SoS has yet to be created in a continuing construction or reconstruction of a female lyrical tradition.

To (re)construct a tradition of women's literature is to write a story of experience to which the woman reader of canonical texts can refer. In that sense, Model 1 and Model 2 depend on Model 3. Model 3 enables the reader to move *towards* a new canon rather than reacting *against* an established one. The reader-as-a-theologian thus gives up her (un)easy position of a critical outsider. However, in questioning her identity as a theologian, the reader tends to seek anchorage in determining her own and other women's sexual identity. As Carol Christ notes, looking back on her writing of *Diving Deep and Surfacing*, 'we wrote as if women's experiences were undifferentiated and universal'.[62]

Leaping upon the Mountains

The fourth reading model seeks to revitalize the endeavours of a female canon in danger of becoming mired in egocentrism and ethnocentrism. The Model 4 reader explores the possibility of questioning her identity both as a theologian and as a woman. The stories of reading thus far, when read as an unfolding continuous story, show an initial movement out of established theological discourse that is frustrated by the determination of female identity. In Model 4 the

61. Cf. 1.2.
62. Christ, *Diving Deep and Surfacing* (2nd edn), p. xii.

reader tries to keep moving. In order to configure Model 4, one could suggest a serial image of the previous figures (Models 1–3). The new canon proposed, in Model 3, comes under criticism. The claim that these new texts can shape, value and direct all women's experiences is rejected (Model 2). This might provoke a shifting and expansion of the new canon (Model 1), or lead to new canon formations (Model 3) which are also criticized, and so on. One problem with visualizing this model as a series of successive models is that it remains a mono-perspective. The images proceed one after the other as if in a motion picture, thus creating an illusion of movement. The individual images have nevertheless been captured, as conventional photographs, from a stationary point. Accordingly, the representation cannot do justice to the reader's movements, which are both circular and linear. Whereas these movements succeed one another not only chronologi-cally but also as memories, they are nearly simultaneous. The photo collages by the British visual artist David Hockney depict the fourth reading model perfectly. Inspired by cubism, in these 'joiners' he attempts to overcome the restrictions of 'one-point perspective' in order to come closer to the way we actually look at things. It is not that we do not see everything in focus. We do, but not with one eye and not in one viewing. In looking, movement and memory play an important part. Hockney criticizes photographic 'realism' for reduc-ing the role of the viewer to a theoretical point. To illustrate the rever-sal of perspective at which Hockney aims, I reproduce 'Place Fursten-berg', one of Hockney's large composite photographs.

The theory underlying Model 4 is generated by the application of Hockney's theory to reading. In this model the reader is not located in the centre of an interpretative community but she moves, drawing her own circle, in several circles. She reads books circulating in those cir-cles as the holy Scripture. These books effect change in her, or leave her untouched. She is a woman, looking for the woman she wants to be. She is a theologian, formed by but not tied to theological discourse. Theology as a hermeneutics of existence gives up its compliance with a specific religious tradition. The obligatory relativization of the reader's 'own' tradition makes room for a search for new, more com-plex truths. On the one hand, this model is disruptive: it dissolves the boundaries of interpretative communities. On the other hand, by its openness the model sustains a promise of a more universal, pluralistic canon.

In the proposed Model 4 criteria for selection, tradition- and author-related criteria do not restrict choices but explicate ranges of account-ability. Furthermore, criteria generated by the functions theology

David Hockney, 'Place Furstenburg, Paris, August 7, 8, 9, 1985' Photographic Collage 43^{1}/$_{2}$ × 61^{3}/$_{8}$" © David Hockney

claims to fulfil assume a prominent position. Thus, in this model the criteria for choosing texts could be:

1. Appealing to the senses (criterion of emotivity);
2. naming the unnameable, the other reality and the reality of the other (reality-related criterion);
3. helpful in answering the questions, *With whom do you believe your lot is cast?/ From where does your strength come?*[63] (criterion of opinion);
4. clear and expressive of a moving consciousness (text-inherent criterion);
5. written as re-vision[64] (criterion of tradition);
6. written by an author the reader has chosen to trust (author-related criterion).

A model 4 reading of the SoS is an experiment in discarding single-point perspectives. The question is, how to prevent differentiations of the reader from becoming abstract extrapolations generated by and belonging to classified readers. Regardless of but not in a manner unrelated to my being a woman theologian, I ask myself: What touched and changed me in reading the SoS? What consequences might the acknowledgment of this text as a source of theology have for the development of theological discourse?

Let me name just one insight developed: this song is not 'about' eroticism and sensuality; it *is* erotic and sensual. It enables the reader 'to *see* more, to *hear* more, to *feel* more'.[65] The first four verses in the Song of Songs already appeal to four senses: hearing in the 'song of songs', touch in the 'pull me', smell in 'oils' and taste in 'kisses':

> The Song of Songs, which is Solomon's. Let him kiss me with the kisses of his mouth! For your love is better than wine, your anointing oils are fragrant, your name is perfume poured out; therefore the maidens love you. Draw me after you, let us make haste. The king has brought me into his chambers. We will exult and rejoice in you; we will extol your love more than wine; rightly do they love you (1.1-4).

שחורה אני ונאוה in v. 5 immediately challenges us to look more carefully than usual. I interpret the words 'black and beautiful' in this line as a coordinated arrangement rather than as an opposition. The woman does not deflect attention from her black appearance. Rather, she lures us into noticing hues—the tents of Kedar, the garments of Solomon—and then redirects our glance toward the cultural connotation of 'black'. I perceive 'black' here as an erotic allusion to her love life and an invitation to take another look, this time with a view to

63. See n. 1 above.
64. Rich, 'When We Dead Awaken', pp. 33-49.
65. Susan Sontag, *Against Interpretation* (London: André Deutsch, 1987), p. 14.

catching her eye. In the first four verses, the constant alternation between direct and indirect speech and the switching between subject and object create a movement that can be sensed but not observed. The female persona talks about and with the girls, about and with the male persona and from within and to herself. Sometimes she speaks in the first person plural to involve the man or the girls or the reader (the listener). While the linguistic context never seems this way, it *is*. Like in Hockney's image of memory, the immediate past remains present.

While the images and transitions in SoS 1.1-6 may be explained as movements in time, spatial motions figure elsewhere in the SoS. Rejecting the idea that descriptions are given from a single viewpoint leads to the explanation of some SoS settings and shifts, commonly regarded as impossible or abrupt, and to a new interpretation of 2.8-9.

קול דודי הנה־זה בא מדלג על־ההרים מקפץ על־הגבעות

דומה דודי לצבי או לעפר האילים

הנה זה עומד אחר כתלנו משגיח מן החלנות מציץ מן החרכים

(behold, there he stands behind our wall of boulders, staring through the windows, blushing through the foliage—trans. for v. 9b by author).

All the commentators I consulted regard the image of the beloved as leaping upon the mountains, bounding over the hills, as a case of poetic licence. But if one takes into account that both lovers are in the countryside, and that the description is given from the moving perspective of the female I-figure who is working in the vineyard, the image is not so much an expression of poetic license as of realism. This reading conflicts with conventional translations of v. 9, as it is for instance presented in the Revised Standard Version:

> Behold, there he stands behind our wall, gazing in at the windows, looking through the lattice.

This translation suggests that the woman is sitting at home. However, I would argue, this translation is biased.[66]

---

66. The word כתל* is a hapax legomenon. Koehler and Baumgartner trace the word from *katallu* in Akkadian, meaning 'wall (of a house)'. I suspect that from here חלונות ('windows') relates back to the wall of a house. While חלון ('window') is a standard Hebrew word, the preposition מן ('from') is unique in association with משגיח. Moreover, the plural 'windows' is strange with respect to looking inside a house. Elsewhere, in the descriptions of Abimelech (Gen. 26.8), the mother of Sisera (Judg. 5.28), Michal (1 Sam. 19.12 and 1 Chron. 15.29) and Jezebel (2 Kgs 9.30), looking through their windows to see inside or outside, respectively, we find the expression בעד החלון and the verb השקיף ('look downward'). Admittedly, my

The Hebrew text recalls the image of a flirtation between a woman guarding the vineyards and a shepherd passing with his flock. Both are outside and in motion. As she occasionally glances up from her work, the woman sees her lover in a different place each time. I imagine that whenever he approaches, she gets the other women working with her in the vineyard to attract his attention. As Trible noted, work and play intermingle in the SoS. I believe that locating the woman in the vineyard, for instance, eliminates the justification for the general consensus of attributing 2.15 to a third speaker. Rather, the female persona, to whom I attribute this verse, interrupts her lover and responds to his challenge with a provocative burst of energy.

For the Model 4 reader, the theological value of the SoS lies in its eroticism, explained as an effect of the 'cubistic' quality of this text. As a theological source, the SoS might serve more than overcoming a vanishing sexual taboo, more than a broader vision of sexuality. The moving consciousness of its I-persona might provoke a disruption of the logocentrism of theological discourse. This discourse may induce sensitivity to visual and tangible qualities and to smelling and tasting the unknown. It may provoke a theology aimed not at finding universal truths, but at connecting 'common, acute particularity'.[67]

The logocentrist perspective depends on a vast but also fictitious point: 'if you try to walk up that point you'd never get there, it's like the end of the rainbow!'[68] Reversing this old 'one point perspective' has major theological consequences:

> In the old perspective you are totally rigid. The furthest point from you is theoretically infinity, which means that if the infinite is God, it's always a long way away. You never get there. One hundred per cent of

---

translation of 'foliage' for חרכים is speculative. This word appears nowhere else in the Hebrew Bible, except for the root חרך in Prov. 12.27. Martin Buber translates the verb in Proverbs as 'disturb', but the noun in the SoS as *Gitter* ('lattice'). Koehler and Baumgartner report the meaning as unknown in Proverbs but suggest *Gitterfenster* ('lattice window' in the SoS, which they mysteriously trace to a root meaning *wackeln, beweglich sein* ('shaky, being movable'). Supposing this last meaning of 'being movable' is accurate, would it account for both Buber's Proverbs translation and my translation of the SoS passage? Unlike bars or a lattice (in front of a window), the leaves (of a vine?) are generally in motion. My suggestion that the hapax כתלנו refers to a wall of boulders also explains the plural of חלונות ('windows'): the woman's lover stares through the holes in the wall, he 'blushes' through the foliage (or, through the openings).

67. Rich, *The Dream of a Common Language*, p. 8
68. Joyce, *Hockney on Photography*, p. 101.

our images in the world are like that. When you reverse the perspective, that point is movement, you're moving. Infinity then is everywhere, including in you, which is far more interesting theologically, isn't it? God is then within us, and actually we are a part of God.[69]

To Conclude

I shall leave it at that. The scope of this article precludes a more detailed discussion of the individual models, and a more comprehensive reading of the SoS. I have nearly eliminated here readings from *Twenty-One Love Poems*. As a result, my explanation of the extent to which my readings of the SoS result from intertextual readings of this song with modern literature may leave something to be desired. I have been unable to cover the remarkable resemblance between Rich's poetry and Hockney's philosophy of photography more thoroughly: Rich is 'dreaming the film-maker's dream but differently'.[70] So be it. Hopefully, I have demonstrated that notwithstanding the nature of theology's discourse, shifting from identity-as-fate towards identity-as-force-for-change, so remarkably present in Rich's poetry, is helpful in resisting the apparent splitting of theology from women. It brings us 'into another scene of choices', concretized in four options for reading as a feminist theologian.

The suggested reading options appear to increase in complexity as my story of reading unfolds. The order in which I have presented the options seems to suggest a hierarchy, from the worst to the best option. This, however, is *not* my intention. The usefulness of each option, or model, depends on the contexts of reading. The first model fits feminist vicars; the second and third will suit university teachers who either want to integrate women's religious studies into theological curricula, or claim an autonomous status for such studies. The fourth model is meant for dialogic situations among equals. The opening up of established canons, and the formation of alternative ones, can contribute fruitfully to creating situations in which open dialogues can take place.

69. Joyce, *Hockney on Photography*, p. 109.
70. Adrienne Rich, *The Will to Change: Poems 1968–1970* (New York: W.W. Norton, 1971), p. 49.

'MY VINEYARD, MY VERY OWN, IS FOR MYSELF'

Daphna V. Arbel

Introduction

Lack of consistency and uniformity are one of the most prominent features of the SoS, as many scholars have noticed. It contains diverse love poems, different in length, literary form and content. The plots of these poems are unclear. They make references to various locations, presented from different perspectives and voices. These features of the SoS have long puzzled scholars. They posed various questions regarding the identity of the writers, the nature of this text and its levels of meaning.[1]

In this paper I wish to suggest that such varying characteristics of the SoS are not an obstacle for understanding this work but a guide to its interpretation. One way to approach the multi-level complexity of this work is to read the whole text as a woman's inner and personal discourse.[2] In the discussion to follow I suggest a possible inter-

---

1.   See discussion and bibliography in M.H. Pope, *Song of Songs: A New Translation with Introduction and Commentary* (AB; New York: Doubleday, 1978), pp. 40-48; R.E. Murphy, *The Song of Songs: A Commentary on the Book of Canticles or The Song of Songs* (Minneapolis: Fortress Press, 1990), pp. 3-105. For a treatment of the religious dimension of the Song, its unity and its archetypal images see F. Landy, *Paradoxes of Paradise: Identity and Difference in the Song of Songs* (Sheffield: Almond Press, 1983). For a study of the poetic technique of the SoS see R. Alter, 'The Garden of Metaphors', in *The Art of Biblical Poetry* (New York: Basic Books, 1985), pp. 185-203. For a literary study of the SoS see M. Falk, *Love Lyrics from the Hebrew Bible: A Translation and Literary Study of the Song of Songs* (Sheffield: Almond Press, 1982). For treatments of various aspects of the SoS from a feminist perspective see articles and bibliography in A. Brenner (ed.), *A Feminist Companion to the Song of Songs* (Sheffield: JSOT Press, 1993). For an intertexual reading of the SoS see A. LaCocque, *Romance She Wrote: Hermenueutical Essay on the Song of Songs* (Harrisbury, PA: Trinity Press International, 1998).

2.   On female authorship of the SoS see discussion in LaCocque, *Romance*, pp. 39-53. For a detailed distribution of female and male voices in the Song in A. Brenner, 'Women Poets and Authors', in Brenner (ed.), *Song of Songs*, pp. 87-91.

pretation of the SoS as the poetic expression of the inner dreams, emotions and thoughts of one individual woman. All these are presented in a variety of voices, and acted out in a range of settings and in parallel sequences.

The woman in the Song of Song appears to describe a process in which she reflects upon her feelings of love and attraction towards her lover. In her imagination she observes herself in possible encounters with him. In these encounters she takes on different roles, both masculine and feminine. She places herself in various locations, pictures herself in manifold situations, and predicts social and cultural reactions to her acts. To present these aspects, the writer seems to select several poetic voices and to develop various parallel situations. The writer, on the one hand, appears to have no intention of organizing all images into a unified portrayal of characters. She makes no effort to develop all occurrences into a linear and sequential plot. On the other hand, she does not present these varied depictions as isolated units. The writer seems to control the various descriptions of her fantasies, to stand behind them, and to weave them together. By so doing the Song becomes a unified composition of self expression.

Nature of the Account

Although the actual identity of the poet remains concealed, scholars have convincingly argued that a female authorship of the SoS is conceivable.[3] The woman speaker tells the story and recounts its events through her eyes.[4] Evidence derived from several words and phrases suggests that the writer does not intend to describe events that occurred in reality. She does not, as well, tell dreams that she has experienced. Instead, she appears to describe her fantasies and give expression to a series of mental images and occurrences constructed in her imagination.[5]

Two specific situations demonstrate the nature of the account in the SoS. Before the writer details a specific episode in which she is

3. Cf. LaCoque, *Romance* and Brenner, 'Women Poets'.
4. F. van Dijk-Hemmes, 'The Imagination of Power', in Brenner (ed.), *Song of Songs*, p. 162.
5. Chaim Rabin suggests seeing the entire Song of Songs as a woman's fantasy: 'The Song of Songs and Tamil Love Poetry', *Studies in Religion* 3 (1973), pp. 205-19. Cf. H. Fisch's treatment of the dream passages discussed below: *Poetry with a Purpose: Biblical Poetics and Interpretation* (Bloomington: Indiana University Press, 1988), p. 89. It seems to me, however, that the imaginary quality colors the whole SoS.

searching for her beloved, she states: 'Upon my bed at night I sought him ... ' (3.1).[6] This description presents her solitary search in the empty streets of the city at night. Such a search by night is highly unrealistic, considering the accepted norms of the writer's patriarchal society.[7] Thus her introduction, 'upon my bed at night', is necessary. It characterizes this experience as a mental search in which she is not passive, as in a dream, but active, as in a personal process of imagination. In a similar fashion she states: 'I slept but my heart was awake' (5.2). She gives the impression of a particular state of mind in which her heart, or inner feelings and thoughts, were active.

Two leading interpretations of these verses suggest that such descriptions relate to either dreams or realistic situations.[8] It seems, however, that a different view is possible. The writer is not simply the receiver of dreams which she reports later. Nor is she simply a recorder of real events. Instead she is an active author, describing her own experiences that are constructed on an inner level. She turns her gaze inward and allows herself the freedom of self expression. She recounts primarily the imaginary structures of her heart. In addition to her references to 'her heart' in 5.2, she repeats the term 'soul' (נפש) several times (1.7; 3.1-4; 5.6).[9] She thus makes references to an inner realm of emotions, feelings and thoughts. She also recognizes the power of her imagination which directs, and perhaps dictates, developments and descriptions at certain times: 'Before I was aware, my fancy set me ... ' (6.12).

It is in the realm of the imagination that the writer presents her descriptions in the SoS. She does so perhaps for the sake of self reflection and, also, for the sake of exploring and expressing various optional patterns of behavior and feelings. She introduces a wide range of thoughts, feelings and dreams concerning the fulfillment of love. Ideal romantic emotions, passionate erotic desires, confusing fears and hesitations, yearning and longing for closeness with the lover are embodied in various parallel images. A sensual erotic woman, a hesitant young girl, a protected virgin, an admired lover, a

---

6.   All quotations are from *The Holy Bible*, New Revised Standard Version.

7.   On the women in patriarchal, biblical society see G. Lerner, *The Creation of Patriarchy* (New York: Oxford University Press, 1986); R. Biale, *Women and the Jewish Law* (New York: Schocken Books, 1984).

8.   For example Murphy, *Song of Songs*, pp. 145, 165; Pope, *Song of Songs*, p. 511; Rabin, 'Tamil Poetry'; Fisch, *Poetry*.

9.   For a discussion of the centrality of the soul in the SoS see D. Deckers, 'The Structure of the Song of Songs and the Centrality of *nepeš*', in Brenner (ed.), *Song of Songs*, pp. 172-96.

seductive dancer are some of these images. It seems that the writer presents the contents of her imagination freely and openly. She takes the liberty of avoiding fixed gender roles and attitudes, allowing for multidimensional female characters to surface.[10] Various roles are acted out in monologues and dialogues. Conflicting images of both males and females are juxtaposed, and a wide array of hypothetical situations are developed in several parallel scenes.

Imaginary Scenes and Leading Roles

I

In her opening lines, the writer immediately expresses her inner thoughts and wishful longing: 'Let him kiss me with the kisses of his mouth' (1.2). She does not, it seems, speak directly to her lover. Instead, she presents an inner monologue in which she describes in words several connected associations. It appears that each thought stems from a previous one in a series of associations. For example: 'Let him kiss me with the kisses of his mouth. For your love is better than wine, your anointing oils are fragrant, your name is perfume poured out, therefore maidens love you' (1.2-3). It seems that one stream of thought strings together three items: terms of love, liquid and scent. Thus she moves from 'kisses' and 'love' to 'wine', to 'anointing oil' that is 'fragrant' and 'perfume poured'. She concludes again with the theme of love.

In this scene the woman proudly declares her physical beauty. With great confidence she states: 'I am black and beautiful, daughters of Jerusalem, like the tents of Kedar' (v. 5). Such a positive declaration does not prevent her from revealing other feelings of hesitation. She allows herself to express self doubts. She is even defensive: 'do not gaze at me because I am dark, because the sun has gazed on me' (v. 6).[11] This attitude, expressed in the opening scene, will color the rest of the text, in which we find free expression of the different inner fantasies and conflicting attitudes of a woman who is observing and analyzing her own feelings of love.

10. On understanding complexities and diversities of gender beyond fixed categories see N. Schoer and E. Weed (eds.), *The Essential Difference* (Bloomington: Indiana University Press, 1994); E. Graham, *Making the Difference: Gender, Priesthood and Theology* (London: Mowbrays, 1995).

11. For a different reading of this verse see Falk, *Love Lyrics from the Hebrew Bible*, p. 110.

II

The first scene is in the countryside, a natural setting. The writer, in the first image of herself, is a shepherdess. She is a sensuous young woman who addresses her beloved directly. She asks: 'Tell me, you whom my soul loves, where you pasture your flock, where you make it lie down at noon?' (v. 7). She is youthful, dynamic, with no hesitations. In this scene her beloved responds warmly. He gives her directions to their meeting place, attesting his admiration of her as well as his deep emotional involvement: 'If you do not know, O fairest among women, follow the tracks of the flock and pasture your kids beside the shepherds' tents' (v. 8). Their mutual love is permitted and joyous: 'My beloved is to me a bag of myrrh that lies between my breasts. My beloved is to me a cluster of henna blossoms in the vineyard of Ein Gedi' (vv. 13-14). Their union with each other and also their union with nature is celebrated: 'Our couch is green. The beams of our house are cedar; our rafters are pine' (v. 17). Metaphors of fertility and fruitfulness are associated with this scene, such as flocks, kids, vineyard, myrrh and henna blossoms.[12]

III

How different is the next scene! 'He brought me to the banqueting house, and his intention towards me was love' (2.4). A new mood and changed images of the lovers and their relations are quite obvious. In contrast to the countryside, they meet in a 'banqueting house'. They did not plan this meeting together. Instead, the woman, led by a man, is brought inside. The presentation of their love is different as well. In contrast to the previous mutual relationship, now only the man's intention is mentioned. For the sake of love he brings his woman lover into the banqueting house. Traditionally this setting would be associated mainly with men and, possibly, with drunkenness and a loose atmosphere.[13] Unlike the first scene, in which the shepherdess is a part of the larger realm of nature, in this scene she is in a place where she does not quite fit. She does not seem to belong to this public male domain.

It seems that the writer deliberately creates this scene in which she plays another role. Yet when she expresses her feelings in these

12. On the metaphorical imagery of the SoS see C. Meyers, 'Gender Imagery in the Song of Songs', in Brenner (ed.), *Song of Songs*, pp. 197-212; Alter, 'Garden of Metaphors'.

13. Compare, for example, Est. 5.18; 7.2, 7-8; Prov. 23.20-21.

circumstances, she does not portray herself as being misled or mis-
treated. She sees herself as an equal participant in the events and
states her fulfillment of passionate love: 'Sustain me with raisins,
refresh me with apples, for I am faint with love' (v. 5). She goes on and
relates her lover's affection for her even in this situation. She focuses
on both the sexual and the emotional aspects of their encounter: 'O
that his left hand were under my head, and that his right hand
embraced me' (v. 6).

IV

In another possible scenario, the woman is the initiator of erotic love.
'Under the apple tree I awakened you' (8.5b), she recounts. She
imagines herself in this wishful situation as bold, passionate and active:
'If I met you outside, I would kiss you and no one would despise me.
I would lead you and bring you into the house of my mother and into
the chamber of the one who bore me. I would give you spiced wine to
drink, the juice of my pomegranates' (8.1-2). She ignores all negative
connotations traditionally attributed to women who initiate sexual
activities.[14] Instead she is open and proud, expressing neither shame
nor secrecy. It is interesting to note that, parallel with the previous
scene, in this occurrence as well the writer emphasizes feelings of
tenderness and caring as part of the lovemaking. She intentionally
repeats the same lines: 'O that his left hand were under my head, and
that his right hand embraced me'.

V

The opposite role is also an option. The woman writer gives expression to her hesitations and doubts. In contrast to her image of a daring
passionate woman, she also casts herself as a more modest and shy
character who is not ready for love. This woman does not open the
door to her beloved when he begs her. In fact she tries to avoid a

14. Compare, for example, Prov. 7.9-12; 8.1-4; Hos. 2.4-12; Ezek. 16.36-37. See
F. Landy, 'The Song of Songs', in R. Alter and F. Kermode (eds.), *The Literary Guide
to the Bible* (Cambridge, MA: Harvard University Press, 1987), pp. 315-18; van Dijk-
Hemmes, 'The Imagination of Power'; T.D. Setel, 'Prophets and Pornography:
Female Sexual Imagery in Hosea', in Brenner (ed.), *Song of Songs*, pp. 143-55. On
the views of the prophets Hosea, Jeremiah and Ezekiel regarding women's sexuality see discussion in R. Weems, *Battered Love: Marriage, Sex, and Violence in the
Hebrew Prophets* (Overtures in Bibilical Theology; Minneapolis: Fortress Press,
1995). Compare, for example, the priestly conception of impurity connected with
the sexual act in Lev. 15.17-18.

direct meeting, giving excuses and explaining: 'I had put off my garment; how could I put it on again? I had bathed my feet; how could I
soil them ?' (5.3-4).[15] In this scene she continues to express her feelings
openly, admitting contradictory emotions. Ready and yearning now
to unite with her beloved she does open the door only to find that he
had already gone: 'I arose to open to my beloved, and my hands
dripped with myrrh, my fingers with liquid myrrh, upon the handles
of the bolt. I opened to my beloved, but my beloved had turned and
was gone' (vv. 5-6).[16]

VI

Other passages present desperate feelings of loss, loneliness and pain.
Describing herself seeking her lover alone, in the empty streets of the
city, in the middle of the night, the writer acknowledges such emotions. Feeling forsaken and not being answered, she describes her
seeking but not finding: 'I sought him, but found him not. I called him
but he gave no answer. I will rise now and go about the city in the
streets and in the squares I will seek him whom my soul loves' (3.1-2).
She imagines fear, contempt, criticism and even violence when she
helplessly roams the streets: 'Making their rounds in the city the sentinels found me; they beat me, they wounded me, they took away my
mantle, those sentinels of the walls' (5.7). The guards' hostile response
to the woman's untraditional behavior is acknowledged and pre-
dicted in the writer's thoughts.[17]

The immediacy and ultimate importance of the meeting is emphasized when the writer appeals to her friends, the daughters of
Jerusalem, to help her in her search: 'I adjure you, O daughters of
Jerusalem, if you find my beloved tell him this: I am faint with love'
(5.8). In a different scene, in a more optimistic fashion, the writer calls
upon cosmic powers such as the winds: 'Awake, O north wind, and
come, O south wind! blow upon my garden that its fragrance may be

15. For a discussion of this scene from a different perspective see I. Pardes, ' "I
am a Wall, and My Breasts like Towers" ': The Song of Songs and the Question of
Canonization', in Pardes, *Countertradition in the Bible: A Feminist Approach*
(Cambridge, MA: Harvard University Press, 1992), pp. 118-43; Falk, *Love Lyrics in
the Hebrew Bible*, pp. 123-24.

16. On the physical and emotional dimensions of this scene see P. Trible,
'Love's Lyrics Redeemed', in Brenner (ed.), *Song of Songs*, pp. 100-20; Falk, *Love
Lyrics in the Hebrew Bible*, p. 124.

17. On the brothers' role and image see Pardes, 'I am a Wall', pp. 140-42;
LaCocque, *Romance*, pp. 53, 180-84. Compare a different use of the brother image
in SoS at 8.1.

wafted abroad. Let my beloved come to his garden, and eat its choicest fruits' (4.16).

VII

In contrast to her helpless or fragile image, the woman appears in other scenes as most powerful, forceful and even dangerous. Using metaphors of architecture, she is compared to two major capital cities: Tirzah, in the northern kingdom and Jerusalem, in Judea. Metaphors rooted in army life and language express these aspects too: 'You are beautiful as Tirzah, my love, comely as Jerusalem, terrible as an army with banners'. Her lover, being overwhelmed by her, tries to avoid a direct encounter: 'turn away your eyes from me, for they overwhelm me' (6.5).[18] The powerful image is also emphasized by associating her with uninhabited remote places and with untamed, majestic wild animals: 'Come with me from Lebanon, my bride; come with me from Lebanon. Depart from the peak of Senir and Hermon, from the dens of lions, from the mountains of leopards' (4.8).[19]

VIII

Once again contrasting images are permitted. In her imagination the writer appears as a young virgin: 'A garden locked is my sister, my bride, a garden locked, a fountain sealed' (4.12). She acknowledges her traditional world, her role within her social group and immediate family, and presents this aspect as well. The writer places her brothers in their patriarchal role as her keepers: 'We have a little sister, and she has no breasts. What shall we do for our sister, on the day when she is spoken for?' (8.8). She also presents them as feeling responsible for her moral behavior and chastity: 'If she is a wall, we will build upon her a battlement of silver; but if she is a door, we will enclose her with boards of cedar' (8.9).[20] The door and the wall must be guarded in the mind of the brothers, who plan to prevent the woman from defying them. The woman defines herself in reaction to them. Confronting their limited and blind views, she declares her maturity and independence. She transforms their images and re-uses them as metaphors to declare her sexuality and power : 'I was a wall, and my breasts were

18. On dangerous and awe-inspiring aspects of feminine beauty see Murphy, *Song of Songs*, p. 177.

19. On the imagery and metaphors see Meyers, 'Gender Imagery', pp. 201-12.

20. For readings of this see Pardes, 'I am a Wall', pp. 139-42; Falk, *Love Lyrics in the Hebrew Bible*, pp. 49, 123; Murphy, *Song of Songs*, pp. 198-99.

like towers'. She then explains her perspective, linking maturity to her peaceful relations with her beloved: 'Then I was in his eyes as one who brings peace' (8.10).

IX

King Solomon's bride is another role which seems to be considered during the imaginary journey. 'Look, it is the litter of Solomon! Around it are sixty mighty men of Israel' (3.7). It appears that royal roles are assigned to the two lovers in this scene. The woman, perhaps, sees her beloved as the most well-known king and herself as his chosen bride. Thus she describes the inside of his palanquin and mentions specific details: 'He made its posts of silver, its back of gold, its seat of purple; its interior was inlaid with love' (v. 10). In addition, it seems that the traditional role of a bride is recognized indirectly by using the term 'bride' (כלה) in several passages (4.8-10, 12) or, possibly, by describing wedding processions or rituals (4.8).[21] It is obvious, however, that such a role is not fully developed, perhaps because it was one most familiar, realistic and well known to the writer, if she was a woman. Thus it was irrelevant to develop a personal fantasy about it.

X

A physical description of the woman's body, as seen from the eyes of her beloved, is presented in a most positive way. Shame, disgrace or concepts of sin are not associated with these descriptions at all. The body is celebrated because of its beauty and grace. Attention is given to the face and to other features of the female body.[22] Lovingly, the male beloved describes his female beloved in praise: 'How beautiful you are, my love, how very beautiful!' (4.1). He continues to outline in vivid metaphors the features of his beloved's body, eyes, hair, teeth, lips, cheeks, neck and breasts, concluding: 'You are altogether beautiful, my love; there is no flaw in you' (4.7). A similar description occurs in two more sections in which the woman's body in respected and adored (1.15-16; 6.8).[23]

21. On the absence of a matrimony theme in the SoS see Trible, 'Love's Lyrics', pp. 119-20; LaCocque, *Romance*, pp. 7-8.
22. On comparisons to the *waṣf* tradition of praising the physical body of the beloved see M. Falk, 'The *waṣf*', in Brenner (ed.), *Songs of Songs*, pp. 225-33; A. Brenner, ' "Come Back, Come Back the Shulammite" (Song of Songs 7.1-10): A Parody of the *Waṣf* Genre', in Brenner (ed.), *Song of Songs*, pp. 234-57.
23. On the concept of the body in the Bible see discussion and bibliography in

The woman sees the body of her beloved in a similar manner. Using many analogous terms she describes him, admiring and appreciating the physical aspects of his being. When her women friends ask: 'What is your beloved more than another beloved?' (5.9), she goes on to praise him, describing his head, locks, eyes, cheeks, lips, arms, and legs. In addition to the physical attraction, the description seems to reflect as well the mutual friendship between the two lovers. The woman concludes her portrayal of the beloved by stating: 'This is my beloved and this is my friend, O daughters of Jerusalem' (v. 16), making a connection between a physical and emotional appeal.

According to both the female and male perspectives, the beloved is distinguished as the chosen by all people. Thus the physical attraction does not stand in isolation but is created, perhaps, by the subjective eyes of the beholder. The man states: 'Sixty are queens, eighty the concubines, and maidens without number. Unique is my dove, my perfect one' (6.8-9). The woman, in a similar fashion says: 'My beloved is all radiant and ruddy, distinguished among ten thousand' (5.10).

XI

A different image is presented in the dance scene (ch. 7). The woman is now a dancer, performing before a group of people, exposing her body as a dancer before a demanding audience. They seem to 'look upon the Shulammite as upon a dance before two armies' (7.1). A Brenner reads this unclear phrase as a depiction of a scene in which the Shulammite is called on to perform a dance between two rows of spectators.[24] The audience is probably loud and the atmosphere not very solemn. They ask her to perform again and again: 'Return, return, O Shulammite! Return, return, that we may look upon you' (7.1). The intimacy of the previous description is replaced in this scene. The previous description presents mainly visible parts of the body in a modest fashion, from the head downwards. In contrast, the woman dancer exposes her naked body which is described as an object, starting from the feet and proceeding upwards. References to intimate parts, such as thighs, navel, belly and breasts stand in

H. Eilberg-Schwartz, 'The Problem of the Body for the People of the Book', in H. Eilberg-Schwartz (ed.), *People of the Body: Jews and Judaism from an Embodied Perspective* (New York: SUNY Press, 1992), pp. 17-46; G. Anderson, 'The Garden of Eden and Sexuality in Early Judaism', in Eilberg-Schwartz (ed.), *People of the Body*, pp. 47-68. On the question of body and gender differences see E. Grosz, *Volatile Bodies: Towards a Corporeal Feminism* (Bloomington: Indiana University Press, 1994).
    24. See analysis and discussion of this scene in Brenner, ' "Come Back" '.

contrast to previous depictions of her body. The writer seems to choose such an image, in addition to the previous ones, in order to express yet another aspect of the woman's character. She appears to be also non-conformist, promiscuous, provocative and perhaps humorous.[25]

XII

Playing an important part in the woman's fictional reality are images of the mother and the daughters of Jerusalem. These feminine images seem to be in her mind when she dramatizes herself in various situations. The mother is often associated with love-making. The woman prefers to bring her beloved into her 'mother's house, and into the chambers of she who conceived me' (3.4; 8.2). Even in regards to the male lover (8.5) and to King Solomon (3.11) the mother image is needed. It seems, that by invoking this image of the mother in the context of sexual passion, the writer introduces her wishes for support, security, familiarity and approval.[26]

Friendship with women, fictional or real, is another dimension which the woman explores. She describes herself as helpless at times, getting support from her female friends, the daughters of Jerusalem.[27] At other times she seems to direct them by introducing her conclusions about love. It is interesting to note her repeated message which is often linked to her descriptions of love-making: 'I adjure you, O daughters of Jerusalem, by the gazelles or the wild does: do not stir up or awaken love until it is ready' (2.7; 3.5; 8.4). It seems that such a conclusion reflects a basic attitude of the SoS. The writer's descriptions intend to express her own quest, her optional choices, possible reactions, and conflicting feelings about love. Such a subjective and personal quest reflects her own process of becoming aware and learning concepts of love. She seems to realize, however, that it is impossible to reach objective and universal conclusions about love and lovers' attitudes towards it.[28] Thus she states clearly in different stages of her discourse: 'Do not stir up or awaken love until it is ready'.

25. See Brenner's reading in, ' "Come Back" '.

26. On the mother's house see Trible, 'Love's Lyrics', pp., 115-16; C. Meyers, *Discovering Eve: Ancient Israelite Women in Context* (New York: Oxford University Press, 1988), esp. chapter 6; Meyers, 'Gender Imagery', p. 209.

27. On the flexible role of the daughters of Jerusalem see Murphy, *Song of Songs*, pp. 150, 171, 173.

28. On the issue of subjective–objective identity see, for example, J. Lacan, *Ecrits: A Selection* (trans. A. Sheridan; New York : PAJ Publication, 1977), p. 4.

Conclusion

The diversity of voices, images and characters in the SoS appears to represent a particular personal way in which the writer treats the question of love and its fulfillment. By bringing to the surface thoughts, dreams and images built within herself, the writer presents a process of self-reflection. She imagines conflicting situations, casts herself and others in contrary roles, and juxtaposes various attitudes towards love, passion and intimacy. Not insisting on playing a fixed role in a linear and consistent development, she truly explores her individual approach to love in light of conscious and unconscious social and cultural constrictions. Deliberately she acknowledges varied options, possibilities and hypothetical situations and examines herself in relation to them. Her literary integrity, however, is clear. Her voice reverberated in all scenes. She moves in pastoral, urban and regal settings in her imaginary personal journey of seeking; yet, all her movements seem to reflect and stem from her basic perspective: 'My vineyard, my very own, is for myself' (8.12).

This page intentionally left blank

Part II

SPECIFIC READINGS: ALLEGORIES AND FEMINISTS READINGS

UNLIKELY BEDFELLOWS: ALLEGORICAL AND FEMINIST READINGS OF SONG OF SONGS 7.1-8*

Fiona C. Black

The various descriptions of the woman by her lover in the Song of Songs have proved difficult for interpreters over the centuries. Imagery drawn from the worlds of nature and human endeavour (architecture, war) makes little sense when applied to the female form as literal and, it is often presumed, complimentary description. Interpreters have been somewhat uneasy about the descriptions, either because (in the case of earlier readers) they encounter the female body in an erotic context, or because they find the strange presentation of a supposedly desirable woman repelling rather than attractive. Scholarly curiosity and unease have resulted in a number of different interpretive strategies: allegory, the search for ancient Near Eastern parallels, and—often with humorous results—far-fetched over-explanations of the 'poetic' comparisons in the text. Efforts to try to understand the images or to subvert their descriptive nature construct the body in these texts in a particular way, so that, when read as a description of the female form, the body described seems distorted and compromised.

In this paper I consider the problem of interpreting the Song's imagery from a gender-critical perspective. I compare and contrast two feminist readings of one of the descriptions of the female body, Song 7.1-8 (Athalya Brenner, Carol Meyers),[1] with two mediaeval allegorical readings of this same text (Rashi, Nicholas of Lyra).[2] Song

---

* Verse numbers follows the *BHS*.

1. Athalya Brenner, ' "Come Back, Come Back, the Shulammite" (Song of Songs 7.1-10): A Parody of the *waṣf* Genre', in Athalya Brenner and Y.T. Radday (eds.), *On Humour and Comic in the Hebrew Bible* (Sheffield: Almond Press, 1990), pp. 251-76 (reprinted in Athalya Brenner [ed.], *A Feminist Companion to the Song of Songs* [A Feminist Companion to the Bible, 1; Sheffield: JSOT Press, 1993], pp. 234-57; all citations are taken from the second printing); Carol Meyers, 'Gender Imagery in the Song of Songs', *HAR* 10 (1986), pp. 209-23 (reprinted in Brenner [ed.], *A Feminist Companion*, pp. 197-212; all citations are taken from the second printing).

2. Rashi, *The Megiloth and Rashi's Commentary with Linear Translation* (trans.

7.1-8 describes the body according to a specific order (from the feet upwards),[3] commenting on feet, thighs, stomach (or vulva), breasts, neck, head, nose, eyes and hair. Objects of comparison range from jewels to various military paraphernalia to animals. This text presents a detailed and concentrated image of the female form and gives a strong (perhaps the strongest in the book) impression that the woman is on display—an object of viewing.[4] The four readings I have chosen are disparate in their perspectives and intentions, and so their respective interpretations of this unusual text are naturally quite different. Despite this, they are, however, strikingly similar in their figuration of the female body.[5] I use allegory's fanciful and distorted images to identify problems of interpretation which I think affect feminist critical readings.

Avraham Schwartz and Yisroel Schwartz; New York: Hebrew Linear Classics, 1983), pp. 129-40; Nicholas of Lyra, 'Chapter Seven' from the *Postilla Litteralis in Canticum Canticorum*, in Denys Turner, *Eros and Allegory: Medieval Exegesis of the Song of Songs* (Cistercian Studies Series, 156; Kalamazoo: Cistercian Publications, 1995), pp. 403-406. Nicholas was a French, Franciscan monk, writing in the late thirteenth and early fourteenth centuries. His work is known for its important contribution to the mediaeval debate on the nature of allegory. Turner's *Eros and Allegory* is invaluable for its combination of important mediaeval texts, some of which are hard to come by; I rely on his selection and translation of Nicholas's commentary.

3.   Song 7.1-8 (or part thereof) is often assessed by biblical scholars as a *wasf*, a description of the body according to certain conventions, such as order of body parts. I do not look at the imaging of the woman within this generic framework, and I will not involve myself in the debate on where the boundaries of the *wasf* lie. The description of the actual body parts seems to me to end at v. 8. See Marvin H. Pope, *Song of Songs* [AB; Garden City, NY: Doubleday, 1977], pp. 67, 142-44 for some discussion and bibliography.

4.   There is some suggestion that the woman is dancing for an audience, either for her lover alone or a group of men. The phrase כמחלת המחנים is cryptic and has been the subject of much discussion; see, for example, Pope, *Song of Songs*, pp. 601-606 and Brenner, 'Come Back, Come Back', p. 245.

5.   I am aware of the potentially unfair comparison of two allegorists whose work is of crucial importance in the history of mediaeval interpretation and two feminist critics, whose excellent work is representative of a diverse but still developing discipline. My selection of these four readings is not by chance. Nicholas and Rashi were chosen because they represent two traditions of allegory on the Song (Jewish and Christian), Nicholas being one of a very few Christian scholars whose commentary is not homiletic and which actually proceeds up to the seventh chapter of the Song. Likewise, though there are a number of feminist studies on the Song of Songs, Brenner and Meyers are, to my knowledge, the only two specifically concerned with how the imagery of the body in the Song of Songs should be interpreted.

Feminist critics, like other biblical readers, have to negotiate imagery that is unclear or cryptic, but also encounter in these texts a problem of another kind. The manner in which the female body is described is potentially ridiculous or comical; as a description of a body, it paints an unflattering picture. This imaging has implications for the woman in the text, in terms of the way her body is viewed and in terms of her freedom from being objectified. A ridiculed and objectified woman might not be a problem for feminist critics *per se*, especially if it is something they mean to expose and debunk. But for those feminists who celebrate the woman in the Song as an autonomous creature who articulates her own story and seems to control her own sexuality,[6] the way her body is imaged and objectified poses a potential problem to their estimations of the book. The challenge that this imagery poses in these terms, has, to date, largely been ignored by feminist critics. Even the two feminist readings I look at here, both of which concern themselves with how to interpret the images, do not take up the challenge because of the way they are oriented towards this text.

The objection can be raised that the images that describe the female form are *poetic* language; to speak of them as literal description would be to miss the point. But scholarly dis-ease with the language and subsequent scrambling to settle the meaning of the texts reveal that these readers have not been able contentedly to excuse this language as 'poetic' and forget about it. Scholars have commented on the nature of the imagery variously as 'comical and puzzling', 'bizarre, if not grotesque', or 'grotesque'.[7] If the language were simply excused

---

6.   This seems to be the consensus of opinion among feminist critics of the Song of Songs. See, for example, Athalya Brenner, *Song of Songs* (OTG; Sheffield: JSOT Press, 1989), p. 90; Athalya Brenner, 'On Feminist Criticism of the Song of Songs', in Brenner (ed.), *A Feminist Companion*, pp. 28-37, esp. pp. 28-29; Phyllis Trible, *God and the Rhetoric of Sexuality* (Philadelphia: Fortress Press, 1978), p. 161. Renita Weems, 'Song of Songs', in Carol Newsom and Sharon Ringe (eds.), *The Women's Bible Commentary* (London: SPCK, 1992), pp. 156-60. Ilana Pardes, *Counter-traditions in the Hebrew Bible: A Feminist Approach* (Cambridge, MA: Harvard University Press, 1992) agrees, but with reservations (pp. 118-19, 128); Fokkelien van Dijk-Hemmes, 'The Imagination of Power and the Power of Imagination: An Intertextual Analysis of Two Biblical Love Songs. The Song of Songs and Hosea 2', *JSOT* 44 (1989), pp. 75-88; reprinted in Brenner (ed.), *A Feminist Companion*, pp. 156-70, esp. pp. 169-70, sees the freedom of the woman in the Song as redemptive of the oppression of the woman in Hosea 2.

7.   Marcia Falk, *Love Lyrics from the Hebrew Bible: A Translation and Literary Study of the Song of Songs* (Sheffield: Almond Press, 1982), p. 81. Falk quotes Richard Soulen, Leroy Waterman and M.H. Segal, respectively.

as poetic, then these kinds of evaluations would not be necessary; nor would the imagery be such a repeated site of scholarly visitation and inquiry.

It is a fortunate coincidence that some biblical scholars have called the imagery grotesque, since, as a literary construction, the grotesque provides a useful lens through which these readings of the descriptions of the female body might be viewed. Grotesque figuration is all about registering and negotiating unease with certain subjects or events. It depends upon sudden juxtaposition, the startling presentation of the unexpected, and a particular presentation of images that play on human attraction to the comical/ridiculous and/or the repulsive/ugly. Grotesque figuration allows, then, for the portrayal of things that might not comfortably be portrayed, such as the female figure in an erotic context—most especially in a biblical text. And, since its recognition is ultimately a readerly activity,[8] it will reveal a certain readerly unease with something in a text.

In light of the difficult nature of the Song's imagery and the interpretive tendency to cover it up or modify it, allegorical interpretation of the Song of Songs proves to be elucidating and entertaining reading.[9] Allegories represent one extreme of fancy footwork around the imagery in this text in the interpretive tradition. Allegorical interpretation of the Song (especially Christian) is often stereotypically described as suppressing the eroticism of the book and interpreting away that which offends its theological sensibilities (for example, the female body and the presentation of it in an erotic context).[10] In its effort to deal with these subjects—to present something that causes unease in an alternative manner—allegory figures the female form in such a way that it takes on many characteristics of the grotesque.

Allegorical and feminist readings of the Song of Songs are unlikely bedfellows. The comparison of these approaches, however, provides a

8.   Grotesque figurations will have a number of elements in common, but, ultimately, whether something is grotesque or not will be subject to whether or not the person reading about it or viewing it sees it as such (so Margaret Miles, *Carnal Knowing: Female Nakedness and Religious Meaning in the Christian West* [New York: Vintage Books, 1991], pp. 161-62).

9.   Allegory is meant to refer loosely to the traditional means of interpretation of the Song by Jewish and Christian communities. Here, various aspects of the Song, such as the identities of the lovers (even specific body parts) and their activities, are interpreted so that they might conform to certain theological themes.

10.   The stereotype is usually justified, though caution should be exercised in making simplistic blanket generalizations, especially when mediaeval hermeneutical interest in *eros* is, as Turner shows (*Eros and Allegory*), a complicated matter.

useful way to reconsider the problem that the text presents for feminist readings in its description of the female body. But allegory, tar-
nished as it is with the 'fanciful twists and turns' of Jewish and Christian 'spiritualized interpretation',[11] tends to be ignored by 'critical
biblical scholarship'[12] on the Song.[13] If allowed back into the realm of
'scholarly' discourse, though, allegorical readings of Song 7.1-8 reveal
some interesting similarities with feminist readings. Both approaches,
in trying to negotiate the image of the woman in this text, result in
readings that confuse the physical properties of the protagonist's
body and compromise her sexual freedom—both significant features
of the grotesque. In this essay, I use the grotesque as a heuristic device
in an effort to account for the distorted and ridiculous natures of the
bodies constructed by the readers and as a means of uncovering what
unease the readings exhibit or suggest. I look first at the pictures
created, then I consider whose interests (i.e. whose pleasure or
enjoyment) these resulting constructions serve, and finally, I ask
whether or not and to what degree the readings compromise the
woman's sexual freedom. By way of conclusion, I look at other
options for feminist critical interpretation of imagery of the female
body in the Song of Songs.

The 'Perfect One'

Rashi's interpretation[14] of Song 7.1-8 reveals two different, though
likely not mutually exclusive concerns, cultic and didactic. The
woman (identified as Israel) is associated through her specific body
parts with various cultic furniture and scholarly endeavours, and she

---

11. Meyers, 'Gender Imagery', p. 209.
12. Meyers, 'Gender Imagery', p. 209.
13. This is understandable to a large degree, but allegorical readings should
not be ignored because of their overtly ideological perspective, in the same way
that any viable resource should not be ignored in the exploration of an issue as
important as how to interpret the Song's imagery.
14. Though known for his interest in *peshat*, the literal meaning of the text,
Rashi's work on the Song of Songs is primarily allegorical. For a discussion of
peshat and *derash* see Benjamin Gelles, *Peshat and Derash in the Exegesis of Rashi*
(Leiden: E.J. Brill, 1971), esp. pp. 3-35, 81-85. There is, also, an interesting
hermeneutical relationship between Rashi and Nicholas of Lyra: see Eugene
Merrill, 'Rashi, Nicholas de Lyra and Christian Exegesis', *WTJ* 38 (1978), pp. 66-79;
Turner, *Eros and Allegory*, pp. 115-16, 387; and Jeremy Cohen, 'Scholarship and
Intolerance in the Medieval Academy: The Study and Evaluation of Judaism in
European Christendom', *American Historical Review* 91 (1986), pp. 592-613.

tends to be appreciated by Rashi for these, and not for her beauty or sexual appeal.

Rashi begins with the woman's feet, which, though viewed literally as feet, [15] are allegorized and given cultic and historical significance: Israel's feet were fair specifically as they made pilgrimage to Jerusalem. Rabbinical tradition is used to explain the woman's jewel-like thighs (ירכים): the phrase refers 'to the holes of the drainage pits [beneath the altar] [used] for the libations...[fashioned] round like a thigh.'[16] The woman's navel שררך[17] is said to be like a marble basin for bathing.[18] 'The allegory', Rashi reveals, 'is to the Chamber of Hewn Stone, which is situated in the navel of the earth',[19] and from which instruction flows as plentifully as drink from the basin the Song describes.[20] Rashi interprets שושנים in v. 3 as a hedge of roses which fence the woman's stomach. He notes that 'not one of them breaches it to enter',[21] and offers an analogy to further understanding. Like the bridegroom on the night of his marriage, any 'one of them' (Israel's possible suitors) might be barred from consummating the marriage if his bride says to him, 'I have seen a drop of blood the size of a mustard seed'.[22] If she is menstruating, then, he must resist temptation, just as, Rashi observes, one tempted to pick fruit must resist if he is advised that the fruit belongs to someone else. The woman's breasts are the two tablets of the Law, and/or the king and high priest. Her neck refers to the Temple and the altar (as did her thighs).

The woman's eyes come next in the description. Rashi interprets their tearfulness and proximity to the gate to mean that Israel's sages, when they sit at the gates, engage in calculation of the seasons and the constellations, their wisdom flowing as pools of water.[23] Rashi understands the word אף (nose) to mean face.[24] The connection with

15. Though Rashi's reading is primarily allegorical, the literal does punctuate his reading of Song 7.1-8 at three points: the feet, the nose and the breasts.

16. Rashi, *The Megiloth*, p. 131. In various places in this commentary, such as this one, the translators have added words to clarify Rashi's. I mark these with square brackets.

17. 'Navel' is the translators' term (Schwartz and Schwartz).

18. Rashi, *The Megiloth*, p. 132.

19. Rashi, *The Megiloth*, p. 132.

20. The next verse, which compares the stomach to a heap of wheat, does not further this comparison for Rashi. He says only, 'which all need' (i.e. the wheat, presumably to eat); Rashi, *The Megiloth*, p. 132.

21. Rashi, *The Megiloth*, p. 132.

22. Rashi, *The Megiloth*, p. 133.

23. Rashi, *The Megiloth*, p. 134.

24. Relying on the literal meaning, Rashi observes, 'I cannot explain it ... [as] a

the tower of Damascus signifies either the greatness of Israel (visible from the tower), or the limit to which Israel's 'face' (i.e., its territory) will extend. The head (Carmel) signifies the phylacteries, worn so that nations may identify Israel and be afraid. The braid of the woman's hair (דלת) refers to Nazarites' hair, beautiful through the fulfilment of precepts. [25] Finally, the tresses in which the king is caught refer to the laces with which girdles are tied, or, alternatively, they refer to the fact that YHWH is bound to the people in love.[26] Rashi sums up the picture of the woman with his interpretation of vv. 7-8 and uses Dan. 3.3 as an intertext. Rashi identifies the clusters of a palm tree in v. 8 as Daniel, Hananiah, Mishael and Azariah, 'who were for you like breasts from which to suck'.[27] The woman's breasts, now doubled in number (from v. 4), take on identities of their own in the form of great men of renown in Israel's history, and, oddly, they nourish her, instead of the reverse.

'The Parable of the Beautiful Woman'

Nicholas of Lyra's allegorical[28] interpretation of the text presents a woman who is an interesting mixture of the Church and Christ. The woman is not to be looked at and admired, but is rather described as a vehicle (the Church) which both embodies the attributes of Christ and the means by which the people of God might be created/sustained.

---

term [denoting] a nose, neither with respect to the simple meaning nor with respect to the allegory, for what praise of beauty is there in a nose, large and upright like a tower?' He reasons that אף refers to the face, specifically the forehead, for the forehead follows the eyes in the reverse anatomical order of this poem, and the forehead is the face's 'most distinguishing feature' (Rashi, *The Megiloth*, p. 134).

25. Rashi, *The Megiloth*, p. 135.
26. Rashi, *The Megiloth*, p. 135.
27. Rashi, *The Megiloth*, p. 137.
28. Nicholas provides in separate readings both a literal and an allegorical interpretation of Song 7.1-8. In his literal reading, it is clear that Nicholas appreciates the physical beauty of the woman and is well aware of her sexuality and promise as an object of desire. Only two elements, namely her belly and her breasts, are appreciated not so much for their beauty but for their physiological function. This interpretation anticipates Nicholas's allegorical reading, where he interprets the woman's body parts as various aspects of the Church and/or the physical body of Christ (she is a 'Type of New Testament' [Turner, *Eros and Allegory*, p. 403]), thus concentrating on the body's capabilities for childbirth and child rearing. For a discussion of Nicholas's hermeneutic, particularly his invaluable contribution to the debate on the allegorical interpretation of scriptural texts, see Turner, *Eros and Allegory*, pp. 89-113, 381-92.

The meeting of the thighs heralds the coming together of Jew and Gentile in one church (Christ is the craftsman who made one of the two people). It follows, then, that the woman's belly ('within which a child may be conceived') illustrates that the Church is fertile in children, begotten, of course, by Christ (Nicholas adds that this is spiritual conception, not fleshly). The woman's breasts are the two Testaments from which these children draw milk, an attribute reiterated in Song 7.8.

Is this vehicle worthy of such procreative responsibility? The other parts of her body seem to suggest she is. Her feet are protected by sandals which, Nicholas goes to some pain to point out, are made from the hides of dead animals and are reminiscent of the martyrdom of Christ. She stands erect in justice and is drawn up to the height of devout contemplation. Her belly is encircled by (marital) chastity. Her neck signifies faith, which is strengthened by charity, and therefore supports her crowning glory, her head, which is Christ. The woman/Church's head (Christ) is like Carmel, fertile and abundant in harvest. Her/his—for there is, at this point, some mixing of gender apparent here—eyes are filled with mercy and her/his nose reveals the power of discernment; it is able to sniff out believers and unbelievers ('as the nose discriminates between foul and fresh smells').[29] Finally, the hairs of her/his head are the apostles, who, 'for love of Christ the king...were dyed in the red of their own blood by the prize of martyrdom'.[30]

Fightin' Words

Carol Meyers's treatment[31] of the woman's body in Song 7.1-8 is quite cursory, partly because it comes in the context of a broader discussion on imagery in the Song of Songs. Rather than discussing Song 7.1-8 in its entirety, Meyers looks only at the specific images in vv. 4-5, those that describe the breasts, neck, eyes and nose. Meyers's woman, in other words, will consist of her facial features and her breasts; she is missing[32] feet, thighs, stomach/womb (vulva?), and head. Her construction is also 'out of order' in terms of the text's order of discussion. Meyers is not interested in the woman's physical appearance,

29. Nicholas in Turner, *Eros and Allegory*, p. 406.
30. Nicholas in Turner, *Eros and Allegory*, p. 406.
31. Meyers, 'Gender Imagery'.
32. Missing, that is, with reference to the biblical text and the other readings considered here.

particularly her beauty, but instead seeks the woman's empowerment through the imagery that describes her. [33]

Meyers observes that the imagery that depicts the facial features is taken from the world of the military/architectural. She sees the comparison of the nose to a tower in Song 7.5 as building on more complex imagery which was introduced in relation to the neck in Song 4.4. She explains that the military advantage of the מגדל (tower) in Song 7.5 is its proximity to Damascus, which means that it is strategically situated to overlook the city.[34] The tower image is also used in Song 7.5 to describe the woman's neck. This, Meyers posits, is 'derived from the world of military structures' and enhanced by its companion image of the eyes as pools, which are situated next to the gate of the בתרבים. The pools are 'most likely artificial pools—reservoirs—constructed for military, not agricultural purposes'.[35] The gate Meyers views as 'part of the military defenses of a city' and also as a public place where men would frequent.[36] Finally, Meyers mentions the woman's hair (v. 6), even though it does not fit into her groups of military or faunal imagery. This serves as another example of the 'reversal of conventional gender typing' in that the 'most powerful human', the king, is imprisoned by the woman.[37]

The woman's breasts (v. 4) are part of a different group of images (faunal), which are generally associated with 'wildness, danger, might, strength, aggressiveness',[38] and other 'masculine' traits. The breasts are likened to gazelles, which, Meyers notes, are actually used to describe both the man and the woman in the Song. She thus

33. For a discussion of Meyers's evaluation of the implications of the imagery in the Song of Songs, see 'Gender Imagery', pp. 217-21 and *Discovering Eve: Ancient Israelite Women in Context* (Oxford: Oxford University Press, 1988), pp. 177-81. Meyers's argument is that in 'masculine' imagery which is used to describe a female subject, one can see a 'underlying subculture' where women are not subordinated, but may even dominate certain aspects of life ('Gender Imagery', p. 220). She briefly outlines two types of images, faunal and military/architectural and concludes that they bring about an unexpected reversal of conventional stereotypes; these images are 'metaphors for power and control which suggest female attributes' ('Gender Imagery', p. 213). Meyers believes that the attributes expose the power that women had (as opposed to the authority of men) in various aspects of life (e.g. domestic, social—'private' life) and reveal the interdependence of both sexes.
34. Meyers, 'Gender Imagery', p. 214.
35. Meyers, 'Gender Imagery', p. 214.
36. Meyers, 'Gender Imagery', p. 214.
37. Meyers, 'Gender Imagery', p. 218.
38. Meyers, 'Gender Imagery', p. 216.

differentiates: 'for the female, the tenderness and softness, and perhaps suppleness of these young animals have led the poet to use them in a simile celebrating the attractiveness of her breasts'.[39]

A 'Mixed Bag'[40]

Athalya Brenner's interpretation of the description in Song 7.1-8 is facilitated largely through her understanding of the context in which this text is placed: the protagonist is dancing for a group of spectators.[41] She observes that the audience is 'probably active and noisy, slightly drunk perhaps', and the dancer is subject to a 'running commentary' where the commentator is encouraged to be 'flippant' by other spectators, who are probably also male.[42] There is no 'wooing' or 'adoring' voice here, 'but a close scrutiny of a present, live woman in a public performance'.[43]

Brenner makes little comment about the first two body parts discussed, the feet and the thighs. These are described (and masked) by clothing and/or comparison to various 'artefacts'.[44] Then, the vulva is the correct understanding of שׁרְרֵךְ, the subject of 7.3b. Brenner also notes that אַל יֶחְסַר הַמֶּזֶג suggests not only the free flowing wine, but

---

39. Meyers notes, 'the grace and free movement of these wild creatures would seem to underlie the poet's choice'—for the description of the male ('Gender Imagery', p. 216).

40. Brenner, ' "Come Back, Come Back" ', p. 252.

41. Brenner's intention in her article is to account for the odd description of the woman in this text. She notes: 'by the end of the poem, we still have no idea what the loved person looks like, in the sense that no *complete* image is communicated' ('Come Back, Come Back', p. 235; italics Brenner's). She believes that it is not a photographic type of image that is relayed, but something that reflects the emotional state of the speaker and draws in the reader's sense and emotions (p. 235). Brenner argues that if we change our perspective slightly while reading, we might understand Song 7.1-10 as a parody of two previous descriptions (*wasfs*) in the book. In this way, then, Brenner's reading does not resist the text unflattering and ridiculous imaging of the female body. She sees that the image is blatantly honest about the woman's unattractive state, so poking fun putting her on display for the amusement of many.

42. Brenner, ' "Come Back, Come Back" ', pp. 245-46.

43. Brenner, ' "Come Back, Come Back" ', p. 246.

44. Brenner, ' "Come Back, Come Back" ', p. 246. The rest of sumably does not benefit from such cover. Brenner urges that whether or not the woman is clothed is not as important as no the comment on the woman's vulva (p. 247)

also the 'womb's juices'.[45] The stomach and lilies are next (7.3c-d), lilies signifying the woman's pubic hair. Brenner's subsequent comment is striking: 'It appears that the dancing damsel is far from slim'.[46] She summarizes, less timidly, 'the dancer is, frankly, fat, her belly in dance motion is big and quivering, much like an unstable mound of wheat. She looks comical; her body inspires pithy comments'.[47] Brenner notes that much scholarly energy has been expended on the attempt to explain the comparison of the woman's breasts to gazelles. She reminds us of the context of this description— the woman dancing—and observes, 'The dancer is in constant motion. Together with the rest of her body, her breasts move fast, much like frolicking fawns. This is titillating, but might look ludicrous as well.'[48]

Brenner turns next to the facial features. The comparison of the woman's neck to a tower proves difficult, and Brenner eventually defers to ignorance of the context.[49] The eyes are also the subject of an equally 'opaque' image. She observes that 'the public water places outside the gates of Heshbon...were used for drinking, watering of animals, washing bodies and clothes, and clearing debris. Their waters were probably turbid rather than serenely limpid.'[50] For the nose, Brenner relies on the assumption that its 'Lebanese proportions' were probably no more attractive then as they would be today.[51] Finally, the woman's hair is not richly dyed as other commentators suggest, but 'wet with perspiration, much like packs of thread in the dyeing vessels'.[52] In sum, Brenner calls this woman a 'mixed bag':

45. Brenner, ' "Come Back, Come Back" ', p. 246. This double meaning is then characteristic of a type of joke that is exclusive to those who hear it and experience its context (p. 247).

46. Brenner's comment that the woman is 'far from slim' is based on the ˋ˗ˢᵉʳvation that the wish to see this text as complimentary might condition the
ᵗion of the woman's large size as the subject of an 'adoring remark'
ˋ, Come Back" ', p. 247).

' "Come Back, Come Back" ', p. 248. Brenner points out that these
ᵗures that are covered (p. 248). Curiously, as Brenner observes,
of the body that the text calls beautiful. This might be a
ʳ an insightful discussion of desire and exposure of the
Pardes, *Countertraditions*, pp. 134-38.
ˋme Back" ', p. 248.
ˋne Back" ', p. 249. This is surprising, since
ˋ context which informs her interpretation

' ', p. 250.
ˋ" ', p. 250.
ˈk" ', p. 252.

> True, she dances well and suggestively (v. 2a). Her thighs are like artistic jewels (2b), her vulva guessed to be generous (3a-b)—so far on the credit side. On the other hand, her belly is fat and jumpy like her breasts (3c, 4), her neck is (disproportionately?) long, her eyes by now turbid, her nose outsize (5).[53]

She points out that there is 'no reason to assume that the picture she [the woman] now presents is aesthetically captivating'.[54]

Making a Spectacle[55]

When read as physical descriptions of the female body, the four readings of Rashi, Nicholas, Meyers and Brenner all reveal, to use Brenner's words, less than 'aesthetically captivating' women. The readings surely do not solve any mysteries posed by the cryptic imagery in the text, and, if they once acknowledged that the text was a lover's (complimentary?) description of a loved one, there is no sign of this now. What has happened to the human figure described in this text?[56] In the pursuit of their particular interests, the readings either take the focus off the erotic/sexual nature of the description or obscure the woman's body image; ultimately, therefore, they imply a certain unease with the body described in this text. The grotesque provides a useful lens through which to view this distorted, uneasy figuration of the female form.

The grotesque is elusive, slippery.[57] It has been widely studied, but there is little or no scholarly consensus on its nature, and attempts to define it are often as vague as the thing itself. One might describe it as an artistic or literary convention, marked by difference or a sudden juxtaposition of incongruous elements. It might also be seen as that

---

53. Brenner, ' "Come Back, Come Back" ', p. 250.

54. Brenner, ' "Come Back, Come Back" ', p. 252.

55. Mary Russo begins her definition of the grotesque by citing the familiar phrase, 'she is making a spectacle out of herself'; *The Female Grotesque: Risk, Excess and Modernity* (London: Routledge, 1994), p. 53. In this case, the readers make the spectacle, not the woman in the Song.

56. Of the four readings, it will be apparent that only Brenner's is ultimately concerned with the (human) image that remains. Though different from the other three in her analysis, her reading will be investigated, like the other three, for the implications that it has for the imaging of the female form.

57. One can speak of the grotesque as either an authorial or readerly construction. In the case of the latter, it may well be that the author has not intended his or her work to be grotesque. My investigation into this literary device is in terms of a readerly response, not as an inquiry into authorial intent.

which displays 'an attempt to control and exorcise the demonic elements in the world',[58] or as 'the expression of the estranged or alienated world'. In the latter, 'the familiar world is seen from a perspective which suddenly renders it strange',[59] and this strangeness is often achieved by a jarring clash of opposites—usually the comic and the terrifying (hideous, or ugly). Grotesque forms depend upon this clash, and if it is resolved, the impression of the grotesque ceases to be maintained. Readers or viewers cannot negotiate their responses to grotesque figures or events, and the grotesque persists because of the sense of unease it produces.[60]

The human body is a frequent and ideal target for grotesque depiction, since exaggerated or extreme characterization of the human form, to the point where physical abnormality is highlighted, makes it both funny and frightening. The depiction of the human body as grotesque includes a variety of elements, among them, giant size, hybridization, exaggeration and caricature.[61] In addition, the grotesque body is the changing, unfinished body that moves beyond its own limits—in Mary Russo's words, the 'open, protruding, extending, secreting body, the body of becoming, process, and change'.[62] One of the results of this kind of figuration, notably features such as hybridisation and exaggeration, is in effect to dehumanize the

58. As summarized by Philip Thompson, *The Grotesque* (The Critical Idiom; London: Methuen and Co., 1972), p. 18.

59. Thompson, *The Grotesque*, p. 18.

60. In adopting the theoretical perspective of Kayser, I ally myself with critics who tend to focus on the unease of the grotesque, rather than those who side with Bakhtin, who insists on the liberating and comic effect of the grotesque. The reason for this at this point is not to deny Bakhtin's invaluable contribution to the discussion, but to take advantage of the important insights of Miles and Russo, who illustrate that the grotesque becomes very un-funny once its implications for the female gender are realized (see below).

61. So Miles, *Carnal Knowing*, pp. 155-58. I use Miles's work in what follows because of her clear and concise definition of the grotesque, useful for the confines of this essay, and her discussion of gender (see below). Miles's study uses material gathered from the Christian artistic tradition. It is therefore important to exercise caution in applying her insights to literary texts—though her work is based on Bakhtin's study of Rabelaisian literature—especially those which are not generated in the same cultural and historical milieu as the art which she studies. For more detailed studies of the female and the grotesque, see Mary Russo, *The Female Grotesque*, and on the related concept of the abject, Julia Kristeva, *Powers of Horror: An Essay on Abjection* (trans. Leon S. Roudiez; New York: Columbia University Press, 1982).

62. Russo, *The Female Grotesque*, pp. 62-63. Russo follows Bakhtin.

described target, both by combining the human with the non-human (usually various parts of animals) and by disallowing functional integrity.[63] Exaggeration and caricature are useful in establishing the connection to humour, and, as Margaret Miles points out, caricature has a particular connection to the fetishising of the body and the revelation of a 'social consensus on what is to be avoided'.[64]

Whereas scholarly discussion of the grotesque has included the topic of sexuality, Miles criticizes its neglect (particularly Bakhtin's) of the subject of gender.[65] She observes in the works she studies that the female body and the grotesque are intricately bound together.

> The association of the female body with materiality, sex and reproduction makes it an essential—not an accidental—aspect of the grotesque. The socially constructed *différance* which means that male and female bodies are not only physically different, but also hierarchically arranged and asymmetrically valued underlies the literary use of woman's body as the primary figure of debasement...[66] Figured as Eve, the perversely bent rib, every woman was seen as essentially grotesque, though the revelation of her hidden monstrosity could be prevented by her careful adherence to socially approved appearance and behavior. The function of this figuration was to identify, define and thus to stabilize a feared and fantasized object. Grotesque figuration contributes the bonus of laughter, permitting relief of tension; the simultaneously feared and desired object becomes comic.[67]

Miles sees that the volatility of the female form is the one essential aspect that ensures its suitability for grotesque depiction. This is particularly visible in female reproduction and all that it encompasses (sexual organs, physiological abilities/changes, female sexuality):[68] 'In menstruation, sexual intercourse, and pregnancy, women's bodies lose their individual configuration and boundaries'.[69] Thus, the bodies of prostitutes (the 'body shaped by lust, the permeable body that produces juices and smells')[70] are exemplary in their volatility.

63. Miles, *Carnal Knowing*, p. 161.
64. Miles, *Carnal Knowing*, p. 155.
65. See Miles, *Carnal Knowing*, esp. pp. 145-68, 221 n. 24.
66. Miles, *Carnal Knowing*, p. 150.
67. Miles, *Carnal Knowing*, p. 152.
68. Miles, *Carnal Knowing*, p. 153. Quoting Bakhtin, Meyers observes that, specifically in the mediaeval period, '...female reproductive functions...were...the quintessential terror that must be ' "conquered by laughter".'
69. Miles, *Carnal Knowing*, p. 153. Miles follows Bakhtin, who finds intercourse, birth and death to be the ultimate grotesque elements.
70. Miles, *Carnal Knowing*, p. 153.

Rashi and the Grotesque

If one tries to imagine that Rashi's reading depicts the body of the woman in the Song, a ridiculous and incomprehensible picture emerges. On two human, female feet are precariously balanced drainage pits for an altar, the Chamber of Hewn Stone, a fence of roses, the two tablets or the king and high priest—or, alternately, Daniel, Hananiah, Mishael and Azariah. Her head confuses her gender, for s/he wears phylacteries, a Nazarite's braid, and, for a peculiar final touch, is coifed with girding laces. Rashi's construction is thus a giant woman with a human-sized male head and/or an extremely innovative dress sense.

The giant size,[71] confused and hybridized body and the playing with gender in this reading fit the pattern of the grotesque, but Rashi's discussion of vv. 2-3 makes an even stronger impression of it. In v. 2, חמוקי ירכיך is usually translated as 'curved parts of your thighs';[72] it has also been rendered 'hidden parts of your thighs',[73] which seems very suggestive, especially considering the direction in which the description proceeds.[74] If we entertain the possibility that the vulva, which appears in v. 3, is intimated here—either by the notion of 'curved' or 'hidden' thighs—latent vaginal/menstrual imagery is made evident. The similarity of חמוקי ירכיך to the drainage pits of the altar, then, becomes one in function, in addition to shape, for both may carry away blood. The vaginal/menstrual imagery continues in the next verse with Rashi's emphasis on washing. It is continued with Rashi's prohibition against penetration and compounded with the final analogy to the bridegroom and menstruating bride.

Miles has pointed out the links between the changing nature (reproductivity) of the female body and the grotesque. Though the

---

71. Miles, *Carnal Knowing*, p. 146.

72. חמוקי is a hapax legomenon. Pope connects it to חמק (see 5.6; *Song of Songs*, p. 615).

73. Rashi, *The Megiloth*, p. 130.

74. Indeed, this prefigures the reference to שררך in v. 3, which Rashi sees as the vulva—as is obvious from the context in which he discusses it—though his translators render it as 'navel' (Rashi, *The Megiloth*, p. 131). Many commentators read 'vulva' here. See Pope, *The Song of Songs*, p. 617. Pope's discussion of Arabic cognates is also interesting: one (*sirr*) denotes 'secret' or 'pudenda' (p. 617), which makes a nice connection to the 'hidden parts' of the thighs in v. 2. The noun אגן should also be mentioned here in discussion of menstrual imagery. Pope cites Exod. 24.6, where אגנת (pl.) describes bowls for throwing blood on the altar (p. 618).

discussion of המיקי ירכיך in Rashi's text may be interpreted positively, in that sacrifice, an important cultic act, is here located in the female form, such a reading is implausible given Rashi's historical and theological milieu. What seems more likely is that vv. 2-3, read with their vaginal/menstrual imagery, allow for the tempering of Rashi's identification of the woman's body with significant cultic elements, thus, with an assertion of the very unsuitability of this creature for this identification.

I am suggesting that Rashi's reading might potentially undermine its own theological agenda. Why might this be important? It is clear that this constructed woman with her cultic paraphernalia serves Rashi's theological agenda well. But another issue arises if we think of the woman's desirability. Rashi, doubtless aware of the possibilities of reading Song 7.1-8 as a literal description of the body (notably in two places, the feet and the nose), may have found a beautiful and desirable woman in a *biblical* text problematic—consciously or unconsciously.[75] According to Rashi's reading, this woman's purpose is not for procreation—the opposite is implied—so the dangerous possibility that she is as her lover sees her—a desirable woman—persists. As a deterrent, Rashi gives us an odd looking woman whom a prospective lover is unlikely to find appealing. The suggestion that she is menstruating makes it absolute, moreover, that should anyone desire her, her body prohibits the consummation of that desire.

Does Rashi's reading consider the woman's own sexual desire and autonomy? A sexually autonomous woman could, after all, be just as dangerous as a sexually desirable one. There is a certain amount of ambiguity surrounding this issue, since, on the one hand, the reference to her sexual organs illustrates her impenetrability. In this instance, abstinence is not a matter of choice for the woman, but for the man, who must avoid sexual contact with her. Furthermore, the analogy to the fruit and ownership of the trees implies ownership of the woman, at least in sexual terms. On the other hand, however, the reference to the woman's Nazarite's braid (and the girding laces?) suggests celibacy; here abstinence would be a matter of *her*[76] *choice*, rather than be dictated by the unsuitability of her body. Though it is uncertain who actually controls the decision, the message is clear: this

75. Rashi's identification of Solomon with the deity 'to Whose relationship with His people Israel this book belongs' (Gelles, *Peshat and Derash*, p. 85) reveals a concern that the literal, erotic sense of this book be circumnavigated.

76. But then, at this point is it any longer a female body, since the imagery is patently male?

woman is not going to be sexually active. Rashi's reading de-sexualizes the woman by ensuring that she is safely removed from any context that is even faintly erotic.

Nicholas and the Grotesque

Nicholas's allegorical woman is also removed from her erotic context, albeit by means different from Rashi's. In Nicholas's construction, we see the same kind of figuration of the body as Rashi's, the same denial of her body's sexual appeal/desirability and the same erasing of her own opportunity for sexual expression. Though Nicholas's historical and theological context was different from Rashi's, he would have been under similar pressure to endow this text with theological significance, but to be wary of its (read: the woman's) erotic nature.[77] The grotesque again provides a useful lens through which to view Nicholas's reading.

Nicholas's woman is volatile: she gives birth to all believers of Christ, and thus from her emerge vast numbers of people, fathered spiritually. She nurses these children, and hence the suggestion of clusters of breasts in 7.8 is entirely appropriate, as so many offspring would require more than two. This woman must be enormous: she can be mother to the world (as evidenced by the coming together of Jew and Gentile) and can feed all her children; her breasts can also be the two Testaments and all they contain; she is as tall as devout contemplation and justice (however tall these may be); by her own neck she supports Christ; and her nose, eyes and head are huge in terms of their theological significance. Nicholas's woman has been de-humanized, for her procreative powers are super-human and her features gigantic.

Then, like Rashi's construction, there is the curious transfer of sexual identity from female to male, as Nicholas discusses the facial and capital features. Nicholas is aware of the change, for he switches from feminine to masculine pronouns, but shows no interest in the difficulty that this presents for the constructed image. With the exception of the hair, the woman's face and head represent Christ's, so that we have a curious hybrid of a divine/human male head on a female body. When put together with the incongruous elements of the rest of her body, we see that this woman fits the pattern of the grotesque.

---

77. Perhaps even more so. See Turner, *Eros and Allegory*, pp. 37, 83-84, 136, 151, and, for Nicholas's ingenious hermeneutical 'solution', pp. 114, 137-38.

Like Rashi's woman, Nicholas's construction is an ideal vehicle for the presentation of his theology, but less promising when looked at in terms of a woman to be desired. It is only in fragments that the woman's body seems to have any sexual currency, as her capable vagina and ample breasts illustrate. But her enormity is frightening, not alluring, and her purpose is to manufacture children. She is a giant factory for Christ, not a sex object.[78] Her marital chastity, thankfully, keeps her safely restricted to one man (Christ), who does not even use her sexually as one might expect. Furthermore, the incorporation of Christ into her body as her head (she is both Christ and the partner of Christ), makes her an odd hybrid of man, woman and deity, likely less an object to be desired and more something to be feared—any prospective lover's gaze in the eyes of the 'whole' woman would be met by the eyes of Christ.

What of her own desire and sexual autonomy? If this woman is not the object of desire, could she be the one desiring—another 'dangerous' possibility? As with Rashi, there seems to be some ambiguity in Nicholas's reading around this idea. On the one hand, her body's sexual use is for procreation and there is little to suggest that this is a matter of her own choosing: she is clearly a vehicle for multiple births, not a woman who wants a large family. She is, moreover, sexually responsible to someone with whom she has only 'spiritual' relations. Thus, any suggestion that she might exercise her own sexual license is negated by the assertion that she is chaste in a sexless marriage. These factors suggest that there is little opportunity for the woman's personal sexual expression. On the other hand, however, her chastity does leave some question of her autonomy open. The issue then is whether her chastity is an expression of her own self-discipline or her partner's celibacy.

Meyers and the Grotesque

The constructed image in Meyers's reading is even more ridiculous than Rashi's and Nicholas's. The woman is gigantic, like the others, but compared with the text and the other readings, she is also incomplete, having only nose, eyes, neck, hair, breasts. The king is imprisoned in her hair; her neck and nose are towers; her eyes are military reservoirs. These features float about unrestrained (there is no head), in proximity only to two graceful and supple gazelles: a

---

78. Or is she a giant sex object? Even given that 'big might be beautiful', Nicholas's woman is surely too large to be considered human.

jarring hybrid of imagery, some of which is said to be alluring and desirable, the rest imposing, if not frightening. Moreover, due to Meyers's emphasis that most of the images are masculine, this woman's gender is confused.

The image constructed through the hybridization of the woman's body, her giant size and the mixing of gender, fits the pattern of the grotesque. In addition, parts of her are sexually connoted (the breasts are 'alluring') and thus volatile—another grotesque feature. Interestingly, since other body parts are not sexually connoted, a tension exists in this body between the sexual and the non-sexual so that it is not fully either. This tension is also expressed by the possibility of another grotesque feature in the body, permeability. At first glance, Meyers's construction of military towers and pools seems impermeable: physically, its military defences cannot be penetrated. In figurative (sexual) terms, it is impermeable, having no vulva, and thus it is non-sexual, non-reproductive. Meyers's description of the breasts, however, contrasts sharply with the body's other features (military, imposing). Supple and alluring (soft, attractive) means permeable, physically (penetrable defence) and figuratively.[79]

The juxtaposition of the military and faunal imagery and Meyers's interpretation of it has implications for whether or not the woman constructed is desirable and then, accessible. On the one hand, the (in)complete image does not seem promising—breasts, neck, nose, eyes, hair. If a man[80] is thinking of having sex with a woman, would he not miss the rest of her? Moreover, would he find all of these comparisons stimulating: are military paraphernalia sexy?[81] But does the moment when the body becomes supple and alluring offset the military imagery, swinging the balance in favour of desirability? Or, does it merely confuse the issue—in terms of desire, is it both desirable and not desirable (repulsive?) simultaneously? Then, depending on what the reader decides in terms of desirability, there remains the question of whether or not this body is attainable. The message behind most of the imagery is surely that the woman pictured is

79. I would suggest that, ultimately, the opposition permeable/impermeable is too simplified for the grotesque. That is, the play between the two—the inability to be concretely one or the other—is all the more grotesque in the confusion and uncertainty it causes in the reader.

80. I read here, and throughout, following the Song's pattern, where the desired relations are heterosexual.

81. There is a disturbing connection that can be made between desire and war, and in these terms, the woman's body could be construed as especially desirable.

inaccessible, like the strongest of military defences. However, the permeability of the body through its sexual allure, makes it available and
attainable. Thus, it seems as though no one response can be sustained
since the terms of the description are mixed—there is always
something to subvert the other. And this is the stuff of the grotesque.

Meyers intends, in her reading of the imagery in the Song, to
establish the power (autonomy) of the protagonist (over against the
authority of males in the public sphere). Because of the erotic content
of the Song, the investigation of the potential for sexual power (or
autonomy) is a legitimate subject of inquiry.[82] Does, then, Meyers's
woman have any sexual autonomy? Since this reading mostly
removes the woman from her erotic context, the most basic answer to
the question is that the protagonist's sexual autonomy is a non-issue;
it is rather ignored. However, this is to consider her autonomy as a
woman. If, as I have suggested, there is some gender play in this
reading, which renders the woman mostly male, the question is more
plausible, as biblical males generally have more say in their sexual
pursuits than women. Moreover, the protagonist is inherently, mili-
tarily powerful, and though this does not have to refer to sexual
power, it could.

Meyers's reading is clearly different from Rashi's and Nicholas's
theologically motivated configuration of the woman in Song 7.1-8.
Her work does not reveal the same kinds of theological concerns, nor
is she mandated theologically to repudiate the female body and
female sexuality—in fact, just the opposite. Yet, in Meyers's reading,
one can observe a grotesque construction similar to Nicholas's and
Rashi's and thus, I think, an unease about the female body and female
sexuality. I suggest that Meyers's attempts to establish a locus for
power in the woman's body[83] leave her uneasy, with an image that
cannot satisfy. She subverts her reading by reminding her readers

82. See *Discovering Eve*, pp. 165-68, 178, 180.

83. The question is, does Meyers's constructed body reverse expected gender
stereotypes, as she wished to show? As I have mentioned, it seems that her use of
'masculine' and 'feminine' imagery in part relies on her own gender stereotypes in
addition to the 'biblical' ones she elucidates; this is particularly evident with
respect to the woman's breasts. Here, Meyers seems to have asked the question,
'how might a gazelle resemble a breast?' (or, 'how might a breast resemble a
gazelle?') and answered accordingly. Her reading of the breasts, then, is actually
more in line with stereotypes about women's breasts than about masculine
imagery used to describe women. This poses a problem for Meyers's reading in
that she must reinforce modern stereotypical descriptions of women (which she is
trying to subvert) in order to account for a puzzling image (the gazelles).

that there is something 'feminine' and desirable about the woman. Grotesque figuration in this female form witnesses to the unease which Meyers's hermeneutic brings to the text, despite its intentions.

Brenner and the Grotesque

In Brenner's picture one sees a construction that is very different from Rashi's, Nicholas's and Meyers's. Unlike the other readers, Brenner is interested in interpreting the imagery in human terms. Granted, the woman is not necessarily attractive, according to Brenner, but she is all there (a quick check against the text confirms that nothing has been left out). She has a huge nose, turbid eyes, overly-long neck, fat stomach, 'jumpy' breasts, vulva, pubic hair, shapely thighs, feet. She is quite realistic—too realistic, perhaps?

Brenner's reading is commendable because it discourages attempts to view Song 7.1-8 as a serious representation of the female body. It also problematizes the assumption that the description is complimentary, and that, in its context of amatory discourse, it must paint a flattering and endearing picture. But despite its come-clean philosophy, this reading exhibits certain features that render the woman's body grotesque, thereby precluding its being viewed in an attractive, complimentary light.[84] Brenner's constructed woman is the sexual/volatile body *par excellence*; the body with thighs, vulva, 'womb's juices',[85] pubic hair, jiggling breasts—all sexually connoted.[86] And, not only does the reading enumerate and isolate these fragments, it also caricatures them. The breasts move about ridiculously. The stomach is fat and quivering. Song 7.1-8, then, is not an affectionate catalogue of the woman's best bits. This reading of a quivering, perspiring, woman dancing for jeering men secures the connection

---

84. Compliment only scratches the surface: nor can the image be endearing, loving, empowering. Brenner's acceptance and promotion of certain stereotypes should also be observed here: the nose and the body's fatness, for example. She observes, 'there is no reason to assume that the picture [the woman] now presents is aesthetically captivating' (' "Come Back, Come Back" ', p. 252), but is there cause for assuming that it is not?

85. Again, the 'permeable body that produces juices and smells', (Miles, *Carnal Knowing*, p. 153).

86. There are a few parts (nose, eyes, neck, head) that are not as explicitly sexually connoted by Brenner as the rest. However, the complete reading does maintain this sexual context for the woman, seen, for example, in summarizing phrases such as 'a description which anchors desire...in energy and sex appeal' (p. 252).

between her appearance and activity and the ridiculous/funny and repulsive.

Unlike the other three readings, Brenner's does not obscure the sexuality of the protagonist, but emphasizes it. But is this emphasis on good terms? The woman is locked into a setting (the dance) that cements her status as sexual object. What better way to ensure that she cannot exercise her sexual freedom than if she is pinned to her place like a turning doll on a platform? (Brenner does not suggest that she is dancing to satisfy her own interests.) Is she desirable?[87] Brenner thinks that, to her audience, she is, though this desirability is tempered, perhaps by embarrassment or fear, so that it yields to ridicule. Are ridicule and sexual attraction then part of the same condition? Brenner may think so. She observes that it is allowed to poke fun at an object of personal and communal desire in this situation;[88] 'humour is eminently more suitable [than serenity] for dealing with a flesh and blood object of desire.'[89]

Like the others, Brenner's reading follows no identifiable theological mandate. Nevertheless, like the others, the construction of the female body as grotesque here reveals a certain unease with it in terms of its sexuality, specifically as sexuality relates to objectification and ridicule. Ultimately, the image does not sit well with Brenner (and so it should not); she undermines her exposure of the description as parody by claiming that she read under the guise of a male reader. Brenner's apparent complicity in the ridiculing of the protagonist, then, is not what it seemed. Her final aim is to redeem this text, and so she supplements her reading with another: the purview of a female reader. Positing this text has been authored by a woman,[90] she proposes that it is to be sung to a woman before her marriage and it shows that

87. Interestingly, though Brenner relies on some conventional stereotypes to evaluate the woman's 'beauty', she drops them in her evaluation of the audience's desire.

88. Brenner, ' "Come Back, Come Back" ', p. 250. It is especially allowed when the fun-pokers are male. Brenner does not explain this here, but she does address the subject elsewhere ('Women Poets and Authors', in Brenner, (ed.), *A Feminist Companion*, pp. 86-97; 90). She speculates that perhaps, because women take love more seriously than men, they are not as easily able to make it the subject of humour or parody. This, however, seems to excuse men for belittling their 'objects of desire' (as if objectification is not already a problem) on the feeble grounds that they do not take love seriously; it also stereotypes them unfairly.

89. Brenner, ' "Come Back, Come Back" ', p. 253.

90. This suggestion is explored further through work on M and F voices in Athalya Brenner and Fokkelien van Dijk-Hemmes, *On Gendering Texts: Female and Male Voices in the Hebrew Bible* (Leiden: E.J. Brill, 1993).

women are aware that men idealize women's bodies to mask their embarrassment and fear.

But does Brenner's suggestion to read as a woman ameliorate the grotesque figuration I found in her male reading? It is always difficult to see the humour in a parody of the female body, especially here, where it is being expressed to one who is about to become another's wife/property, where the threat of exposure and objectification is real. At the end of her male reading, Brenner cites a Shakespearean sonnet to show that humour about the body can be viewed as affectionate teasing. There is, however, an important difference. In Shakespeare's sonnet, the *male* author, aware of the hyperbolic descriptions of women in his day, will love his mistress, despite her 'faults'. Neither of Brenner's readings, however (male or female), allows the protagonist this security (love). Ultimately, the woman is ridiculed and alienated not only by a group of onlookers (men), but now possibly also by women whose words might couch vituperative criticism. I suggest that Brenner's playing with gender as a reader does not redeem the text or her previous reading, but reaffirms them. In fact, the gender inversion in her readings is rather reminiscent of that in the other three (Meyers's, Rashi's, Nicholas's).

Conclusion

This bedding of allegorical and feminist readings indicates that two very different kinds of interpretation have engendered curiously similar final products: both interpret the imagery that describes the female body in such a way that it figures the woman grotesquely, thereby compromising her body image and her sexuality. The reason for the similarity is not that mediaeval allegories and twentieth-century feminist biblical criticism share any previously undetected critical strategy, or, say, that feminist criticism is really allegory. Rather, I suggest that the similarity occurs because the four readings, like any others I have seen, favour a hermeneutic that insists on their embracing these texts and viewing them in a positive light, a hermeneutic that is, at the same time, entangled, to varying degrees, with the notion that the texts contain positive, endearing descriptions of a loved one. That is, the allegories doubtless embrace (i.e. would never reject the applicability or usefulness of) the texts, using them in their theological enterprise—who would expect any different? Yet, they are fraught with the difficult task of both acknowledging the erotic nature of the text—in human–divine terms—and downplaying the capacity of this eroticism, located in a woman's body, to arouse and excite the reader. Nicholas's and Rashi's readings thus show, in their acknowledgment of the desirability of this body, that they are aware of the fact that the descriptions are meant to describe a real body (especially where literal readings permeate the allegorical). And, the feminist readings also embrace this text, finding in it material that is useful for their feminist enterprise, be it elucidating instances of female power (Meyers) or giving evidence of female voice (though this was not ostensibly the primary point of the study, it clearly informed the reading; Brenner). Moreover, they also wrestle with the nature and degree to which the description depicts a real and desirable body. In all four readings, this hermeneutic and its entanglements are understandable, and might be in line with our expectations of what love poetry ought to entail, but they bring with them negative implications, as I have shown, for the woman whom the text describes.

Given that feminist biblical criticism normally works through an ideology to liberate, and is generally concerned about the objectification of the female body, these implications should be legitimate concerns in feminist readings of a text such as Song 7.1-8. The pressing question is whether it is feasible at all to read Song 7.1-8 without compromising the woman's body image and sexual freedom. Is it possible to interpret these texts in such a way that the bodily and personal integrity of the woman imaged is preserved? Should—could—such a readerly move even be attempted? There seem to be two options for feminist readings of this text and others like it in the Song (4.1-5; 6.4-7). One option is to attempt to preserve the subjectivity and integrity of the protagonist, despite or resisting images that may unsettle, or provoke laughter. This is ultimately what Brenner's reading does, in a bold and capable way. Or, as a variation on the same theme, one could preserve integrity by basing it on, say, power or authority, as Meyers's reading does.

The potentially problematic nature of the imagery, however, is always there, an undercurrent that causes a certain tension for readings that try to establish and/or maintain the integrity of the woman in the Song. And this tension undercuts that integrity; it trips up our dancing Shulamite. I suggest a second option for feminist readers, which is to problematize the imagery, to accept that it depicts a woman as ridiculous, comical, as Brenner did, or even (dare one say it?) ugly, but then to take this one step further. Suppose, for instance, that the texts that describe the woman's body are intended as an impediment to the autonomy that she boldly exhibits. Or, if not so overtly constructed, perhaps it is the case that the female body, so figured, reveals a certain unease on the part of the woman's lover, and hence on the part of the primarily male audience that gazes upon her.

I used the grotesque as a tool for metacommentary. It is even more useful for reading the texts themselves,[91] though its usefulness depends on whether one is willing to entertain the second option discussed above. Viewing the descriptions of the body as grotesque accounts, in the first place, for the odd imagery, the juxtaposition of incongruous elements, and the ridiculous pictures that result. It thus alleviates the need to struggle to make sense of the imagery as endearing or complimentary, as biblical scholars typically have, often by stunning displays of interpretive gymnastics.[92] Moreover, the grotesque, with its juxtaposition of the comic and the terrifying, its bold dancing on the edge of unease, encourages the investigation of such issues as whether the way the woman's body is figured reveals some anxiety about her and her sexuality on the part of the one(s) who describes her. Finally, the very unsettling nature of the grotesque also problematizes the reader's reaction to it—to images that are intended to startle, to mock, to terrify—an important issue for evaluating how we come to view the Song of Songs.[93]

A study of the body imagery in the Song using the grotesque urges the re-examination of a variety of issues that are significant for feminist readings of this text. It challenges, for instance, the sexual autonomy and/or gender equality that the protagonist is reputed by feminists to have. It thus raises the possibility that the Song is not as gynocentric as we thought,[94] and in so doing, risks relinquishing the last positive text (?) for feminists in the Hebrew Bible.[95] These are, I

91. See my PhD thesis, 'The Grotesque Body in the Song of Songs' (University of Sheffield, 1999).

92. Read, for example, among many others, Michael Goulder's attempts to explain the images (*The Song of Fourteen Songs* [JSOTSup, 36; Sheffield: Sheffield Academic Press, 1986]), or see Marcia Falk's acknowledgment of their difficulty in her translations (re-creations?) of the images (*Love Lyrics*).

93. This is particularly important, I think, in light of the many acclamations of the book as a beautiful, desirable text. What is it about it that so attracts us as readers and makes us reluctant to entertain any possibility other than that it is lovely, beautiful literature? See Catherine Belsey, *Desire: Love Stories in Western Culture* (Oxford: Basil Blackwell, 1994) for an interesting discussion of responses to texts (notably fiction) such as this one.

94. Or, perhaps its gynocentrism serves phallocentric purposes. See, for example, David J.A. Clines, 'Why is There a Song of Songs and What Does It Do to You if You Read It?', in Clines, *Interested Parties: The Ideology of Writers and Readers of the Hebrew Bible* (JSOTSup, 205; Sheffield: JSOT Press, 1995), pp. 94-121.

95. The relinquishing of this text may not, in fact, be a big issue for some, but it

think, timely issues, though not to be pursued in order to pronounce this book a 'bad text' for women and the protagonist just another captive of patriarchy: such evaluations would be limited, not to mention frustrating. The gender politics in the Song are surely more complicated than this; expressions of male and female desire are woven as intricately as the voices of the lovers who call to each other.[96] And it is this interplay which we ought to take up and ponder. Complicated, and worthy of consideration, too, is the relationship between the body's figuration, with all that it entails in terms of the viewer's anxieties (or not), and affection or admiration—the lovers' and the reader's. Is it a case of one or the other?[97] A reading which urges the recognition of something ugly, instead of insisting on something beautiful, perhaps merely turns over the coin, but it will significantly affect readers who are enamoured with the Song, its beauty of language and idyllic view of love.[98] And affecting readers is what the Song does best.

would seem that there is a general reluctance to tarnish this book. A refreshingly dissonant voice is provided by Daphne Merkin, 'The Woman in the Balcony: On Rereading the Song of Songs', in C. Spiegel and C. Buchmann (eds.), *Out of the Garden: Women Writers on the Bible* (New York: Fawcett Columbine 1994], pp. 238-55.

96. A study of the Song using the grotesque will also include the woman's descriptions of her lover, less prevalent, but present nonetheless. Looking only at the female body has facilitated this study, but I do not pretend that the conversation should be so one sided. See my thesis, 'The Grotesque Body in the Song of Songs'.

97. I am grateful to Athalya Brenner for asking the question. My suspicion is that it will be useful to entertain these oppositions for a while, in order to explore some of the complexities of the Song's presentation of desire.

98. This feeling toward the Song may account for readerly resistance to deviate from the usually positive interpretation of the book and the glossing over of other troubling moments in it (the beating in 5.7; the anger of the brothers); see Fiona C. Black and J. Cheryl Exum, 'Semiotics in Stained Glass: Edward Burne-Jones's Song of Songs', in J. Cheryl Exum and Stephen D. Moore (eds.), *Biblical Studies/Cultural Studies: The Third Sheffield Colloquium* (JSOTSup, 266; GCT, 7; Sheffield: Sheffield Academic Press, 1998), pp. 315-42.

LUIS DE LEÓN AND THE SONG OF SONGS*

Jane Barr

Remarkably little attention has been paid to Fray Luis de León (1527–91) in the English-speaking world. He does not, for example, have an entry in the *Oxford Dictionary of the Christian Church* (1978 edition).[1] For many scholars, the first introduction to the man and his work is acquired when visiting the University of Salamanca, where one sees the classroom in which he lectured and in which, on returning to resume teaching after almost five years as a prisoner of the Inquisition, he is said to have begun his first lecture with the incomparable words *Dicebamus hesterno die* (or 'Decíamos ayer...,' 'we were saying yesterday'). In his native Spain he is much read and admired, chiefly for his poetry, but also for his meditations on the names of Christ (*Los nombres de Cristo*) and his book of advice to married women, *La perfecta casada* (The Perfect Marriage), a series of homilies linked to verses in Proverbs 31.

The 1920s saw the publication in England of a life of Fray Luis de León by Aubrey F. Bell, a short monograph by James Fitzmaurice-Kelly, and some important studies by E. Allison Peers. Then followed a long period of comparative neglect until the balance was redressed by the appearance of the splendid volume by Colin P. Thompson, *The Strife of Tongues: Fray Luis de León and the Golden Age of Spain* (1988).

The 'Decíamos ayer' anecdote may not be true, but it accords well with what we know of Fray Luis's character. In his *Libro de descripción de verdaderos retratos de ilustres y memorables Varones*, begun in 1599, Francisco Pacheco provides a verbal sketch of his appearance and character.[2] He was of smallish stature, with a large, shapely head and

*   First published in S.E. Balentine and J. Barton (eds.), *Language, Theology and the Bible: Essays in Honour of James Barr* (Oxford: Oxford University Press, 1994), pp. 311-24. Reprinted with permission.
1.   I am informed that this omission is to be rectified in the next edition.
2.   Pacheco's *Retrato* is printed as an appendix to J. Fitzmaurice-Kelly, *Fray Luis de Leon: A Biographical Fragment* (Oxford: Oxford University Press, 1921). See also Rogelio Reyes Cano, ' "Retrato de Fray Luis de León" por Francisco Pacheco', *Insula* 539 (1991), p.1.

broad forehead, and lively green eyes. Quiet and reserved, austere and unsmiling, and of a choleric disposition, he nevertheless showed kindness and tolerance towards friends and colleagues. He was so ascetic in his personal life that most nights he did not sleep on a bed. More important for this study is what we learn about his scholarly reputation. He showed singular acuteness in his pronouncements, and the field of his competence was wide. If Pacheco is to be believed, he was versed in mathematics, astrology, law and even medicine. As for the humanities, he knew Latin, Greek, Hebrew, Chaldean and Syriac as well as any expert in those languages. While there may be some exaggeration here, it is clear, as we shall see, that he was an excellent linguist, and his love for the Greek and Latin classics is evidenced throughout his writings. When in prison, he asked for books to be brought from his library, requesting his Homer, his Aristotle and a copy of Horace and Virgil, 'of which there are a great many'.[3]

Certain of the aspects—the austerity, the asceticism, the choleric temperament, the kindness to intimates, and the mastery of languages—he shared in common with St Jerome, and while there are also great dissimilarities between these two biblical scholars, the linking of their names is not inappropriate. Fray Luis, like Jerome, was deeply concerned with the *Hebraica veritas*, and when he decided to translate the Song of Songs into Spanish, it was to the original Hebrew that he turned, at the same time consulting and comparing the Septuagint and the Vulgate versions. While holding the Vulgate in the highest esteem, Fray Luis did not hesitate to question its accuracy. His temerity in challenging the authority of the Vulgate was one of the chief causes of his imprisonment.

It was in 1561 or soon after that Fray Luis, a professor of Bible at that time at the University of Salamanca, began to translate the Song of Songs from Hebrew into Spanish, with an accompanying commentary. It was his first prose work. It was a daring venture. The vernacular was not regarded as a suitable medium for any learned treatise, and most certainly not for the transmission of the inspired text of the sacred scripture. Later, Fray Luis was to argue persuasively for the use of the vernacular.[4]

3.   Fitzmaurice-Kelly, *Fray Luis*, p. 83.

4.   'Dedicatoria', in *Los nombres de Christo* 1.3. *Obras completas castellanas de Fray Luis de León* (2 vols.; ed. Felix Garcia; Madrid: Biblioteca de Autores Cristianos, 1957), I, p. 687. All translations from Spanish are my own. I am very grateful for the helpful comments of Maria Donapetry, without whose encouragement this essay might not have been written.

> Words do not carry weight because they are in Latin, but rather through
> being expressed with the seriousness that is proper to them, whether
> they be in Spanish, or in French. If, because we call our language
> common (*vulgar*), it is imagined that we cannot write in it except in a
> vulgar and low style, that is a very serious error (*grandísimo error*).
> When Plato wrote in his own language, he did not write in an unsuit-
> able manner about commonplace things; and Cicero likewise in the lan-
> guage which was common in his time. To move nearer to home, St. Basil
> and St. Chrysostom and St. Gregory Nazianzen and St. Cyril... wrote
> the most divine mysteries of our faith of their own native language
> (which the children at that time drank in with their mother's milk, and
> the women stall-holders spoke in the marketplace), and did not hesitate
> to put into their own language what they knew would be above the
> heads of many who understood the language.

Such arguments, however, fell on mainly hostile ears. Not only was
Fray Luis defying long-standing convention in translating Scripture
into the vernacular, but, in proceeding to question the accuracy of the
Vulgate, he was striking at the roots of the Church's faith. Fray Luis
was at pains to point out that his alterations to the traditional text
were *palabrillas*, 'little words', of no import and that his faith in the
authority of the Vulgate text was unshaken. Colin P. Thompson refers
to 'two sharply-contrasted attitudes'—'that of scholars like Fray Luis,
who believed that it [the Vulgate text] contained no error in faith and
morals, and was more reliable than other Latin versions, and that of
those for whom it was quite simply infallible'.[5]

Fray Luis cannot have been unaware of the dangerous waters into
which he was entering when he commenced his translation and exposition of the Song of Songs. He did not, however, intend his
manuscript for public circulation. He wrote it at the request of a nun
in a Salamanca convent, his cousin Isabel Osorio. It was later copied
without his permission and circulated. To a Jerome scholar, the parallels between Jerome and Fray Luis are many. Both delighted in giving
instruction to women of their acquaintance who were dedicated to the
study of the Bible. (One has already been reminded, through Fray
Luis's experiences, of the hostile reception accorded to Jerome's challenge to the infallibility of the Septuagint.)

While translating the Vulgate into another language was a novel
step, to write a commentary on the Song of Songs was to follow a long
distinguished mediaeval tradition. Ambrose, Isidore of Seville, Alcuin,
Bede, Haimo of Auxerre, Anselm of Laon, Bernard of Clairvaux, Hon-

---

5.   C.P. Thompson, *The Strife of Tongues: Fray Luis de León and the Golden Age of
Spain* (Cambridge: Cambridge University Press, 1988), p. 44.

orius Augustodensis—the list could be doubled or trebled. It is not possible to know which of these commentaries Fray Luis might have studied, but it is certain that he was deeply versed in the mediaeval exegetical tradition.

The interpretation of the Song of Songs, on the surface a celebration of erotic love, had posed problems for exegetes since the time of Origen. The influence of St Augustine was strong throughout the Middle Ages. D.W. Robertson, in his introduction to Augustine's *de Doctrina Christiana*, summarizes this well. He quotes Augustine on Cant. 4.2 (Robertson's translation):

> I contemplate the saints more pleasantly when I envisage them as teeth of the Church, cutting off men from their errors and transferring them to her body after their hardness has been softened as if by being bitten and chewed. I recognise them most pleasantly as shorn sheep having put aside the burdens of the world like so much fleece, and as ascending from the washing, which is baptism, all to create twins, which are the two precepts of love, and I see no one of them sterile of this holy fruit (*de Doct. Christ* 2.6).

Robertson goes on to comment:

> The appeal of the Augustinian comparison lies in an intellectual recognition of an abstraction beneath the surface of the language… The function of figurative expression was not to arouse spontaneous emotional attitudes based on the personal experience of the observer, but to encourage the observer to seek an abstract pattern of philosophical significance beneath the symbolical configuration.[6]

Fray Luis was to write a commentary where he specifically concentrates on the *corteza*, the 'bark' or surface of the language, and was to break away from the highly allegorical mediaeval approach where the surface meaning is often ignored and individual words are loaded with symbolism. One example, from Honorius Augustodensis, will suffice to illustrate this:

> Note that seven physical features of the Beloved are praised by the Spouse, namely the seven orders of the elect in the Church. The eyes, those who see what is hidden; the hair, those who, free from their sins, pass through the eye of a needle, that is, the gate of heaven; the teeth, those who correct the wicked; the lips, those who open the secrets of Scripture; the cheeks, those who blush for their own sins and those of

---

6.   D.W. Robertson, *Augustine: On Christian Doctrine* (New York: Liberal Arts Press, 1958), pp. xiv-xv.

others; the neck, those who, by preaching the breath of life or the food of doctrine, administer the joys of eternity; the two breasts, those who are learned in both laws of the two peoples.[7]

Fray Luis's *Prólogo a la exposición del Cantar de los Cantares* makes clear his purposes and it is worth quoting selected passages at some length.[8]

He begins by extolling the love of God, which he says only the blind could fail to recognize, so surrounded are we by his blessings, among which are the Sacred Scriptures, which are marvellously adapted by the Holy Spirit to accord with our nature and language:

Among the divine writings is found the very sweet song which Solomon, king and prophet, composed, in the form of an amorous interchange between two persons, a shepherd and a shepherdess, in which, more than in any other sacred writing, God reveals himself wounded by love for us, with all the passions and sentiments which this state of feeling is accustomed to inflict on hearts that are very soft and tender. And, in brief, all those sentiments which passionate lovers are wont to feel are revealed here so much more sharply and delicately, inasmuch as the Divine Love is so much more living and on fire than earthly love. For this reason, the reading of this book is difficult for everyone, and dangerous for the young and all who are not yet advanced or very firm in the path of virtue [*this was a medieval commonplace*]; for in no Scripture is the passion of love expounded with more force and feeling than here. There is no need in this case to talk of danger [*here Fray Luis refers to the spiritual state of the recipient of his book*]; I shall work hard to deal with the difficulty [*of the Scripture*]—which is great—with such inadequate resources as I possess.

While recognizing an element of danger in the study of the Song, Fray Luis' attitude is far removed from that of Ambrose, who introduces his commentary with *non hic foeditatis incentiva, sed castitatis celebrantur mysteria;...nihil vile, nihil terrenum quaeramus.*[9]

In the next paragraph he goes on to explain that others have dealt with the spiritual meaning, but that he will work only on expounding the *corteza*, the superficial meaning of the text, which, although it is a task of less value (he says 'fewer carats') than the first, is not without its difficulties:

For one has to understand that this Book was originally written in verse, and is all one pastoral eclogue in which Solomon and his Spouse, and at some points their companions, speak in the words and the language of shepherds as though they were all village-dwellers.

7.   Honorius Augustodensis, *PL* 172. 414.
8.   Garcia (ed.) , *Fray Luis*, I, pp. 70-75.
9.   *PL* 15. 1947.

The first difficulty, he explains, arises from the short staccato nature of the utterances of the lovers. Such short sentences are commonly obscure. He then continues:

> The second cause of obscurity is the nature of the Hebrew language in which it is written, which is essentially a language of few words and short sentences, full of a diversity of meanings.

The diversity of meanings of Hebrew words was a strongly held conviction of Fray Luis, and one which influenced him in his translation and exegesis:

> Each language and each people has its own peculiarities of language (*propriedades de hablar*) and what may seem strange and uncouth in one language is beautiful and pleasing in another.[10]

His emphasis on the *propriedad* of language is reminiscent of Jerome. In *Ep.* 106 Jerome states that it is enjoined on a good translator *ut* ἰδιώματα *linguae alterius, suae linguae exprimat proprietate*, and the word *proprietas* occurs several times in that letter.[11]

Fray Luis states his purposes clearly:

> In this book, I am going to do two things: one is to turn the text into our language word for word; secondly, to give a brief exposition, but not of each word *per se*, except in those instances where an obscurity exists in the letter of the text...and I will set out first the translation of the whole chapter, and then its exposition.
>
> As to my first aim, I have tried to conform as far as possible with the original Hebrew, comparing it with all the Greek and Latin translations which exist (and there are many), and I have endeavoured that my translation should correspond with the original, not only in the phrases and words themselves, but also in their tone and nuance, imitating the figures and styles of speech of the original as far as possible in our language, which, indeed, corresponds with Hebrew in many places. [*This perhaps surprising similarity that he discerns between Hebrew and Spanish may have been mentioned here to advocate an increasing use of the vernacular.*]

The *Hebraica veritas* was important for Fray Luis, as it had been for Jerome. But any move to emend the Vulgate in the light of a fresh study of the Hebrew original was viewed with great suspicion in late sixteenth-century Spain. It was believed that the integrity of the original text might have been tampered with by Jews, and the likelihood that Fray Luis had some *converso* blood in his veins was an additional factor.

---

10. He has given as an example of this the likening of a neck to a tower, or teeth to a flock of sheep.

11. *PL* 22. 839.

He defines the role of the translator clearly:

> The translator has to be faithful and exact, and, if at all possible, to
> count the words and replace them with the same number of words,
> neither more nor fewer, of the same type and variety of meanings which
> the originals possessed, but he should not impose upon them his own
> particular opinion as to their meaning, so that those who read the
> translation may be able to understand all the variety of meanings which
> the original supplies, and should be free to choose from these the mean-
> ing that seems best.

And again:

> It is indeed the truth that, translating the text, we cannot maintain con-
> gruence with the original precisely; the character of the sentence and the
> peculiarity (*propriedad*) of our language forces us to add some little
> words (*palabrillas*) without which the meaning would remain quite
> obscure.

Fray Luis does not explain how the translator can choose a meaning
which is so versatile as to enable the reader to choose from within it a
variety of meanings, unless the reader already possesses a knowledge
of the original language. Could it be that, try as he will to translate
only the surface meaning of the text, he is used to words, in allegorical contexts, carrying a considerable cargo of underlying meanings?
Whatever the truth of this, his own method of procedure allows him a
good deal of scope, because he translates each chapter first in a rather
literal way, and then in his exposition elaborates on the bare meaning.

Before beginning his translation and exposition of ch. 1 of the Song
of Songs, he comments on its title,[12] explaining that it is a characteristic (*propriedad*) of the Hebrew language to double a word to indicate a superlative. This was a traditional introductory comment in
mediaeval commentaries and is no proof of Fray Luis's Hebrew scholarship. But throughout his commentary, there are clear indications of
his ability to handle the Hebrew text competently. For his unsophis-
ticated cousin, he does not enter into the complicated problems of the
Hebrew text, but rather adds some background information on a
Hebrew word where this will help her to a greater appreciation of its
meaning; for example, in 1.3, *metiome el rey en sus retretes*, 'The king
put me in his private chamber', he points out that though the Hebrew
verb refers to the past tense, it can also have a future meaning. In 1.5
of *mi viña*, 'my vineyard', he says that the Hebrew possessive has
double force and means *mia remia*, the prefix *re-* having an intensive

---

12. Garcia (ed.), *Fray Luis*, pp. 74-75.

quality in Spanish (cf. 'my own vineyard', REB). Notice that, in his actual translations, he sticks to the letter of the Hebrew.

His translation, in fact, suffers from an excess of literality. In his faithfulness to the original, he commonly omits a copulative verb, and sometimes the sense is obscure. He justifies a lack of grammatical or contextual continuity by explaining that lovers speak in a staccato fashion; asyndeton is accounted for by the lovers' excitement.[13]

If his translation was intended to stand alone, it could be severely faulted. But he intended it to be read with the accompanying commentary, and, in it, he repeats his translation of each verse or part-verse with an exposition.

In this commentary, we move into a totally different world from the traditional highly allegorical mediaeval interpretations. He had begun his prologue to the Son with a paean of love, love of God for man, man for God. The commentary continues in this vein. All the rich imagery exists to fill our hearts with a deeper understanding of this love.

It is true that the twelfth-century commentaries on the Song showed developmental changes, as E. Ann Matter points out. 'The vivid, clear, even shockingly fleshly language of these commentaries describes a flesh-denying spiritual union'.[14]

For Fray Luis, the union is most certainly a spiritual one, but the bodies are real human bodies, teeth are teeth, breasts are breasts, ornaments are for beautifying the wearer. Fray Luis was a poet of great sensitivity. He was an artist, too, according to Pacheco, and this is borne out by his word-pictures of the physical beauty of the lovers, of the landscape, of the jewellery and ornaments the Bride wears. In 1.9, he discusses the meaning of the Hebrew word תרים, which, he says, is in doubt, citing four possible types of ornament it might be, and says that it reminds him of ornaments he had seen in the head-dress of women in old paintings.[15] There is a vivid concreteness in his descriptions, designed to make the scenes more real and vivid for his reader, and thereby, and this is his purpose, to make the love portrayed there more vivid and bring us closer into a union with God.

He succeeds in writing a vivid ecstatic picture of human love which, while erotic, is totally pure. J.N.D. Kelly writes of the 'frankly

13. Thompson, *Fray Luis*, p. 33, suggests that 'Perhaps this was intended to demonstrate in as vivid a way as possible how difficult Hebrew was to translate into any language — including the Latin of the Vulgate'.

14. E. Ann Matter, *The Voice of my Beloved* (Philadelphia: University of Pennsylvania Press, 1990), p. 138.

15. Luis de Leon uses the Vulgate numbering of verses.

erotic imagery' in Jerome's use of the Song of Songs in his letter to the teenaged Eustochium, and of 'feeding her fantasy' with 'exciting images'. One could not accuse Fray Luis thus.[16]

The word-portrait of Fray Luis depicts him as austere and ascetic. E.A. Peers, on the other hand talks of an 'almost total absence of asceticism'.[17] A close reading of the Commentary on the Song suggests there is truth in both these assessments.

It is worth noting that the commentary is rich in allusions to other biblical passages. His classical scholarship also supplies him with illustrations. For example, in commenting on 4.3, he tells us that Aristotle, in his advice on how to recognize a man's qualities from his features, declared that thin lips are a sign of discretion and pleasing conversation.

Some ten years after the writing of this book, and its illicit circulation, Fray Luis was imprisoned by the Inquisition. In the interim, in 1567–68, Fray Luis had delivered a series of lectures, entitled *De Fide*, in which he clearly stated his position on the Vulgate.[18] That there were many variant Vulgate codices, that the Vulgate may not always have made the best choice when the Hebrew text is equivocal, that the Vulgate translation may indeed be wrong at times—these opinions, openly expressed, gave fuel to his critics. His statement that 'there are certain places in Sacred Scripture which, if they are read according to the Hebrew or Greek verity, give stronger confirmation to the tenets of our faith, than if they are read as the Vulgate has them' did little to appease them.

When charges were preferred against him by the Inquisition, his attitude to the Vulgate and his Song of Songs translation and commentary were paramount.[19]

We are fortunate in having a reply (*Respuesta*)[20] by Fray Luis himself to some of the charges written from his prison cell. There he justifies his translation on several points where he had taken issue

16. J.N.D. Kelly, *Jerome: His Life, Writings and Controversies* (London: Gerald Duckworth, 1975), pp. 102-103. See also Jane Barr, 'The Influence of Saint Jerome on Medieval Attitudes to Women', in J.M. Soskice (ed.), *After Eve* (London: Collins Marshall Pickering, 1990), pp. 89-102 (98).

17. E.A. Peers, *Studies of Spanish Mystics* (3 vols.; London: SPCK; New York: Macmillan, 1951), I, p. 260.

18. Thompson, *Fray Luis*, pp. 44-47. There is a useful summary in K. Hölz, 'Fray Luis de León y la Inquisición', *Insula* 539 (1991), p. 6.

19. Hölz summarizes the charges in 'Fray Luis', pp. 7-8. Note the description of Fray Luis' interpretation of Solomon's Song as *carmen amatorium ad suam uxorem*.

20. Garcia (ed.), *Fray Luis*, I, pp. 211-18.

with the Vulgate. The most important concerns the Hebrew words מבעד לצמתך] at 4.1.[21] Fray Luis translates this as *entre tus cabellos*, 'among your locks',[22] as against the Vulgate's *absque eo quod intrinsecus latet*, 'without (or apart from) that which lies hidden within', the context being a description of the dove's eyes of the Beloved. In his commentary for his cousin, he says that he does not understand why Jerome gave this translation, which is different from that of other experts in the language, but also contradicts his own translation in Isa. 47.2, where he translates the same Hebrew word as *torpeza* or *fealdad*, words denoting ugliness. Fray Luis explains why his interpretation must be right. The passage is one of praise for the woman's beauty. Her eyes will sparkle through her hair.

He was later to elaborate on this in his Latin commentary, and in his *Respuesta*, he deals with the fuller argumentation one finds there.[23]

He expresses reluctance to discuss a topic which may be offensive to modest and pious ears (*las orejas honestas y religiosas*), but which he is forced to treat fully because of the accusations of his enemies. He explains that, in his Spanish commentary, it would have been inappropriate to mention such matters, but now he is addressing good and learned men (*los hombres buenos y doctos*) he may speak frankly.

Fray Luis proceeds:

> First of all, I state that whichever of these two ways we translate this passage...in substance, it is the same sentence, and, either way, it seems that the intention of the Holy Spirit is achieved, namely to praise the beauty of the eyes of the Beloved. And if these interpretations differ somewhat, the difference between them does not add up to one iota. [*Rather wittily, in the context, he says it does not matter one* hair].[24] This being so, to say that I take leave of the Vulgate is pure calumny, because I don't take issue with it over a matter which is of any importance, in my opinion.

And again:

21. Thompson, *Fray Luis*, pp. 33-34. Cristóbal Cuevas discusses this passage in his article ' "Estilo del Espíritu Santo": Crítica Textual y Polémica a Propósito de un Pasaje del *Cantar de los Cantares*', *Insula* 539 (1991), pp. 16-18 (17). This issue of that journal is devoted entirely to Fray Luis de León. Unfortunately, it appeared after my article was already written.

22. These locks of hair, he explains, are 'bangs' or fringes on the forehead.

23. I have used the Bodleian's Latin version (Venice, 1604).

24. I am disposed to disagree with Fitzmaurice-Kelly who says (*Fray Luis*, p. 80): 'Humour was one of the few gifts which nature had denied to Luis de León.'

> Secondly, and here I ask the pardon of my listeners, but I do not know
> how to express it otherwise, I say that St. Jerome understood the
> Hebrew word לסתך as being the name given to the shameful parts of a
> woman, just as Castilian has its word for them, and Latin, too; and
> because he did not dare to translate it into Latin using the proper word
> for fear of causing offence to his readers, he employed the circumlocu-
> tion we note'. [*He then points out that Symmachus, too, used a circum-*
> *locution here, and proceeds further to discuss Jerome's comments on the same*
> *word in Isa. 47.2.*]

He continues:

> Three conclusions can be drawn about St. Jerome: one, that he under-
> stood that this Hebrew word means a woman's *pudenda*; two, that he
> accepts that, in the Song, this is the word the Holy Spirit used in the
> same sense; three, that he and Symmachus, to preserve the respect that
> is due to the Holy Scripture, did not translate it with another such word
> in Latin or Greek, but rather with a periphrasis, the one giving the ver-
> sion 'beyond what is hidden' and the other 'beyond what is kept silent'.

Then follows a rhetorical passage in which Fray Luis argues that, if
Jerome and Symmachus felt this word too indecent to be expressed in
their languages, it is extremely unlikely that the Holy Spirit would
have allowed this word to appear in Hebrew. 'Was it less dishon-
ourable, or less dangerous, or less indecent in Hebrew for the
Hebrews to read, than in Latin for the Latins, or in Greek for the
Greeks? Furthermore, if the woman in the Song represents the
Church, could צמתך really have this meaning?'

But, Fray Luis says, it will be argued that, if the Hebrew word has
this meaning, Jerome had no option but to act as he did. But the word
has another meaning, insists Fray Luis, vouched for by Hebrew scholars, namely 'locks of hair or fringes on the temples. I do not think', he
maintains, 'that any censor, even an unjust one, should condemn my
opinion, or should not admit that, in a matter of so little importance
as this, some little words (*palabrillas*) in St. Jerome's translation could
be improved upon'.

He then proceeds to defend his interpretations at points of
difficulty in 7.5 and 6.4, these discussions confirming the impression
that, for Fray Luis, the interpretation which glorifies the beauty of the
Bride, and thereby enhances the beauty of the divine-human relationship, is the right one, provided, of course, that it has good linguistic
backing. He ends his defence with the rueful conclusion that no one
can please everybody; it is sufficient if one can satisfy the majority. He
asks his judges to take into consideration the fact that only a few
scholars have found fault with his work as against the large number
who have approved.

Fray Luis had been imprisoned in March 1572. He was released in December 1576 when the Supreme Inquisition gave orders 'to acquit him, to reprimand him, and to warn him to be more careful in future, and to confiscate the manuscript copy of his Spanish version of the Song of Solomon'.[25]

One can see in the *Respuesta* how Fray Luis was influenced by his theory of a possible plurality of meanings in a Hebrew word. A good example of this is his treatment of the Hebrew word הדר in chapter XV of *La perfecta casada*. He says that Hebrew is fortunate in being able to express so much in one word when it describes women as *la gracia de casa*, for in Spanish *gracia* (grace) is not adequate and we could scarcely appreciate its full significance even if we used many other words, such as *aseo* (neatness), *hermosura* (beauty), *donaire* (elegance), *luz* (intelligence), *deleite* (joy), *concierto* (harmony), *contento* (contentment).[26] A great tribute to the Hebrew language, and perhaps the kind of thing Aubrey Bell had in mind when he reported that 'it has been said of Luis de León that he had a Hebrew soul'.[27]

I have referred to Jerome several times in this article. It is clear from the multiple virtues ascribed to women in the above passage that Fray Luis' opinion of women was very different from that of Jerome. In *The Perfect Marriage*, his wives are still modest, humble and obedient to their husbands, but his attitude is positive and laudatory, and one wonders if he has the refutation of Jerome's attitudes in mind when he says 'God, when he desired man to marry, giving him woman, said: Let us make him a helpmeet like to himself. Hence we are to understand that the natural duty of the woman, and the purpose for which he created her, is that she may be a helper to her husband and not a calamity or misfortune; a helper, not a destroyer'.[28]

25. Fitzmaurice-Kelly, *Fray Luis*, p. 92.

26. Garcia, *Fray Luis*, p. 321.

27. A.F. Bell, *Luis de Leon: A Study of the Spanish Renaissance* (Oxford: Clarendon Press, 1925).

28. Garcia, *Fray Luis*, p. 257.

GO YOUR WAY: WOMEN REWRITE THE SCRIPTURES
(SONG OF SONGS 2.8-14)*

Klara Butting

God's History and Eroticism

> It is quite clear to exegetic science today that the admission of the Song
> of Songs to the canon was not justified with regard to its original
> meaning, for it consists of a collection of love songs, the beauty of which
> might be rightfully admired whereas nothing can be said about the
> theological meaning.[1]

This summary of modern Song of Songs research makes a clean break
with the allegorical exegeses that had formed the interpretation of the
book up to the eighteenth century. The Song of Songs was then
understood as an allegory about God's history with Israel, the Church
or even the single soul. The segregation from the profane world
construction allowed theological exegeses of the Song of Songs. This
method has already been applied in the rabbinic discussion as to
whether the SoS belonged in the canon. It is said that during this
discussion Rabbi Aqiba was strongly opposed to any inquiry about
this Song: 'Heaven forbid! No one in Israel ever disputed that the
Song of Songs defiles the hands. For all the world is not as worthy as
the day on which the Song of Songs was given to Israel, for all the
writings are holy, but the Song of Songs is the Holy of Holies.'[2] From
the very same Rabbi Aqiba another statement has come down to us:
'He who gives his voice a flourish in reading the Song of Songs in the
banquet-halls and makes it a secular song has no share in the world to
come'.[3] The great theological esteem of the SoS is paired with the
prohibition on its festive secular use. This polarization is similarly
reiterated in D. Michel's research survey, quoted above. God's history
and wordly love appear to be incompatible. Eroticism and love

---

1.   D. Michel, *Untersuchungen zur Eigenart des Buches Qohelet* (BZAW, 183;
Berlin: W. de Gruyter, 1989), p. 274.
2.   *Mish. Yad.* 3.5; quoted from R. Gordis, *The Song of Songs and Lamentations: A
Study, Modern Translation and Commentary* (New York: Ktav, 1974), p. 9.
3.   *t. San.* 12.10; quoted from Gordis, *The Song of Songs*, p. 6.

belong in the private sphere and have nothing to do with history or even God's history. However, this construction of reality is contradicted in the Song of Songs.

Love songs are heard in the SoS: the mutual admiration of the lovers and, again and again, their reciprocal call for a rendevouz. Large parts of the SoS are sung by a woman, addressing a group of women as 'Daughters of Jerusalem'.[4] Repeatedly, we hear a woman beseech the Daughters of Jerusalem not to disturb her love (2.7; 3.5; 8.4). These appeals are heard especially when she sings of the affinity with her lover and visualizes their meeting. Hence, it can be assumed that the women grant the lovers access to secret places and make their meeting possible. Furthermore, the woman names her 'mother's house' as a place where she can meet her lover (3.4; 8.2). A space belonging to mothers and daughters becomes apparent in the SoS poems, a place where the singer receives external and spiritual support. The whole SoS can be understood as female literature, as a product of women's culture in ancient Israel.[5] In this dialogue between women and between lovers, biblical tradition has been taken up and changed. The songs give us an insight into a 'song workshop' where 'contextual liberation theology' might have been born.[6] And so we find a new interpretation of Sarah and Abraham's history in the Song of Songs.

Go Your Way

'Go your way', לְךָ לֶךְ! This demand envelops Abraham and Sarah's life.[7] Twice in Genesis we hear this word combination, the form of which—second person singular masculine, in the imperative mode— is unique in the Hebrew Bible.[8]

---

4. 1.5; 2.7; 3.5 (10); 5.8 , 16; 8.4.

5. A. Brenner, *The Israelite Women: Social Role and Literary Type in Biblical Narrative* (Sheffield: JSOT Press, 1985), pp. 46-50; F. van Dijk-Hemmes, *Sporen van vrouwenteksten in de Hebreeuwse Bijbel* (Utrecht: Faculteit der Godjeleeredheid Universiteit Utrecht, 1992), pp. 130-31.

6. Cf. Klara Butting, *Die Buchstaben werden sich noch wundern: Innerbiblische Kritik als Wegweisung feministischer Hermeneutik* (Berlin: Elektor Verlag, 1994), pp. 117-60.

7. F. Breukelmann, *Bijbelse Theologie: Het eerstlingschap van Israel* (Kampen: Kok, 1992), pp. 74-75.

8. This so called '*Davtivus ethicus*'—'I' with the suffix of the second person added to an imperative—'expresses the special connection of the addressed to the action'—W. Schneider, *Grammatik des biblischen Hebräisch*, p. 217, quoted by

YHWH said to Abram:
Go your way from your country and your kindred and and your father's
house to the land that I will let you see... (12.1)

He (God) said:
Take with you your only son Isaac whom you love
and *go your way* to the land of Moriah
and offer him there as a burnt offering upon one of the mountains
which I will point out to you. (22.2)

Abraham is requested to set out and part with the world of his
fathers (Gen. 12.1-9). The destination is a land which God will show
Abraham. The special configuration of this land is part of the second
call to go, starting the story of Isaac's binding (Gen. 22.2-19), a story
whichs forbids the sacrifice of children—no matter what the political
or economic reasons may be—and demands the release of children for
God's history. 'Go your way!' With this call, the way of hope into a
new society is both opened and delimited.

When the singer tells of her lover's call in the second chapter of the
Song of Songs, she confronts herself with this double call from Abraham and Sarah's story for setting out. (The singer says, in the first
person mode:)

2.8 My lover's voice!
there he comes!
Leaping upon the mountains,
skipping over the hills!
9 My beloved is like a gazelle
or a young hart.
Look, he stands behind our wall,
looking through the windows,
peering through the lattices.
10 My beloved spoke, saying unto me:
'Rise up, my love, my beautiful,
and *go your way!*
11 For the winter has passed,
the rain is over and gone.

Breukelmann, *Bijbelse Theologie*, p. 102. Other forms of the same word combination:
Exod. 18.27; Jos. 22.4; 1 Sam. 26.11-12; Jer. 5.5; SoS 2.10, 11, 13; 4.6; Gen. 21.16—
U. Cassuto, *A Commentary on the Book of Genesis*. Part II. *From Noah to Abraham*
(Jerusalem: Magnes Press, 1984), pp. 310-11. Cassuto translates 'go your way' and
adds: 'Go you by yourself, or only those who are united to you in unique relationship, go on the way that belongs to you alone, and leave behind your kinsfolk
amongst whom you have lived till now and who do not wish or are not able to
associate themselves with you in your new way' (p. 311).

12 The flowers are seen in the land,
the time of singing has come,
the voice of the turtledove is heard in our land.
13 The figtree puts forth her green fruits
and the vines in blossom give forth their fragrance.
Arise, my love, my beautiful,
and *go your way.*
14 My dove, in the clefts of the rock,
in the shadow of the cliff,
let me see your face,
let me hear your voice,
for sweet is your voice
and graceful is your face.

Twice we hear the call *'go your way'*, לְכִי לָךְ (2.10, 13). This call, in the second person singular feminine, imperative mode is—like the masculine form in Genesis 12 and 22—unique in the Hebrew Bible. Abraham and Sarah's setting out to the promised land is remembered and, at the same time, a comparable setting-out is expected of the singer.

Moreover, there are further remarkable word connections between this part of the Song of Songs and Abraham and Sarah's story. The SoS describes the 'land', 'our land' (2.12). The aim of the singer's setting-out is so that she *'let* her face *be seen'* (2.14) in our *'land'.* Abraham's promised goal can be seen: 'The *land* that I will *let you see'* (Gen. 12.1). This land, with its blossoms and buds, has already revealed itself in the Song of Songs (2.12). But can the lover, a woman who, like Sarah, is 'beautiful of appearance',[9] let her face be seen in this land?

The Promised Land

In Genesis the character of the promised land is already described at variance with the social structures, according to which a beautiful woman cannot let herself be seen. A land that God will allow to be seen is promised (Gen. 12.1). The development of this promise consists of seven small pericopes that form an inseperable unit, as illustrated below:[10]

12.1-4a 12.4b-7 12.8-9 12.10–13.1 13.2-4 13.5-13 13.14-18

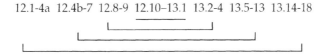

---

9.   Sarah is *'beautiful of appearence'*, יְפַת מַרְאֶה (Gen. 12.11), cf. SoS 2.10, 13 'my *beautiful'*, יָפָתִי; SoS 2.14 'let me see your *face'*, מַרְאַיִךְ.

10.   Breukelmann, *Bijbelse Theologie*, pp. 101-12.

Only at the very end of the ring composition does God fulfill the promise he gave when Abraham set out (12.1-4a), and let him see the land (13.14-18). In the in-between texts the secret of the promised land is unfolded in reflections upon a counter-picture. Framed by the description of the journey to Egypt, from Bet-El southward (12.8-9), and the return journey which is identically described, from the south northward to Bet-El (13.2-4), the pericope situated in the center is the story of Abraham and Sarah's stay in Egypt (12.10-13.1). The land of Egypt is here shown as the antitype of the promised land. Circumstances are characterized by the notion that, in that land, the law of the strongest prevails. Already at the border Abraham describes the order prevailing in Egypt:

> 12.11 When he came near to enter into Egypt, he said to Sarai, his wife:
> Behold, I know you are a woman of beautiful appearance.
> 12 When the Egyptians see you they will say: This is his wife,
> they will kill me, but they will let you live.

Unrestrained demands loom. They are combined with unlimited possibilities of power. The powerful person is free and is right. The destructive force of this disorder first overcomes Abraham. For his part, he finds a weaker object, that is his own wife, and turns her over to the Egyptians in order to further his own vital interests. He passes her off as his sister, thus also rendering her nameless (vv. 14 and 15 of Gen. 12 refer to _the woman_). The verbs 'see' and 'take' make the violent conditions obvious.

> 12.14 When Abram entered Egypt the Egyptians _saw_ the woman, that she was very beautiful.
> 15 The princes of Pharaoh _saw_ her, they praised her to the Pharaoh and the women was _taken_ into Pharaoh's house.

Since the Pharaoh takes what he sees and likes, Sarah, a woman of beautiful appearance (v. 11) cannot let herself be seen. She is taken. To describe God's basic objection to these conditions of violence, Sarah's liberation from Pharaoh's harem is linked to the later liberation of the people from slavery in Egypt. 'YHWH afflicted Pharaoh and his house with great plagues, because of Sarai, Abram's wife' (v. 17). God's last blow against the Pharaoh, starting the exodus from Egypt, can be heard here (see Exod. 11.1).[11] Sarah's liberation from Pharaoh's harem is an aspect of the people's liberation from slavery, a part of the self-revelation of Israel's God.

---

11. The substantive 'plague', נגע is found in the first books of Moses only in Gen. 12.17 and in Exod. 11.1, where it stands for God's blow against all the firstborn of Egypt.

In opposition to the Egypt of Sarah's seizure, God characterizes the land of the future as 'a land that God lets you see'. The secret of the land is found in the sequence of the verbs 'allows to be seen' and 'be seen', 'give' and 'take'. The land can only be seen if God allows it to be seen; it can be taken only if God gives it. Abduction and exploitation cannot dictate the relationship of the people to the land, and towards each other. In this land a woman should be able to appear in public without being seized.

Promised Land—Occupied Land

The authors reacting in the Song of Songs to Abraham and Sarah's story live in the land that was promised to them. In the Song of Songs the blooming land serves not a promised destiny, but as justification for the call to set out. The woman shall set out, because 'the flowers are seen in the land, the time of singing has come, and the voice of the turtledove is heard in our land' (2.12). The blossoming abundance highlights the woman's deprivation—the beloved is neither seen nor heard (2.14)! The social structure of power prevents her departure. In this situation the singer[s] adopt[s] the call for setting out given to Abraham, and make it clear: for the setting out of the singer, for them, the land promised to Abraham is at stake.

This singer who tells of her lover's arrival and the call is separated from her friend. He might overcome all obstacles that are in the way of their love. He *leaps upon the mountains* and *skips over the hills* (2.8). Nevertheless *walls, windows* and *lattices* hinder his coming (2.9). Only eyes and voice continue his movement: peering, looking and speaking, he permeates grated windows (2.9). The social place of a young woman becomes visible. She lives secluded and locked in (cf. 2 Macc. 3.19; Sir. 42.9-14). In Ben Sira a father dreams of a house without windows for the protection of his virginal daughter (Sir. 42.11). In the Song of Songs this order of 'protection' is described from the perspective of the 'protected'. Wall, window and grates characterize the father's world as her prison. The father's house may have dissociated itself from the Egyptian power structures, tried to prevent women from being taken. But the problem of the masculine taking is *not* the one being tackled: it is the possibility of a woman letting herself be seen that is prevented. The woman *is taken* into custody. In the Song of Songs this protective care is outlined in anticipation of the averted violence. Even in her own house the woman is robbed of her possibilities for life.

In the Song of Songs the woman's brothers are the representatives

of the masculine order. They represent the patriarchal order instead of
the father, who does not appear throughout the SoS. In the beginning
and at the end of the book the brothers act as a controlling authority,
thus framing the whole SoS.[12] The intention of this arrangement
might be to show, literarily and literally, the brothers' actual envel-
opment of their sister. It is the brothers who have power of disposal
over their sister.

> 1.6b My mother's sons are angry with me.
> They set me a keeper over the vineyards,
> but I did not keep my own vineyard.

They decide about their sister's work. The singer opposes the economic power of her brothers by making her own decision concerning
the possession she is free to decide about, that is her body. The
brothers compare their sister to a city they have to defend:

> 8.8 What shall we do with our sister on the day when she is spoken for?
> 9 If she is a wall, we will build upon her a battlement of silver and if she
> is a gate we will besiege her with cedar boards.

If the sister is like a wall and lets nobody come near her, they will
decorate the wall with a crown. If the sister opens herself like a door,
they will prevent the entrance with cedar boards. The expression
'besiege', צרר על in the last line is a term referring to the siege of a
city.[13] The defenders turn into besiegers.

The image of war reflects the severity of the conflict the woman
experiences as soon as she tries to break away from the order established by the brothers. The violence she encounters is depicted in the
way her dream about unity with her lover changes to a nightmare.
When she imagines that she rises (5.5) and sets out (5.6) to follow her
lover's call, the town watchmen find her and strike her.

> 5.7 The watchmen going about the city found me,
> they struck me and wounded me,
> the watchmen of the wall stripped my mantle from me.

The watchmen are more closely characterized as 'the watchmen of
the wall'. This suggests an alliance between them and the brothers (cf.
8.9). 'Both male groups watch over the walls in a rather hostile manner!'[14] Perhaps these watchmen conceal a police patrol, quite common

12. J.C. Exum, 'A Literary and Structural Analysis of the Song of Songs', *ZAW*
85 (1973), pp. 74-77.
13. Cf. Deut. 20.12, 19; 2 Sam. 11.1; 20.15.
14. I. Pardes, *Countertraditions in the Bible: A Feminist Approach* (Cambridge,
MA: Harvard University Press, 1992), p. 140. In tracing inner biblical contradiction,

in the Macedonian era during which there was always war or armed peace in occupied cities.[15] But, however historically precise we may picture these figures of a woman's nightmare, it is a fact that these watchmen confront the singer like accomplices of an occupying power. They have a task inside the city. They do not guard the city from outside enemies, but from those within it. In this function they meet the woman. It is not the woman who is protected but, rather, the existing order is protected from her. For the singer of the SoS her father's house has become a prison; the promised land has become an occupied land.

The Promise Is Newly Defined

In the context of the violence that opposes the lovers' longing, the singers of the SoS hear the Torah. They understand the call for setting out to the promised land as a present challenge. To them the promised land is not a past or future place of fantasy to which real life or unfulfilled wishes are transferred. The promise of the land helps their own longing for life. In a present in which the desires of the lovers are not fulfilled, the hope for fulfillment is kept up by its variance with the promise. Here the promise given to Abraham is taken over critically. The opposition to Sarahs becoming an object and being taken over, about which Genesis tells us, is now directed against the Genesis story itself. In that story Sarah is never the subject (!), but serves only as an object depicting the rule of God or that of the Pharaoh (cf. Gen. 12.1–13.18). In the SoS the promise given to Abraham is seen as a pledge for a woman realizing her personality. In the liberating steps taken by the singer, the land promised to Abraham becomes visible. When she sets out she breaks with the existing order and she breaks its hold over the future. The land that God will allow to be seen will be realized when two people hear and see each other, giving and taking without robbing.

Pardes compares the speech made in the Song of Songs concerning female eroticism with prophetic voices. Whatever is done to the Shulamite by the watchmen is threatened by the prophets to happen to Israel depicted as a woman (for example in Hos. 2.2-10; Ezek. 16.36-37): 'A woman who does not maintain her nakedness under cover exposes herself to the danger of being undressed in public' (p. 135). With the description of female eroticism in opposition to the patriarchal restriction in the Song of Songs, this tradition is challenged too.

15. H.-J. Heinevetter, *'Komm nun, mein Liebster, dein Garten ruft dich!' Das Hohelied als programmatische Komposition* (Athenäum Monographien-Theologie, 69; Frankfurt a.M: Athenäum, 1988), p. 108.

Further in the course of the Song of Songs it is described in many pictures that the Shulamite's liberating steps let the land be seen, that God wants to be seen.[16] Her lover discovers in the expressive power of her body the whole glory of the earth (4.1-7; 6.4-7; 7.2-6).[17] The loving man finds with his beloved the land 'flowing with milk and honey' that accompanied, as a future vision, Israel's exodus from slavery (SoS 5.1); and he lets her know that 'honey and milk are under your tongue' (SoS 4.11). He even describes her as a paradise garden (4.12-15), into which Israel will turn according to God's promise.[18] The woman confirms, on the other hand, that her affinity is the experience of Israel's way to the garden of Eden. She takes up the description of the destroyed sex relations from the garden story (Gen. 3.16), and insists that the damage done there is healed because of her association with her male lover. The woman's longing is not answered by the man's rule (such as in Gen. 3.16), but by his longing: 'I am my beloved's, and for me is his desire' (7.10).[19]

There Is a Land where Women Like to Live

In the Song of Songs a friendship, forbidden for a woman, comes into view without a happy end being mentioned. Desires for meetings, hidden possibilities for women, experiences of control and restriction form songs of love and yearning. A collection of love songs is presented. These love songs are full of theology. They tell us how, in so-called privacy, Abraham and Sarah's setting out is taken over and a promise is retold and won for the singers' life. The Song of Songs contradicts the separation of erotic love from God's history. Perhaps it

16. Butting, *Die Buchstaben*, pp. 117-60.

17. In this connection I wish to point out O. Keel's commentary, *Das Hohelied* (Zürcher Bibelkommentare, AT 18; Zürich: Theologischer Verlag, 1986), who emphasizes that in metaphors describing beauty in the SoS the comparisons do not mention form or colour, but the expressivness of a part of the body sung about. So, if the beauty of the woman is praised with this sentence, 'your eyes are doves' (1.15; 4.1), the singer does not mean doves' eyes or dove-blue, but eyes as messengers of peace and love. Especially concerning her beauty, she is not an object that can been seen and judged by colour and form.

18. Cf. Isa. 51.3; 58.11; Jer. 31.12.

19. SoS 7.10 is clearly concerned with this part of Genesis, for 'desire', תשוקה is found in the Hebrew Bible only in Gen. 3.16, 4.7 and in SoS 7.10. 'Her use of the word desire (*těšûqâ*) echoes, in contrast, the divine judgement upon the first woman: "Your desire (*těšûqâ*) shall be for your man, but he shall rule over you"', P. Trible, *God and the Rhetoric of Sexuality* (Philadelphia: Fortress Press, 1987), pp. 159-60.

is thanks to this concealed power of contradiction that the Song of Songs is read in the Synagogue on the Sabbath of the Pesach week. When the liberation from suppression is celebrated, the singer's longing for her lover's kisses is recalled and we are shown a way which is still before us. All spheres of life, eroticism included, have to be permeated by God's liberating power, so that the land can change to a land where women would like to live. This is a land Joke Smit has sung about:[20]

> There is a land, where women like to live,
> where 'woman' doesn't mean subordinate, intimidated, small,
> where women don't compete for men,
> but can be sister and beloved,
> where wrinkles do not stand for loneliness,
> but signs of wisdom, like advisors of the earth;
> where the young women so prepare a life
> where they can reach the forty, sixty, eighty.
>
> There is a land where women like to live,
> where injustice is not the normal course,
> where service is not just restricted to one sex,
> where men don't always take the lead,
> where mother is not just the same as housewife,
> where it is always checked anew who's weak or strong,
> where ev'rybody sees who might need help
> and just five hours work supply tomorrow's bread.
>
> There is a land where men, too, want to live,
> for boys the duty is not stubborness,
> where nobody wins at cost of others,
> where being man means too: take care of others,
> where you don't have to hide your sadness and your fear,
> where jobless men don't think that they are less,
> where women, men don't have to hate each other,
> but go together sisters and brothers now.
>
> There is a land where people like to live,
> to be a child, it is not being in the way,
> and weaker ones are treated with great care
> and foreigners no longer sent away
> and violence is not accepted any longer,
> where ev'rybody comforts you when you are down.
> That is the land where people like to live,
> the land where people do belong together.[21]

20. J. Smit, 'Er is een land waar vrouwen willen wonen', *Teksten 1967–1981* (Amsterdam: Sara, 1984), p. 353.
21. Translated by Ursula Petruschke.

This page intentionally left blank

Part III

THE SONG OF SONGS, PERSONALIZED

'MY' SONG OF SONGS

Athalya Brenner

Introduction

A while ago I was asked to write an article for a volume of autobiographical Bible criticism. This has become fashionable lately—see a recent *Semeia* volume.[1] The basic issues in that kind of criticism are those of identity and personal experience as formative factors in academic work, and the legitimacy [or lack thereof] of subjectivity in Bible interpretation. I agreed to write about my own academic journey as a woman, Jewish, a native Israeli, a mother, divorced, fifty-three (then) years old Bible scholar. This would not have been a particularly happy story: where I come from, feminist Bible scholarship was not considered a worthwhile occupation, still hardly is; it is perhaps more tolerated now but, still and often, with a certain smirk. However, when I came to writing the article something else happened: I found myself writing about the SoS—my favourite Bible book—and about my work on it, an altogether happier story of the reflexivity of life and reading. This version of the article eventually was published in a collection of essays I edited together with Carole Fontaine.[2] I then tried out the essay on several occasions: the Sheffield Seminar (April 1997) was one of them; a department seminar in Amsterdam (June 1997) was another; a presentation in the Twelfth World Jewish Congress (Jerusalem, August 1997) followed. I also talked about this essay with personal friends and colleagues. It turned out to be more important for me—as a critic, a person, an Israeli, a feminist—than I at first realized.

This is how this small essay developed, in stages. It began as a relatively simple if selective and nostalgic account of the mutuality of my

---

1. J.C. Anderson, J.L. Stadley and R.A. Culpepper (eds.), *Taking it Personally: Autobiographical Biblical Criticism* (Semeia, 72; Atlanta: Scholars Press, 1995).
2. A. Brenner and C.R. Fontaine (eds.), *A Feminist Companion to Reading the Bible: Approaches, Methods and Strategies* (Sheffield: Sheffield Academic Press, 1997), pp. 567-79, cf. n. 13 thereof, p. 579.

life and work, against the background of a specific time–class–location culture. It became an occasion for reflections on my own and others' shifting identities and critical positions. It then made me reflect on the nature of my and others' feminism and feminisms in general and on criticism in, do I dare pronounce it, a postmodernist age in a specific location. I am grateful to the people who responded to my reflections, who were interested enough to consider my personal experience without trivializing it. Without these people, I would not have been able to enjoy the voyage of writing this piece so much.

Background

One of the battle cries of feminists from the 1970s onwards has been the demand to distinguish 'women's experience' as an experiential and critical category that conditions, and contributes to, the definition, enactment and perpetuation of gender. The concept 'women's experience' signified, to a large extent, things connected to the essential biological life cycle unique to women—menstruation, birthing, ageing and other sensations and emotions emanating from the body. The concept was also used as referring to the social and societal conditions that program women into F (female/feminine) roles and anticipated F performance.[3] The work of French feminists, especially, reinforced the recognition of F experience as a basic category for women's voices, reading and writing.[4]

With the growing attention to difference and pluralism in the late 1980s and in the 1990s, a single abstracted notion of 'women's experience' has become an ineffectual critical category. Increasing awareness of differences in body, ethnicity, nationality, location, colour, religion, class, age, social circumstances, economics, education, socialization modes and many more factors have contributed to that, as much as the evolvement of multiple sophisticated feminisms meanwhile.

The growing emphasis on the reader's location, coupled with the recognition of difference, allows the [F and M] critic relative theoretical liberty: personal location—including gender—need no longer be

3.   For the term 'F' as referring to female/feminine 'voice', and its counterpart 'M', see A. Brenner and F. Van Dijk-Hemmes, *On Gendering Texts: Female and Male Voices in the Hebrew Bible* (Leiden: E.J. Brill, 1993), esp. pp. 1-11.

4.   For a convenient selection in English translation see E. Marks and Isabelle de Courtivron, *New French Feminisms: An Anthology* (New York: Schocken Books, 1981).

as masked and devalued, as previously, as a factor motivating academic criticism. The pretense to critical objectivity is fast losing
ground, not least because of feminist insistence. And if the category
'women's experience' has lost most of its validity as a *generally* applicable concept for feminists, a wider category of 'personal/autobio-
graphical' has gained and continues to gain relevance. There is a new,
more nuanced, [relative] permissiveness concerning the pertinence of
readerly difference for critical work. Thus the license to be legiti-
mately different, perhaps paradoxically, may encompass *specific* F
experience, even the experience of a single woman such as my own
experience, as well as other personal factors and socio-political factors. In this manner the elderly feminist slogan, 'The personal is the
political', may be put to fresh use.

I Am...

From these general considerations of experience, especially female
experience, and reading processes, I proceeded by asking myself
questions such as, What was/is there, in my life, that makes it *easier*
for me to adopt certain positions in regard to the SoS? In order to
answer, some details of my life history are necessary at this point—
although, to be sure, they are not unique. Many of my Israeli friends
grew up in a similar way. (But, have they have constructed their
life/work stories in a way similar to mine or otherwise? That is an
entirely and altogether separate issue.)

I am undeniably a product of the culture I grew up in. I was born in
Palestine in 1943. My mother and father were immigrants, from
Poland and Lithuania respectively, who came to the 'land' (אֶרֶץ) as
late teenage 'pioneers' (חֲלוּצִים) for ideological as well as practical
reasons in the late 1930s. They came from an orthodox Jewish culture;
they left this culture (although some tribal customs continued to be
observed) to join another orthodoxy, that of Ben-Gurionist Labour
Zionism. Like many others, I grew up on and into a native 'Israeli'
culture-in-the-making of three 'L's: Language, Land, Legion
(resistance to the British mandate, then defense against Arab enemies,
then a national army). My journey into adulthood included a good
urban school, youth movement, army service in the Naḥal,[5] some
time on a kibbutz, university.

---

5.   The *NḤL*, Hebrew נח"ל, acronym for 'pioneering fighting youth', was an
arrangement whereby active army service was combined with agricultural work
on a kibbutz, undertaken in a group of youth movement graduates.

When I was growing up, both popular and 'high' cultures were always bound up with the Bible. This means that the Bible pervaded, as it still does, all levels of life and all life situations: from political justification of acquiring land and defense, to romance, to gender relations to marital status, to literature, to the visual arts,[6] to radio and theatre. (There was no television in Israel until much later; it was introduced in the 1960s). In the case of the SoS, I knew it before I came to realize it was a biblical book. Like many others of my generation, I suppose.

And so, for me, the Bible—including the SoS—has been an important part of my formative years and still is a significant component of my daily existence. It belongs to my life experience, the emotive baggage that goes everywhere with me. I shall now link specific SoS texts to specific and recurrent personal experiences and social activities of my past and present life; then come back to the question, how does this intimate and emotive connection with the SoS affect my academic study of it? And vice versa: How does the SoS, the Bible in fact, affect my non-professional life?

Situations and Activities

Singing

Some SoS-derived songs were so popular when I grew up that they were, and perhaps still are, considered Israeli folk songs.[7] The poems were set to music and sung often, especially in two kinds of recurrent life situations: spring just before and during the time of Passover (from kindergarten on); love and courting. License with the biblical words was often taken: the order of verses was inverted; additions in modern Hebrew were inserted, parts of verses were deleted, verses from various passages were matched together in a new continuum, and so on. Some examples:

אל תראוני שאני שחרחרת ששזפתני השמש...שחורה אני ונאוה... (Do not gaze at me because I am dark, because the sun has gazed on me...[1.6]; I am dark and/but beautiful [1.5a][8])—

אני חבצלת השרון... (I am a rose of Sharon..., 2.1-2),

קול דודי... (The voice of my beloved..., 2.8-9a),

---

6. Reproductions of pictures on biblical themes, or with 'biblical' influence, by Jewish and Israeli artists such as Abel Pan, Reuven Rubin, Nahum Guttman and Mané-Katz, graced many walls of my and my contemporaries' childhood.

7. Translations, unless otherwise stated, are from the NRSV, but follow the chapter and verse divisions of the Hebrew text.

8. Translation for 1.5a is mine.

...הנצנים נראו בארץ (the flowers appear on the earth..., 2.12a)
...יונתי בחגוי הסלע (my dove, in the clefts of the rock..., 2.14).
...דודי לי ואני לו (My beloved is mine and I am his..., 2.16).
...אנה פנה דודך היפה בנשים... (Where has your beloved gone, O fairest among women?..., 6.1)

Even now, when the SoS is taught in an Israeli university or college setting, more often than not a humming noise would be heard: one of the students, often quite un-selfconsciously, has started to sing one or the other of the poems studied.[9]

Dancing

...אל גנת אגוז ירדתי ('I went down to the nut orchard', 6.11). This passage was known to most, not only as a song but also as a dance, an Israeli 'folk' dance—that is, a dance for Saturday night gatherings, for dancing in the street on the Israeli State's independence day (העצמאות יום), for any joyous occasion. So was the case also with other SoS passages. Some dance troupes, with their distinctive 'folk' style garments, would perform those dances with virtuosity: the rest of us would just do our clumsy best. I still remember the dance steps, the atmosphere, the accordion playing the music, the worry whether I would be invited to dance by a boy or dare ask a boy to dance with me. The provenance of these dances in the SoS was discovered relatively late. To begin with, they were just 'our' dances, originally Israeli and native.

Landscapes and Hikes

The ethos of hiking as a means for establishing a relationship with the land, indeed, for appropriating it, was exemplified by God's order to Abra[ha]m, קום התהלך בארץ לארכה ולרחבה כי לך אתננה ... ('Rise up, walk through the length and the breadth of the land, for I will give it to you', Gen. 13.17). Trips combining geography, history and archaeology were an important part of the school curriculum, youth movement, leisure activities and the army period. And they always, always included some relevant HB passages quoted *in situ*. Masada is linked for me primarily with Josephus Flavius;[10] En-Gedi, first visited on the same school trip, today and at all times is the place where a woman's

9. It should also be mentioned that many poets who write in Hebrew customarily incorporate biblical quotations into their poetry. When such poems are set to music they enrich the SoS-derived stock of Hebrew songs, particularly love songs. An example which comes to mind is Leah Goldberg's poem entitled 'Come, Bride', recently set to a music and made popular by the singer Ahinoam Nini.

10. *War* 7.8.2–9.2.

voice says in my head, immediately and without hesitation, אשכל הכפר דודי לי בכרמי עין גדי ('My beloved is to me a cluster of henna blossoms in the vineyards of En-Gedi', SoS 1.14). This is so simply because there I *heard* this verse for the first time; and every time I reread or hear it, I automatically have the En-Gedi of that first encounter rise up into my consciousness—and other snatches of memory relating to that trip, that specific time. This is my primary memory of the place, superimposed on by later trips and other readings. Thus Jerusalem, among other things, is the territory of the 'daughters of Jerusalem'. The 'Tower of David' has a woman's image hanging over it, and her neck is encircled by metallic jewelry (4.4). In the 'Sharon' and the 'valleys', appropriated by hiking in the past and now frequently traveled by car, חבצלת השרון ('rose of Sharon') and שושנת העמקים ('lily of the valleys'; both in 2.1) float into my mind often (I start humming the songs), even before I see the flowers so named. Granted, place names like the Hermon, Lebanon, Gilead, Carmel have other biblical connotations too; but, because the SoS was sung and heard on the radio so much and so often, the special primary flavour remains.

Nature, gardens, food

The word 'pomegranate', Hebrew רמון, occurs 47 times in the HB. The contexts are varied: from cultic ornaments[11] to place names[12] to a human name[13] to, perhaps, a god's name.[14] All these appear to be secondary usages statistically. The chief denotation of the word is the tree, a native to the region like olives and other vegetable foods.[15] When I look at the pomegranate trees in my garden I do not think about silver pomegranates on priestly garments. Neither do I think about other cultic applications, or about place names. It is the SoS pomegranates, six times used in the SoS in metaphors for skin colour and wine-drinking,[16] which come immediately to mind, together with the verses they are part of. Hair is described in terms of a herd of goats sliding down a hill (4.1; 6.5). I have seen it so many times. I still see it sometimes. The colour, the movement, even the texture come to me in a compact image; there is no difficulty and no need to work at

11. Exod. 28 and 39 (in the tabernacle); 1 Kgs 7; 2 Kgs 25; Jer. 52; 2 Chron. 3 and 4—in the Jerusalem temple.
12. In Joshua, Judges, Zechariah 14, 2 Chronicles.
13. In 2 Sam. 4.
14. 2 Kgs 5.
15. Num. 13.23; 20.5; Deut. 8.8; Joel 1.12; Hag. 2.19.
16. SoS 4.3, 13; 6.7, 11; 7.13; 8.2.

converting verbalization into visualization: when I do see goats going down the hill and have to stop my car to let them pass I recite the relevant verses to myself, automatically. The metaphor is immediately effective for me because I have experienced its referent so many times.

I could cite more examples for illustrating how the SoS, for me like for other Israelis of the same generation and circumstances, is an intimate and personal part of my life. But this is hardly necessary. It was and still is impossible not to recall, sing, dance, recite SoS passages in daily life and recurrent life situations: because I am a native Israeli. Because I had a certain kind of childhood and upbringing and growing up and young adulthood in Israel at a specific time in history and with specific ideologies. Because the SoS (more, perhaps, than any other biblical book) was part of my [pop] culture before it became Bible for me. Because I study the Bible for a living.

The Personal and the Academic

In the past ten years I have studied the SoS, taught and written about it extensively.[17] My imagined personal intimacy with this collection of love lyrics is therefore relevant to my critical work with and on it. For example, here are a few points.

Is the SoS One Poem or a Structured Collection?

Scholars are divided on this issue. Basically, two contrastive positions are advocated. A. The SoS is a unified composition, with two [or three] lovers—a female lover and a male lover [or two male lovers]—engaged in a series of courting, dialogues, monologues, meetings and departures.[18] B. The book is an anthology of love lyrics, from various times and locations, with many figurations of female and male lovers. The whole is unified structurally, through the efforts of capable editors (or an editor). There are several variations on these two basic

17. At the risk of self-advertising, here is a partial list of my work on the SoS: *The Song of Songs* (Old Testament Guides; Sheffield: JSOT Press, 1989); ' "Come Back, Come Back the Shulammite" (Song of Songs 7.1-10): A Parody of the *wasf* Genre', in J.T. Radday and A. Brenner (eds.), *On Humour and the Comic in the Hebrew Bible* (Sheffield: Almond Press, 1990), pp. 251-76; A. Brenner (ed.), *A Feminist Companion to the Song of Songs* (Feminist Companion to the Bible, 1; Sheffield: Sheffield Academic Press, 1993); 'To See Is to Assume: Whose Love Is Celebrated in the Song of Songs?', *Bib Int* 3.1 (1993), pp. 1-20; and more—in Hebrew, Dutch and German.

18. J.C. Exum, 'A Literary and Structural Analysis of the Song of Songs', *ZAW* 85 (1973), pp. 47-79; F. Landy, *Paradoxes of Paradise: Identity and Difference in the Song of Songs* (Sheffield: Almond Press, 1983).

positions but, fundamentally, one of these two positions would be adopted by any given scholar.

I agree with those who view the SoS as a *collection* of love lyrics, editorially strung together (option B.). There are many reasons I can cite for this choice: formalistic, linguistic, stylistic, contextual—to name but several. All these reasons are no doubt worth bearing in mind. But I suspect that, unconsciously at best, something more is at play for me. I came to know the SoS as individual poems, indeed, as fragments (with no knowledge of the whole, at the beginning and for years). I incorporated components of it into my early life long before I knew of the biblical book itself (it was not on the school syllabus as such; it took years before I recognized it as a unity at Passover night; it turned out to be various songs and dances, individually performed). This must have, somehow, conditioned my interpretive position at least in part—although I am hardly aware of it most of the time.

The SoS is Exactly What its Title Indicates: Songs, Not 'Poetry' for Recitation
I am deeply aware of the singability, so to speak, of SoS constituents. This is how I met such constituents or components to begin with, as *songs*, poems set to music. Some of these songs were encountered first or foremost as dances. My experience makes it absolutely clear to me that the SoS is *not* there primarily for recital as 'poetry': it is there for *singing*. Fortunately, Rabbi Aqiba agrees with me, although indirectly: 'Rabbi Aqiba says, He who trills his voice with the Song of Songs in drinking houses and makes it a kind of song [has no portion in the world to come]'.[19] It seems, then, that these songs were *sung*, primarily; and that the legitimation by allegorization programs of Judaism— and Christianity—concerning this collection of love songs required that they become recited poems instead of songs; that is, that the songs be divorced from their original mode of performance,[20] a mode I imagine as not dissimilar to the kind of SoS performance I grew up with.

Erotic Love Lyrics, Not an Allegory: The Erotic Nature of the SoS
The 'Israel' I grew up in—urban, educated, lower-middle-class, chauvinistic, insular, non-orthodox religiously, orthodoxly socialist, mildly aware of gender problems—promoted an understanding, from a very early age, that the SoS is about *love*—erotic and physical as well

19. *t Sanh.* 12.10 (my translation).
20. See also tractate *Kalla* 1.4, 6: 'He who reads a verse in the SoS and turns it into a kind of song… brings a flood to the world'; and similarly *b. Sanh.* 101a.

emotional. The two aspects of love, the material and non-material, were easy to image as inseparable. Imagining that an allegorical meaning—of divine/human love, historical or mystical; of any kind of Jewish or Christian or scholarly approach—is the *primary* or even a coexistent 'original' meaning of the SoS leaves me with genuine puzzlement, even embarrassment. Nothing will convince me that, to begin with, the SoS was conceived of as an elaborate allegory of religious passion, be it the passion for a goddess[21] or for a male mono-theistic god of whatever definition. I cannot even agree that, primarily, *both* heterosexual human love and divine/human love are indicated.[22] SoS allegories are interesting critically and culturally and a worthy subject of study. However, I find it implausible that the original significance of the biblical text is a 'hidden' significance, that the SoS text is anything else but what it declares itself to be by its contents: songs of love and love-making between heterosexual humans.

Sitz im Leben

At the beginning of this century it was fashionable to imagine the SoS as a set of wedding poems, or songs to be performed during a pro-longed (perhaps seven days, as in the case of Samson, Judg. 14) wedding feast.[23] Indeed, a wedding of King Solomon is mentioned in the SoS (ch. 3), although this is an isolated feature. In my life experience, such songs are sung in non-wedding situations. This undoubtedly influences my view, based on additional criteria, that the songs are *love* songs rather than *wedding* songs. The many lovers of the SoS end (8.8) exactly where they started (1.2): running after each other, running away from each other. Indeed, secondary wedding usages of this non-wedding material are made. For instance: the Jewish orthodox wedding ceremony is notorious for the bride's oral passivity. But my female cousin arranged with the Rabbi that, at a certain point in the ceremony, she addresses to her partner the words אני לו דודי לי ('my beloved is mine and I am his'). Beautiful, but a secondary utilization.

21. M.V. Pope, 'Metastases in Canonical Shapes of the Super Song', in G.M. Tucker, D.L. Peterson and R.R. Wilson (eds.), *Canon, Theology and Old Testament Interpretation: Essays in Honor of Brevard S. Childs* (Philadelphia: Fortress Press, 1988), pp. 312-28.

22. Cf. R. Murphy, *The Song of Songs: A Commentary on the Book of Canticles or the Songs of Songs* (Hermeneia; Minneapolis: Fortress Press, 1990).

23. See M.H. Pope, *Song of Songs: A New Translation with Introduction and Commentary* (AB; Garden City, NY: Doubleday, 1977), pp. 141-45.

Female and Male Voices

Somehow, most of the SoS songs I have heard throughout my growing years were sung by female singers (of oriental origin—Beracha
Zefira, Hannah Aharoni, Shoshana Damari, to name but a few). Most
of the lines chosen for musical settings were female first-person lines.
I wonder, without reaching a conclusive result, how much that conditioned my current feminist positions. It seems to me—and not only to
me[24]—that female voices in the SoS are stronger, more self assured,
more confident, more articulate than male voices. Why this is so is
less than clear at the present stage of SoS study. Various possibilities
are considered: that the SoS is primarily a female composition; that in
it female voices are allowed expression, as also in other cultures, such
as Egyptian[25] and Tamil,[26] in pre-nuptial situations within the
patriarchal frameworks; and so forth. And I cannot ignore the suspicion that my own search for the likelihood or feasibility of women's
voices in the SoS[27] is influenced by my upbringing and life history as
well as by feminist convictions adopted in later life.[28]

24. For instance, A. Brenner, *The Israelite Woman: Social Role and Literary Type in
Biblical Narrative* (Sheffield: JSOT Press, 1985), pp. 46-58, 138; P. Trible, *God and the
Rhetoric of Sexuality* (Philadelphia: Fortress Press, 1978), pp. 144-65; van Dijk-
Hemmes in Brenner and van Dijk-Hemmes, *On Gendering Texts*, pp. 71-81.
J. Bekkenkamp and F. van Dijk-Hemmes, 'The Canon of the Old Testament and
Women's Cultural Traditions', in Brenner (ed.), *A Feminist Companion to the Song of
Songs*, pp. 67-85.

25. M.V. Fox, *The Song of Songs and Ancient Egyptian Love Songs* (Madison: University of Wisconsin Press, 1985).

26. C. Rabin, 'The Song of Songs and Tamil Love Poetry', *JBL* 89 (1973), pp. 27-
37; A. Mariaselvam, *The Song of Songs and Ancient Tamil Love Poems: Poetry and
Symbolism* (AnBib, 118; Rome: Pontifical Biblical Institute, 1988).

27. Cf., for instance, Brenner and van Dijk-Hemmes, *On Gendering Texts*.

28. I am well aware of the fact that what is banal for me is not equally banal for
others. For instance, one of my best friends roughly shares many growing-up factors with me: age, place of birth and residence, gender, school, youth movement,
army service, economic circumstances. However, her parents came from Germany
and were not motivated by Zionist ideology. Hence, her native tongue was German, the early literature she came into contact with was primarily the Brothers
Grimm's stories in the original language rather than Bible and Jewish stories in
Hebrew. Thus, these two variables made a great difference—at least until those
differences were leveled by shared cultural factors in our early twenties. Upon
reading this article, my friend remarked: 'But, for me, this is not banal at all; and
while I share some of your sentiments and critical insights about the SoS, still
others do not belong to my personal experience'.

Humour in the SoS

I think that in certain SoS passages, such as ch. 3 (Solomon's procession and wedding)[29] and ch. 7 (the Sulammite's dance),[30] a certain kind of humour underlies the descriptions. This view is certainly easier to adopt when the Bible, including the SoS, is viewed as a cultural artifact in the wider sense, from a non-orthodox place, rather than from an orthodox high seriousness; it is also easier to recognize when coming from a non-religious culture, where a more flippant attitude is allowed even in contexts of love and human relationships.

So What?

Do I assess my perspectives on the SoS as privileged, academically or otherwise? Yes and no. As a Jewish Israeli woman of a certain age, background, culture and temperament, I am mindful of certain privileges that are mine: the privilege of having been born in a 'Palestine' that very soon became an 'Israel', of having Hebrew as a native tongue, of having grown up in Israel, of having grown with the Bible in the special sense I have tried to recapture here. But these privileges, by themselves, neither validate nor invalidate my interpretations of the SoS and of other Bible texts, although they do give me and the likes of me a certain edge. The point of this semi-confessional stuff is that the acknowledgment of personal, autobiographical experience legitimates difference while, paradoxically and at the same time, it also validates concord. It is a fact that my interpretive positions vis-à-vis the SoS are not idiosyncratic. Other people, whose background and interests and circumstances are different from mine chronologically, spatially, politically, gender-wise, may—and do—share the same views that I hold. These 'others' are undoubtedly influenced by *their* life experiences, whether they admit it or choose not to; still, a certain grid of consensus can and is usually reached—although, certainly, one might question how valid any consensus is and how long it lasts. You do not have to be a feminist, Hebrew-speaking, Israeli woman of a certain age to ponder the predominance of female

29. J.W. Whedbee, 'Paradox and Parody in the Song of Solomon: Towards a Comic Reading of the Most Sublime Song', in Brenner (ed.), *A Feminist Companion to the Song of Songs*, pp. 252-62.

30. Brenner, ' "Come Back, Come Back" '. For a critique of my position in that article, on the grounds that I view the dancing woman as a grotesque figure, thus not a helpful image for feminist identification—see now F.C. Black, 'Unlikely Bedfellows: Allegorical and Feminist Readings of the Song of Songs 7.1-10', in this volume, pp. 104-29.

figures in the SoS; you do not have to be that woman, or a woman at all, to speculate about this fact's significance. You can come to such and other views via other routes. Eventual agreements—even if invalidated by future criticism, changes in cultural emphases or fashions in criticism—are rendered all the more convincing when coupled with the notion of acknowledged, accepted plurality and cultural difference between interpretive communities and individuals. Or are they? Identities are dynamic; if interpretive assessments are bound up with identities, as I believe they are, and identities shift continuously, no wonder that scholarly opinions shift. And if agreement is reached on certain topics, over and beyond different starting points of personal experience, perhaps there are even certain things 'in-the-text', so to speak, to facilitate such agreement?

But this exercise in reading critique and (self) criticism does not end for me here, certainly not after I have discussed it with friends and colleagues. And this brings me back to the mutuality of personal and political experience and the Bible, of experience and the SoS, which for me and for numerous other Israelis is a fact of life. On first writing this essay I operated from within the meta-experience of nostalgia. I chose, unconsciously, to invoke an Israel of my childhood through lenses of fondness and idealization—after all, this world is to a large extent gone by now. From this perspective military security, the army, hatred of our Arab 'enemies' and 'neighbours', and discrimination against non-Ashkenazi Israelis did not play a major role in my experience, hence seemed irrelevant to my academic views on the SoS. This was certainly in the nature of significant omissions and, in addition, is detrimental to my work. Let me explain why. Like so many Israelis, I am mindful of security concerns but minimize their effect in my daily life, including my work. I repress and suppress. This suppression prevents me, for instance, from fully understanding the nature of SoS love not only as joyful and idyllic but also as dark, threatening, depressing, suffering,[31] which is exemplified by military and wild-life imagery.[32] In short, it prevents me from seeing a fuller picture. It enables me to minimize things less pleasant. It serves my typically 'Israeli' attitude of ignoring those parts of the Bible—and they vary from person to person—which do not suit my academic or socio-political purpose in any particular moment.

Another point is that of Orientalism. When I grew up 'my' Israel, as

31. For instance: SoS 3.1-4; 5.6-7; 8.6-7.
32. Cf. C. Meyers, 'Gender Imagery in the Song of Songs', *HAR* 10 (1986), pp. 209-23. For a critique of Meyers's essay see now Black, 'Strange Bedfellows'.

I described it in the first versions of this essay, was dedicated to ideal-
izing Oriental culture on the one hand; and to discriminating against
oriental Jews, oriental culture, Arabs and Islam and anything 'Levan-
tine' on the other hand. The idealization was cultivated in both low
and high culture: in music, art (the Bezal'el school), literature, folklore,
lower-register language usages like curses and much besides.[33]
Simultaneously, from the 1950s, the Oriental Jew, not to mention the
Arab, became the non-differentiated butt of the predominant Israeli
culture, high and low. Most of 'us' (first-generation Ashkenazi Israelis,
children of 'veterans') had no difficulty in maintaining a double standard: in viewing SoS and similar biblical images of women (especially)
as Oriental beauties—this represented romance and exotica—whereas,
in our daily lives, we cultivated other images of oriental women (and
men) from a standpoint of cultural superiority. Consider, for instance,
the song 'Simona from Dimona' (singer: Yisrael Yitzhaki, 1950s). The
SoS utterance שחורה אני ונאוה ('I am dark and/but beautiful', SoS 1.5a),
which is incorporated into the song in praise of a beautiful Oriental
Jewish female immigrant, was by and large ignored in 'our' culture,
outside the song. Consequently, the utterance became a scream that,
by stages, has developed into a political factor in our lives. While I do
not remember myself as ever being overtly prejudiced about Israeli
'minorities' (read: Oriental Jews, new immigrants, Arabs), neither do I
remember having made the connection between the two (the SoS and
'life'). Regrettably, I do not see that I, personally, learnt a preventive
lesson from the SoS concerning this adoption of a double standard—
as I should have.

And all this is just one example. No wonder that I chose the SoS for
an autobiographical piece! It is less 'political' than other biblical
books. I could practice the art of denial so much better here, say, than
in a piece about Joshua or Deuteronomy—in spite of being of Labour
party background and persuasion, then and now. This is not how a
feminist, presumably committed to socio-political justice in her work
and life, should have chosen to view the mutuality of her past life and
present work. But this is what I initially and effortlessly did.

The SoS 'daughters of Jerusalem'[34] are presumably, within the
framework of the book, 'insiders': urban, sophisticated, fair. The

33. A good illustration of this point is the recent exhibition in the Israel
Museum (Jerusalem) called קדימה, 'To the East', whose subject matter is precisely
the influence of the oriental in Israel as a state-to-be and state, and the ambiguities
of orientalism in all areas of life since the beginning of this century.
34. SoS 1.5; 2.7; 3.5, 10; 5.8, 16; 7.14; perhaps also 6.9.

female voices appealing to them for testimony, help and support—
including the dark beauty's voice—are probably the voices of
'outsiders', of 'others'. Most readers will identify with those 'outsider'
voices of the female 'others', the female lovers-in-the-text, rather than
with the silent, conventional, skeptical or tardy (6.1-2) voices of the
'daughters'. The female lovers' voices are closely studied by academic
interpreters; they marvel at these voices' lack of conventionality (as in
3.1-4). And yet, that same community of interpreters, in the Israel of
my youth and later years, would continue to marvel at these 'proto-
feminist' voices while, at the same time, refusing recognition to the
voices of feminists in their midst, in their own country. The 'other'-in-
the-text was adopted as their own; the feminist 'other' in their life and
work continued to be suspect: the double standard, so it seems,
extends to all 'others'—including Orientals, Arabs, women, feminists.
No integration of the personal, political and academic was ever
achieved—not in the Israel I grew up in; possibly not in the academic
Israel of biblical studies now.

My autobiography has taken me, between writing the first version
of this essay and the current one, to an appointment in Amsterdam: I
now live in two countries, move from the one into the other frequently. 'Things that can be seen from here cannot be seen from there',
as an Israeli song says;[35] and vice versa. The shift in personal circumstances facilitates new perspectives: physical relocation undoubtedly
is clearly functional in readerly activity. Recognition of this personal
factor, among others, probably facilitates an understanding of critical
work: this seems a cliche; perhaps, though, it should be stated in the
present context.

To conclude. My life, my personal circumstances and history, affect
my work: it so happens that they also enhance my enjoyment of the
SoS and the Bible. The SoS, the Bible, affect my life. I remind myself
again and again of this two-way traffic, of this inter-subjectivity of
text and reader, reader and text. If my awareness of the intervention
of personal circumstances is an efficient sentinel; if awareness of
emotional and critical processes helps; if my willingness to admit the
bias created by my banal life history is of any value, if confession of
experience is a safeguard against allowing that same experience too
much weight—then this self exposure can be of value not only to me.
It can also be of a limited value to other interpreters who would bring
their primary and secondary experiences and life histories, possibly

---

35. 'דברים שרואים מכאן לא רואים משם'. This is from a popular song performed
by the Israeli singer Judith Ravitz.

very different from mine, to their own reading and work. They can reconstruct *their* SoS. And, who knows, this sometimes happens, our different Songs may intersect. Or they may not.

THE VOICE OF THE TURTLE: NOW IT'S *MY* SONG OF SONGS

Carole R. Fontaine

Long Ago and Far Away...

Once on an elementary school field trip to Crandon Park Zoo in Miami, Florida, I sought out a zookeeper to ask him why the tortoises and turtles were so quiet. He looked startled by this child's question, to say the least. I told him earnestly that I had been waiting for the turtles to speak for some time, but not a sound did I hear. When asked *why* I thought the turtles should be speaking, I replied as any good Fundamentalist child is taught to do, 'Because the Bible says so! "The voice of the turtle is heard in our land'. He was nonplussed: uneager to disagree with biblical logia, unequipped with biblical translation skills, he finally fell back on his own expertise. In all his many years of keeping the tortoise and turtle corral under his watch, he told me, he had never heard any one of them speak in a voice.

I remained troubled by this glaring discrepancy between the Infallible Word and the Living World. Eventually, I sought out my Sunday School teacher and asked my turtle question. She was shocked and surprised (and also had no relevant information to offer); her only comment was, 'You're just a child! You shouldn't be reading THAT!'

Such an experience perhaps destines a thoughtful child to pursue biblical studies as an adult, though I cannot say that I recalled this story until asked to respond to some of the issues concerning the Song raised in the current volume. I think it is fair to say that the Song of Songs does *not* figure heavily (sic!) in Fundamentalist presentations of the Bible as a Rule for Life; indeed, were I not an avid reader, I would never have known from anything I heard among the Southern Baptists that the book even existed. No Bride of Christ was ever called forth to love her Master (how Catholic!), no Gazelle ever searched for his Dark Beauty (how heathen!); no Dark Beauty ever spoke to her lover out of unbearable yearning (how sinful!). One can well understand why the Southern Baptists, now so well known for asking Christian women to 'submit gracefully' to male authority, would not include such an explosive set of little ditties in its regular study of the Church's Holy Books. The lovers in the book seem to operate outside the parameters of marital control, maidens work outside the home, and there is *no* mention whatsoever of the Beloved bearing fine Christian children to her mate.[1]

I was born in 1950 in Ohio. My parents moved to Florida in 1956 for a variety of reasons, and there the story of my tango with textual inerrancy began. Why my non-religious Yankee mother chose to deposit me at a Southern Baptist church on Sunday mornings I will never know;[2] I did not object because I found out quickly enough that good performance in memorizing Bible verses frequently resulted in being given food, so I complied. I am sorry to report that the Southern Baptist church in Miami still seems fairly representative of what women who take the Bible seriously in that denomination must contend with, even though I am describing a church of 30 odd years ago. I wonder now, even as I struggle with the continuing effects of childhood malnutrition, whether the physical crumbs I received were worth the spiritual famine that accompanied them. And yet, the texts I read openly or secretly have formed a tapestry of images which still comes quickly to my mouth and hands, when I teach, when I weave or illuminate manuscripts. Perhaps it is true that even in the worst of settings, the liberating impulse of some biblical texts still finds a way to deposit seeds of divine discontent with the status quo into the soil of the reader's soul. Certainly, the Song did that for me.

As my family slipped relentlessly down the social scale in the 1960s,[3] a New Thing began to happen in the South: those black and beautiful—and poor—had begun to wonder what it meant to be 'an American', and soon there was a clamor for equal treatment before the law. A sign of Satan's work, my all-white Baptists solemnly intoned, just like rock-n-roll ('jungle music') or a Catholic (Kennedy) in the White House. My marginal neighborhood, much against its will, became slowly integrated by African-Americans, and then almost wholly segregated as 'white flight' to lighter pastures swiftly took

1.   Being fine Christian women who bore fine Christian sons was considered to be the *only* occupation in which a faithful woman could engage. Having fulfilled this basic requirement, she might sometimes accompany her husband into the mission field, but no other opportunities were presented or (supposedly) desired.

2.   Neither mother nor father were Baptists or Christians of any sort. Go, figure.

3.   My mate and best friend invites everyone to note that, health problems and complaints aside, I *am* a perfect representation of the 'American Dream': up from the ghetto in one generation. (Hubba, hubba!)

place. We remained, having nowhere else to go, and given the racist climate of the South, then as now, my presence in the one white family in the midst of a first African-American, then largely Haitian neighborhood marked me for every kind of exclusion.

By the time I was a teen, I was familiar with the worst aspects of street life: heroin, prostitution, violence, gambling, hunger, abusive police—the works. The white church I had attended turned its back on my neighborhood, and engaged in major 'conniption fits'[4] when I brought black neighbors to church, ending my participation in that denomination by the age of 16. Now, street preachers with hair wooly-white like 'El-the-Kindly's', and Pentecostal store-fronts, plus or minus snake-handlers, formed the backdrop of my religious universe, along with the stories told to me by the communities of Jews on Miami Beach whom I met when I was old enough to flee to the ocean.

I early on realized that standing by windows—a familiar motif from the Song and elsewhere—was a dangerous activity when illegal transactions were taking place outside. I sought shelter in the very smallest, innermost chamber of our house, used for storage: totally protected from gun-fire, with the added bonus that I could fit comfortably inside the room and my parents couldn't, I had found my cleft in the rock. Though short on fresh air, my 'room' became a study and a studio. It contained three items for reading: A King James Bible, an unabridged dictionary, and *The Treasury of Children's Best-Loved Folk Tales*. I read them all. Repeatedly. I confess that my grand eight-year-old's plan of reading the entire Bible, straight through, hit a few snags when I came to Leviticus. I stopped only long enough to read Ruth (it was short), and then headed for the New Testament, since my church had made so clear that this was really The Good Part. How and why I eventually found the Song I cannot say, but I remember the page and the passage which fell open before me:[5]

> My beloved spake, and said unto me,
> Rise up, my love, my fair one, and come away.
> For, lo, the winter is past, the rain is over and gone;
> The flowers appear on the earth;
> the time of the singing of birds is come,
> and the voice of the turtle is heard in our land;
> The fig tree putteth forth her green figs,
> and the vines with the tender grape give a good smell.
> Arise, my love, my fair one, and come away! (KJV, 2.10-13)

4. A mostly Southern condition.
5. In Fundamentalist folk religion, such occurrences are imbued with meaning.

I was forever hooked. I see now that this invitation song so beauti-
fully reached out to the hungering child I was with the most potent
themes: the lure of escape, the scent of food, the promise of no more
rain.[6] The Song's congruence with the folk tales (which were my other
companions in those days) were not lost upon me even then: the
Prince's call to Rapunzel trapped in her impenetrable tower; the
abandoned Hansel and Gretel enticed and delightedly munching on
the glittering gingerbread of the witches' hut in the secret place of the
wood; the battle goddesses of love and beauty from the Iliad,[7] a
search that might take a girl 'East of the Sun and West of the Moon' in
the seeking-and-finding motif so prominent in Hausmärchen. And the
Song held so much more: lush descriptions of fruits, banquets so full
of good things that juices ran down the lovers' chins; clear fountains
running with cool water[8]—was this really *our* world the lovers were
describing, and not Heaven? And best of all for the now-skeptical
Fundamentalist I was teaching myself to be, these objects of desire
were *in the Bible!* Daydreams of deliverance and dessert could take on
an almost sanctified kind of aspect: perhaps someday someone would
counsel even me to 'come away!' and enjoy a life I knew existed by
report, but of which I had no experience.[9]

An artist, even a baby one without training or tools, can only read
for so long, before the eyes and hands assert themselves to displace
the tyranny of the verbal. Early attempts at sculpture were thwarted
by a lack of materials, and a lack of medical care when I nearly sliced
my finger off using a dull knife. Butter, though easy to carve, melted
like…well, butter in my little room;[10] soap was not much better since
the adults of the house *would* keep using it, even after it had been
carved. The first wood block I attempted had suggestive grain, so I

6.   In the sub-tropical region of South Florida, it rains every day from 2.30 to
4.00 p.m. or thereabouts, causing the molds and allergens to flourish even as it
brings cool breezes from the ocean across to the Everglades.

7.   Mythology is first cousin to folk tales in the old Dewey decimal system, so
my *Treasury* was liberally sprinkled with classical mythology. Later, I found the
same beloved stories shelved side by side in public libraries.

8.   The poor had well water in our part of town, rather than 'city water', so we
were frequently without water. To this day, I never use plumbing with some sense
of thanksgiving.

9.   And so it was. Without my knowing it, Enrico Rodriguez, my Cuban high-
school guidance counselor applied for scholarships in my name and sent me away
to college, where I discovered any number of interesting things in my newly white
world. A thousand blessings on your head, Mr Rodriguez!

10.   Authorial license here: it was margarine.

began on a 'horse' among Pharaoh's chariots—or a Trojan horse, I couldn't decide which—with a lovely headdress. The effort was so successful that when I ran out of wood after finishing the project, I began on the only wood left, which happened to be the storage shelves.[11] When thwarted by the materials and the Philistines who actually wanted to wash with their soap, eat their butter, or have their shelves remain standing, I moved onto the more acceptable female art of needlework. No problem in materials there, since my mother 'took in' sewing. And no problem in the subject matter either: 'Arise, my love, my fair one, and come away!'

Never having seen an illuminated manuscript, and spurning the pedestrian 'sampler' models thought appropriate for young girls, I carefully printed my text onto wholly unsuitable yellow satin (but it was *so* pretty and looked just like the sun that must be shining somewhere in my passage), and began to embroider it lovingly. I devised the idea of adding flowers, capital letters surrounded by vines and strange critters of four legs (I had no referents for gazelles at that time) in order to cover the prick marks the needle kept making in the satin every time I pulled my threads of red and blue and purple up through the cloth. I had no idea what I would do with the piece as I embroidered, nor did I ever complete it, even though years later when in graduate school, I could still lay my hands upon it at any time.

Things continued to change around the Song and me. Eventually I grew too big to fit in my hideout, and I emerged, though my world was no more safe than before. I was old enough to take the bus to public libraries (where poor children living outside of some imaginary boundary line were required to make outrageous deposits against theft in order to receive a library card, so I had to read on-site until a teacher intervened and paid on my behalf).[12] And I loved the Song more than before, because it had always been *free* and available to me, whatever my economic status.

Not only my size had altered so that, like Alice who blithely obeyed the 'Eat Me!' command, I towered over my previous retreat; outside the world was altered, too: the 'routine' of street life had shifted as my neighborhood became filled with Haitian immigrants. I learned first

11. Unfortunately, my knife was confiscated once the beginnings of the design had become visible.

12. The English title of Claus Westermann's book, *God's Angels Need No Wings* (trans. David L. Scheidt; Philadelphia: Fortress Press, 1979), is entirely accurate in this writer's experience. Out of nowhere, willy-nilly, deliverance *would* keep on coming.

hand that there was a worse thing than being too pale in the midst of
darkness: being *too dark* could be a handicap, too. In the color-biased
pecking order of the Caribbean hodge-podge of ethnicity, those
whose skin color was darker than a 'brown bag'[13] were openly
derided by anyone of lighter skin color—and most Haitians are very
dark indeed, a rich blue-black hue of shadow and smoke. As I would
walk to the bus-stop, I was often in the company of 'the girls'—little
Haitian whores younger than me (anywhere from 12 to 18 years
old)—who were sassy and fearless and forward. Only in rethinking
my utter comfort with a Dark Beauty who, though scorned by others,
proclaims herself the darkest and most beautiful of them all, did I
come to realize that the Daughters of Jerusalem will always be linked
for me to those clusters of 'girlfriends', themselves calling out rude
and challenging remarks as the men drove by to select one for their
use. Their lives were heartbreaking but their loves were fierce, perhaps for that very reason. A girl might well be called upon to describe
her *young, Haitian* boyfriend to the girlfriends, and the comparison
always worked to the disadvantage of the economically superior, old
white 'johns' who were their main daily fare. They heaped scorn on
the men who chose them, favoring instead the boys of their own
choice. That this was the age of the 'girl groups' of Motown singers
contributed to my sense of the singing of women about their loves.[14] I
can hear them now, crooning and sighing for love, hoping their lus-
cious young men would come to them as swiftly as a gazelle (though
they didn't put it that way, of course).

The Haitian girls and their world brought many other illustrations
of the Song as well. Like Dark Beauty, they also knew what it was to
be beaten for their very accessibility; they were all too familiar with
the vice and the violence of those 'watchmen' who went about the city
in their patrol cars. But they knew their own power, too: when you
live in the same neighborhood where a militant VooDoo priestess
lives, and you see the fear she inspires—*even* in the Miami police
department!—you do not naturally assume that women are powerless
and weak. Far from it: when such a woman dances to her god and

13. As recently as ten years ago, the 'brown bag' test was still being used by
employment agencies to turn away applicants who were not 'front-office, All-
American' material (white)—so much for the 'New South' they keep telling us
about!
14. I am thinking here of the Girlfriend back-up vocals in songs like 'Leader of
the Pack', 'Back in my Arms Again', 'My Boyfriend's Back'. The general theme is
usually, 'What is your beloved more than another...?' to which the lead singer
makes spirited reply.

calls the spirit of the *loa*, she is both militantly imposing *and* desirable, as the circle of celebrants chants and urges her on. While scholars debate ultimate meaning and context of the Song, I have come to understand that, for me, it is these experiences which have supplied the sub-text against which I have appropriated the Song as my very own, a true and genuine reflection of part of my early experiences which my current social context invites me to repress, deny or cut away. I still read the Song wearing dark glasses, and I carry the Daughters with me wherever I go: the Baptists may have failed me; the girlfriends never did.

Then and Now: What Does it Matter?
I have repeatedly complained to my scholar friends that the current penchant for autobiographical criticism clearly disadvantages those of us who hail from the unacknowledged worlds our cultures deny. Around the seminary where I teach, it is fashionable to 'share' one's 'spiritual journey'; I have taken to telling students that those who want to share mine should come equipped with Dramamine and buckle up, because the trip is a bumpy one. I live in a world now where my early experiences would be almost unimaginable—were it not for the knife scar on my index finger and the art based on the Song hanging on my walls. Yet, as Brenner's article on the same topic suggests, when we share what counts to us with others, we learn how not to let it count for *too* much. My experiences are anything but universal (for which I am very glad), but they are meaningful to me, and have impacted the way I read and construe meaning. With that multicultural predisposition in mind, I make the following comments on our current volume:

2. To Plot or Not to Plot?

Current scholarly dispositions eschew fitting a rigid plot-grid over the Song, whether it be one of Israel's vestigial fertility goddess (be she Asherah, Anatyahu, Ishtar, Atargatis, Shekinah, Hokmah or whomever) and her kingly partner, the old Victorian drama of rustic love choosing between a king or a shepherd (we know they are the same thing), or a god wooing *his* Synagogue or Church (we are rightly suspicious of this extrinsic meaning as *the* original meaning). It is usually assumed that those who see the Song as a unified composition are the most likely to want to find a plot in it, but other options exist, even for those critics holding (as I do) that the Song is a collection of erotic poetry with oral origins.

Though it is true that the book opens and closes with the Beloved speaking words of desire and invitation, I do not agree that no 'plot-like' movement has taken place or that desire is wholly deferred. Who defines what is acceptable as a 'plot'? Only heroic battles fought and won, or are there other, more *female* options, perhaps? I am thinking here that if we define stories of female lives by the same criteria as the male heroic tradition uses, female characters in patriarchal texts will hardly seem like whole persons, much less like effective protagonists who have moved through conflict and complication to resolution. A plot-line for F stories is more like a spiraling circle, or a crocheted sock, with a pattern of action punctuated by outward delays, inner delights and daydreams, looping back on to the action male culture permits and deigns to report. And so reading the Song in this way, we see that the brothers of ch. 1 have been rightly answered by Dark Beauty in ch. 8. The woman who was scorned for her color in chapter one has been called blessed by queens and concubines by the end;[15] the Dark Beauty sick with love in the beginning has been sated and fed; the Dancer described by others re-turns to describe her own attributes with pride. These shifting interchanges of fear and longing, seeking and finding, dialogue and daydream, set up a plot-like rhythm which not only roams the eroticized landscape of the Holy Land, but plumbs a full range of possibilities of satisfaction.

That the Song leaves us where it began, with the woman calling for her lover, is the strength of its 'demi- plot', not the sign of its absence, but this plot is a spiral rather than a straight line. The Beloved calls *again* because she knows what it will be like; we join her yearning because she has taught us to prefer her version of him above all others. This spiraling ending leaves us open to receive the next episode of love, if only in our dreams. The Song does not actually end; its words stop, but the feelings evoked by the songs drift on the scented air. We do not need to posit a unified poem to appreciate how skillfully the collection has been woven together into a bricolage, a demi-plot of interplay between call and answering echo.[16]

3. Now about that Action Motif...

Much has been made of the 'seeking/finding' motif by scholars of every stripe, including the present one.[17] We correctly relate it not just

15.   Though they *have* lightened her skin (6.10).

16.   Or 'type' and 'antitype', in the most original meaning of those literary terms.

17.   See my critique of Qoheleth's search, based on the Song of Songs, in

to the woman's dream experiences of chs. 2 and 5, but also to the man's search for her, and the lovers' search for privacy and satisfaction. It also plays a key role in most theological/allegorical readings of the Song, since it is not just the Bride who searches for her Divine Mate, but the Divine Mate who seeks out the human partner in this on-again, off-again relationship.

Having said this, I must say that this motif is heard somewhat differently in the modern context of the twisted and violent relations between men and women. What previously sounded like a harmless enough theme can easily be construed as 'stalking', an aggressive act which can be initiated by either partner and has more to do with possession and revenge than heart-felt devotion. While I might have smiled, thinking of the 'boy-crazy' behavior of teenage girls on a 'drive-by' by the boyfriend's house to check on his activities, I confess that even that fairly innocuous behavior takes on dire overtones when played out between a (nearly teenage) government Intern (F) and a President (M) given over to excesses of the flesh. When the sexes are reversed, the consequences are even more appalling: the angry lover with a restraining order and a grudge to settle doesn't just seek and find his beloved in the night. Too often, he also brings a knife, a gun, or some other instrument of patriarchal oppression, and the only effect of the restraining order is to tell us where to find the body. A quick survey of our popular music from the early days of rock and roll down to its present incarnations show us just how much women are socialized to perceive stalking behavior as a sign of affection: 'That'll be the day (when you say goodbye)!' Buddy Holly tells us; 'Every breath you take/every move you take/ I'll be watching you' sings Sting and The Police (!). Throw in 'Silhouettes on the Shade' and a host of other successful tunes and we have a fairly explosive mixture that structures and mirrors the reality of men who peep[18] and women who preen beneath that jealous gaze of self-proclaimed ownership.

Now in the Song, the motif is nicely doled out to most of the players; neither sex (or species) is the sole participant in that seeking/finding, so perhaps it is not the danger it seems when we are

'"Many Devices" (Qoheleth 7.23–8.1): Qoheleth, Misogyny, and the *Malleus Maleficarum*', in Athalya Brenner and Carole Fontaine (eds.), *A Feminist Companion to Wisdom and Psalms* (FCB, Second Series; Sheffield: Sheffield Academic Press, 1998), pp. 137-68.

18. The girls do it, too, in popular music: 'I Will Follow Him'; 'Ain't No Mountain High Enough', etc.

glumly listening to taped testimony or prosecuting attorneys' sum-
mation speeches. Still, we ought to note when a motif has a shadow
side, and not simply approve or appropriate because it remained
harmless in our Song. Elsewhere in the Bible and its world, when men
seek out women, the results can be just as dreadful as those in the
modern world.

4. *Solomon Who?*

The erasure of Solomon, his voice and power, from the current volume occasions little surprise in a feminist critical climate hell-bent on
recovering what shreds of women's authorship, experience or voice
may be had from a tradition by, for and about men. In the same way
we attribute Exodus 15, the Song of the Sea, to Miriam rather than
Moses, Solomonic authorship has been dethroned for more than formal linguistic grounds, though those had already prompted most
critical scholars to date the Song late instead of early. Feminist sensibilities are given to take offense at the wholesale notion of a male
author articulating the words of a love-sick woman, though few
would argue at this point that *only* a woman could have written those
lyrics. Artists of both sexes are more than able to cross gender restrictions as they imagine themselves as the Other, but it is interesting to
see what we the critical readers make of the very same words,
depending on whether we construe them as coming from an F or a M
perspective.

Personally, I miss Solomon, though this may be the lingering effect
of a specialization in wisdom literature. He *is* there in the Song, even
if only as a catchword (catchking?) used by our editors to bring
coherence where little exists. But thinking of the all the women in the
world with this Bible on their backs, those who are unlikely to be
reached by critical feminist hermeneutics as practiced in the elite
academies, it is the very presence of Solomon and his supposed
authorship which enables them to *read* the Song at all. For them, in
their world of entrenched restrictions legitimated through a supposed
divine curse on all womankind redeemable only through child-bear-
ing, the Song is no luxury, but a necessity. Trapped in a context where
Hosea is considered 'the prophet of Love', let Solomon be king and
poet, if that ascription keeps this little jewel within their view. Socialized to male authority and classic female biological roles as their destiny, the Song *does* represent a 'Holy of Holies' for conservative
women, their best expression of what a heterosexual relationship

might be. Even if a reading of the Song in such circumstances only serves to exacerbate a nascent dissatisfaction with the state of affairs as they find them, at least the Song liberates some future hope for equal relations and a suggestion of female solidarity.[19]

5. *Beautiful and Black as...?*

Even as Solomon has been excised from having any real presence in the Song as read by feminists, so, too, the Shulamit is typically read with little consideration of color/race. This is odd, since the Dark Beauty's skin color is a theme within the text itself. Marvin Pope's translation takes considerable space to discuss the implications of the vocabulary for 'negritude', and the various (usually negative) meanings assigned to it by rabbis and church fathers alike.[20] Whether caused by neglect, outdoor exposure, or hardened sinning, the image of the Black Beauty has usually merited comment by learned readers of the faiths. Granted that *this* interpreter comes from a neighborhood where a common descriptive folk saying 'black as the Queen of Sheba...'[21] was current which may account for some hypersensitivity on this issue, I still wonder what has made modern readers *so* color-blind, preferring to spin out a tale of class conflict between urban and rural women.[22] It certainly cannot be because these issues of race have been settled in the lived contexts of most of the critics! Though the Bible is not explicit on this topic, later traditions connected the Queen of Sheba with the songs of the Shulamit, as have artists through history.[23] How is it that *we* skip over that connection, we who refuse

19. One could argue just as easily that the idealized relations in the Song work to intensify women's misery (rather like emulation of the Virgin Mary) by presenting them with a biblically based portrait to which their lives and relationships could never measure up.

20. Marvin H. Pope, *The Song of Songs* (Anchor Bible; New York: Doubleday, 1977), pp. 307-18.

21. And we hadn't even read Josephus, Ginzburg or Yeats ('Solomon to Sheba'; 'Solomon and the Witch')!

22. I do not necessarily disagree with this reading of ch. 1, but in the majority of the Song, the Daughters of Jerusalem do not seem actively hostile or dismissive of the Shulammite.

23. Roland E. Murphy, *The Song of Songs* (Hermeneia; Minneapolis: Fortress Press, 1990), p. 121 (cf. n. 9); see also my 'More Queenly Proverb Performance: The Queen of Sheba in Targum Esther Sheni', in Michael L. Barr (ed.), *'Wisdom, You Are my Sister': Studies in Honor of Roland E. Murphy, O.Carm., on the Occasion of his Eightieth Birthday* (CBQMS, 29; Washington, D.C.: Catholic Biblical Association, 1997), pp. 216-33. For a survey of art on Sheba and Shulamit, see Dorothie Sölle,

to be tamed by classical historical-critical protocols?

One analogous point of contact, it would appear to me, is the dilemma of unraveling the meaning of the 'Black Goddess', be she Isis, Diana of Ephesus, Demeter, the Black Ishtar, the Hittite Shaushga, or Mary, 'Mother of God'. Here again, explanations range from the 'natural' (statues made dark by the aging of their materials, or pollution) to the 'allegorical' (the Black Madonna as representative of the Gentile Church—marked by an original foreignness [reflected in skin color] but beloved by God—which supplanted the unrepentant Synagogue). The Church's assumption of the Dark Beauty into a 'type' for the Virgin Mary goes mostly unmentioned by feminist interpreters (for historical-critical reasons?). But there is another relevant archetype that lurks in the shadowy unconscious of Mary of Nazareth's mythic genealogy: the Great Mother goddess and her many cults throughout the ancient Mediterranean and Near East. Why do the very real and complex references to goddess iconography embedded within the Song not merit more attention from feminists? From her frightening eyes, her battle imagery, to her gazelle-fixation, imagery for the Dark Beauty is readily contextualized with reference to these traditions. Is it a 'reformist' fear that keeps feminist readers from saying the 'g-word',[24] even in a text where goddess worship may be directly relevant, lest the Church and Synagogue be scandalized into agreeing with Jeremiah and Ezekiel about the dangerous heterodoxies of our foremothers? If so, then it is time to lay down that terror of the Night, for the defenders of religious patriarchy, swords on their thighs, have already made their opinion on this matter quite clear. No matter the clarity of our scholarship, the impeccable nature of our footnotes, the prophetic quality of our critique, we remain only women in their eyes, and unrepentant, unsubmissive ones at that. Already branded as heretics by conservatives, we should consider a more spirited claiming of the freedom of inquiry that belongs to that marginated group.

One might counter, of course, that as feminists, we are far beyond fond hopes of uncovering any golden matriarchies or unproblematic ancient cults that can liberate.[25] I might be impressed that Inanna is

Joe H. Kirchberger, and Herbert Haag, *Great Women of the Bible in Art and Literature* (Macon, GA: Mercer University Press and Eerdmanns Publishing, 1994), pp. 194-205.

24.   She Who Isn't (much regarded in biblical studies).

25.   Carole R. Fontaine, '"A Heifer from thy Stable": On Goddesses and the Status of Women in the Ancient Near East', in Alice Bach (ed.), *The Pleasure of her Text: Feminist Readings of Biblical and Historical Texts* (Philadelphia, PA: Trinity

the guardian of prostitutes—but then, She had better be, hadn't She?— since women slaves in her temple could be loaned out to brothels and as temple slaves were seldom freed.[26] Indeed, feminists have learned to be far more cynical about the options available to women when official goddess cults inscribed biological destiny for human women on a cosmic plane.[27]

And *yet*—given the amount of ink lavished on the patriarchal god(s) in praise of his *motherhood* or female aspects, the defense of God the Father as an adequate deity for women, the alleged feminist leanings of God the Son, Jesus of Nazareth, not to mention the trope of 'Paul the Feminist' (!), I continue to be a bit suspicious of the silence that greets the work of archaeologists, philologists and feminist thealogians with their abundance of concrete, tangible references. We often speak of the uniqueness of the Song of Songs within the biblical canon; we ought instead to point out that it is certainly *not* unique within the broader context of goddess-worshiping societies, with convergences which range from the level of genre to repetition of individual motifs, from abrupt shift in speakers and scene to graphic depictions of sexuality. I am not suggesting that we should embrace the 'Sacred Marriage Rite' hypothesis, or even that there is a direct correspondence between the presence of goddesses and the status of women or their appearance in love lyrics. It would simply seem that where comparative materials or a significant female-centered *Nachleben* exist, consideration of them should not be ruled out on doctrinal or ideological reasons, no matter our allegiances.

6. *'Lovingly Wrought...' (RSV, 3.10)*

Like the demi-plot of plea and pleasing which coils through our Song, I find that I too have followed that spiral dance back to my beginnings of sewing, sculpting, weaving and embellishing the Song in my secret chamber. We know that wise-hearted women brought the creation of their hands to adorn the Tent of Meeting in Exodus; weaving was the special gift of the women of the Jerusalem temple to the Goddess worshiped there; the trope of weaving, fabric, color and artifice winds through the Song, too.

Press International, 1990), pp. 69-95.

26. Orlando Patterson, *Slavery and Social Death: A Comparative Study* (Cambridge: Harvard University Press, 1982).

27. Tikva Frymer-Kensky, *In the Wake of the Goddesses* (New York: Fawcett Columbine, 1992).

It has been suggested in this volume that most feminist criticism loses its edgy, critical affect when confronted by the Song.[28] Like doves fluttering by cool streams, we coo when we ought to be howling. Lured by its language, its assumptions of immediacy, its presumption of the female voice, we seem to lose our own. For me, this observation, if true, is another mark of an *inspired* text (however we may understand that term!). We do not simply read the Song; we are changed by it, coaxed and cozened, and left, like Professor Brenner, with a song on our own lips. Shockingly partial to this little book, we are astonished to find ourselves in agreement from time to time with great rabbis and holy monks. *Surely* something has gone a little off—have so many of us been made so sick from (of?) love that we reach for the Song as a thirst-quenching antidote? Surely we must *do* something!

We *are* doing something: our reading as feminist critics changes the Song as much as the Song changes us. One need only look at the level of analysis found in the first *A Feminist Companion to the Song of Songs* as compared to this one; it is not the same Song as before, and that is a Good Thing. A modern chorus of Daughters of Jerusalem, we wonder about the nature of Dark Beauty's love, her sense of self and shame, the role of the gaze and male desire in forming female consciousness. Perhaps some of us would like to mark the text with a somber warning—Caution! Woman in Love Ahead!—and that is certainly warranted in places. But if most of us simply feel like singing and dancing, that is fine, too. We do not seek to speak in a single voice—far from it, and too inappropriate for this demi-drama of voices! Rather, we desire to receive a single justice before the Torah, whom some name 'Law'. We weave a new Song when we read and our readings pierce its threads; why shouldn't we weave one that more women would choose to sing?

On an artistic note, though I have preached on the Song as well as taught it, some of my most potent experiences of it with my students have come from group art projects. A collage piece entitled *Text: His and Hers* was created by the women of Old Testament 509: Introduction to the Torah and Former Prophets, at Andover Newton Theological School in the fall semester of 1997. The topic of the Song was smuggled in under the cloak of Solomon and Sheba, and the following exercise was assigned. I had printed out in Hebrew two textually

28. See J. Cheryl Exum, 'Ten Things Every Feminist Should Know About the Song of Songs' in this volume, pp. 24-35.

'warped' (curved and word-wrapped[29]) versions of 5.2-8 on colored paper, one a creamy parchment-like card stock with brown ink, the other pink card stock with black ink. The bland, 'male' text, just as it appears in the MT, was destined to be mounted on a collage board.[30] I asked for volunteers from among any needleworking women, and receiving four, I proceeded to cut apart the pink text into four horizontal strips. Even so mild a de-formation of the biblical text occasioned some murmuring among some of the students (which let me know I was following after the right shepherd's track). I gave a strip of the pink text to each of the volunteers with instructions that she was to return it to me embroidered. They resisted, expecting more instructions than that: what color? What stitch? What images should they embroider? I told them firmly that it was up to them and any offering was acceptable: we were making tangible 'women's midrash'.

The next week, they dutifully returned their text strips to me: each one different, cunningly woven, unique, a pleasure to the eye. One had used embroidery floss in a variety to colors to create hearts and flowers along the blank edges of her strip; another had used red floss to 'blanket stitch' (looking a bit like bird's feet) across Dark Beauty's dream. One decorated the spaces in between the words with rather misshapen stars; the final wise-hearted one had embroidered over each and every Hebrew word with multicolored ribbon. Some let their strings hang free like strands of hair; others had tucked them under 'properly' with discreet knots. All the women reported that this little project had prompted them to read the Song differently, and that the act of doing their own 'modern' art on the ancient text had been deeply moving in a variety of ways. I took away their offerings to join with the flat text, and they did not see the final product until it was hung for a community art show in the Theology and the Arts' gallery at the Meetinghouse.

To finish the piece, I slit open the male text (*most* satisfying!) at random intervals, and wove through the four embroidered versions, leaving some side edges and ribbons showing, while tucking in others. Because it was, after all, the *Most* Sublime Song, I provided textural, golden collaged borders of vinework and golden threads at the top and bottom of the male text which formed the base work. All

29. This was done to emphasize that even the 'normative' text is itself warped and shaped in the act of reading—always already.

30. Canvas-covered cardboard, coated with gesso or acrylic medium.

this I mounted on collage board, popped into a shadow box, and the 'femmage'[31] was complete.

There was no better representative for me as the critic/artist/reader of how women had changed and have always changed the 'official' texts presented to them by patriarchal authorities. The 'otherness' of our insights, the marginal nature of our readings which nevertheless had managed to assert themselves between and among the spaces, the overlay of our own derived meanings—there were all those critical insights in trembling, textural color: *Text: His and Hers*. That class, more than any other, came to understand the multi-layered nature of exegesis and composition, and the women claimed the right to read in ways I had not seen before.

7. *The Voice of the Turtle, Revisited*

All things spiral back on themselves. Emerging non-Fundamentalist from a chosen, sequestered hiding place like a turtle poking its head from its shell, I recognize why the image of the silent speaking had fascinated me. Shells are well and good when one is under threat, but they are wearisome to carry when the sun is shining and the winter is past.

Most of all, I am struck that my hidden song of *then* has become the shared Song of *now*. I used to listen to Broadway show tunes (checked out from the *big* library downtown!) and sing along in my last phase of closeted art, especially with Richard Kiley (now recently deceased) in *Kismet*, a sort of Arabian Nights fantasy set to classical Russian music. I had noticed that his song with Marsinah, 'This is My Beloved', was very much like the *wasfs* of the Song, though I did not know the generic term back then. The other night I looked up from proof-reading to realize that *Mysteries of the Bible* was playing a rerun on the Song of Songs, in which I had appeared. Now, it was narrator Richard Kiley's voice repeating *my* words on behalf of Dark Beauty, to the television audience—and the voice of the turtle was heard in our land. I realize upon writing this essay that this turtle has indeed found her voice, and it is a Song!

---

31.   This is the traditional name for collage work made by women, emphasizing domestic items.

'YOU ARE BEAUTIFUL MY LOVE':
THE SONG OF SONGS OF WOMEN*

Maria Häusl and Ursula Silber

Preliminary Remarks

'Do you notice feelings of spring?' With this question, in the spring of 1995, we extended an invitation to an 'Awareness Day' for women. The idea arose out of our co-operation between biblical and practical theology at the university level. We wanted to offer a day in which women could discover a bit of the Bible and thereby become aware of their own selves. It was intended to be 'A day I grant myself.'

The primary texts chosen for the day were Song of Songs 4.1-7 and 4.12–5.1. The following report about the day consists of: brief interpretations of the two texts, as used in the study day (sections 1 and 2); a description of the participants (section 3); a report of the procedure as divided into morning and afternoon activities (section 4); and concluding reflections (section 5).

1. Song of Songs 4.1-7

> You are beautiful, my love; you are beautiful.
> Your eyes: doves through your veil.
> Your hair: like a flock of goats
> That are drawn down the mountain of Gilead.
> Your teeth: like a flock of sheep ready to be shorn
> That climb from their washing—
> All bear twins and none is barren among them.
> As a cord of scarlet: your lips
> And your mouth is lovely.
> Like the tear of a pomegranate:
> Your gums behind your veil.

*   First published as ' "Schön bist du, meine Freundin": Das Hohe Lied der Frauen', *BL* 70.2 (1997), pp. 136-42 (trans. Lillian R. Klein and by the authors).

Like David's tower: your neck,
Built as a bulwark
Hung with a thousand bucklers
All shields of mighty men.
Your breasts: like two fawns,
Twins of a gazelle,
Feeding among the lotus.
Until the day breathes
And the shadows become long
I will go to the myrrh mountain
And to the frankincense hill.
You are altogether beautiful, my love,
And there is no flaw in you.

This so-called Song of Description (*waṣf*) reflects the male lover's view of his female beloved. Parts of the body are recognized and described through images from nature. For contemporary readers, many of these images sound foreign and beyond comprehension.

Understanding the metaphors offers a key to understanding the text: you have to clarify the terms of comparison.[1] The parts of the body are not praised for their perfect physical form but because the lover sees in them the wonderful possibilities and devotion of his beloved. Each body part leads him anew to his beloved, and brings the wonder of the whole world to his senses.[2] The pictures of nature must not be interpreted in their superficial meaning; they have a 'deeper' meaning—one that, admittedly, is not readily apparent to contemporary readers because the 'deeper' meaning originates in the ancient oriental world.

With the first comparison, of eyes to doves, the 'eyes' refer to the beloved's glances. In the iconography of the old oriental world, doves belong to the sphere of the Love Goddess. One could translate the first comparison into 'Your glances tell me of your love'.[3] The metaphor associated with the hair recalls the story of Samson (Jdg. 16) as an image of uncountability and implies unusual power and energy. The image of the goat flock (עֵדֶר עִזִּים) strengthens the allusions to 'numerous, uncountable', and adds a fresh lust for life.[4] The rows of teeth (שִׁנַּיִךְ), perfect and intact, like a procession of white sheep (4.2 קְצוּבוֹת, cf. 6.6, רְחֵלִים), lead the lover into a solemn mood and he

1. Cf. O. Keel, *Das Hohelied* (Züricher Bibelkommentare; Zürich: Theologischer Verlag, 1986), pp. 35-39.

2. Keel, *Das Hohelied*, pp. 33-34.

3. In the interpretion of the metaphors, we follow Keel, *Das Hohelied*, pp. 129-44; for the first metaphor cf. Keel, *Das Hohelied*, pp. 130-32.

4. Keel, *Das Hohelied*, pp. 132-33.

recognizes the complete beauty of his beloved.[5] The lips (שִׂפְתוֹתַיִךְ) and mouth (מִדְבָּרֵךְ Q) capture the world of words and language; this remains comprehensible. The 'red cord' (חוּט הַשָּׁנִי) refers not only to the appearance of the lips, but also can be considered a signal of the invitation to love, much like the red cord on the house of the prostitute Rahab (Jos. 2.10).[6] The Hebrew word that is translated as 'gum[s]', רַקָּתֵךְ, is often understood as 'temple[s]', since a 'veil' (צַמָּתֵךְ) is mentioned. A tear in the pomegranate (פֶּלַח הָרִמּוֹן), however, gives a view into the soft interior, which makes רַקָּתֵךְ more appropriate as 'your gums'. The pomegranate, a recognized symbol of life and fertility, is also attributed aphrodisiac properties in the entire ancient Near Eastern world. The image thus invokes also the disturbing fascination of the beloved.[7] If the woman's neck is compared to David's Tower, then the lover discerns an attitude of confident pride in his beloved.[8] That her breasts with their 'nourishing' and live energy are associated with goat kids, conveys security. The image of lotus blossoms (שׁוֹשַׁנִּים) interweaves a further aspect of the renewal of life.[9] This superlative glorification of the beloved is reinforced with the closing lines (vv. 6-7).[10]

2. *Song of Songs 4.12–5.1*

A locked garden: my Sister-Bride
A locked garden, a sealed Source!
Your watercourses: a pomegranate grove
With costly fragrances (fruits)
Of shrubs of henna and nard
From nard and saffron, ginger-grass and cinnamon
Together with all incense plants
From myrrh and aloe
Together with all the best balsam saplings;
You: a garden fountain
A well of flower water
Like the water streams from Lebanon.

Awaken, North Wind, and come, South Wind!
Let my garden disperse its fragrance!
The aroma of her Balsam saplings should flow.
My beloved shall come into his garden,
He shall eat from his precious fruits.

5.   Keel, *Das Hohelied*, p. 133.
6.   Keel, *Das Hohelied*, p. 134.
7.   Keel, *Das Hohelied*, pp. 134-35.
8.   Keel, *Das Hohelied*, pp. 136-38.
9.   Keel, *Das Hohelied*, pp. 138-40.
10. Keel, *Das Hohelied*, pp. 140, 144.

> I come into my garden, my sister, bride
> I pluck my myrrh and my balsam.
> I eat my honeycomb with my honey.
> I drink my wine with my milk.
>
> Eat friends, drink and intoxicate yourselves with love.

The text compares the loving woman to a garden. The first passage describes the garden; in the second, she invites her lover to enter her garden. He answers that he wishes to enjoy the fruits of the garden.[11]

The picture of the garden should not be confused with a nature idyll. Rather, the imagery suggests a carefully laid out and nurtured park.[12] The park's preciousness is suggested by the collection of rare and exotic plants to be found in it. Fascinating plants are present in excess.[13] All of the five senses are accosted; not only by the fruit of the trees but also by fragrant plants and flowers. In such a garden, water—especially valuable in a dry climate such as that of Syria-Palestine—is in great abundance too.

As the fragrance of the garden, caught by the wind, invites the lover, so does the beloved invite her lover with words. Her lover should come to her, into this wonder garden. In his assent, the language of eating and drinking, of honey, wine and milk, strongly suggests an intimate union.[14]

The fascination of and joy in the garden, as presented in this text from the Song of Songs, show themselves to be especially powerful when read, with Phyllis Trible, as a midrash on the narratives of Genesis 2–3.[15]

In Genesis 2 a garden in which plants grow (v. 16) and water flows (vv. 10-14) is laid out (v. 8). A wonderful park emerges; however, it is a garden whose meaning will be changed by the very different intention of the so-called 'Fall of Man' Story. The garden 'locates the tragedy of disobedience in Genesis 2–3. But the garden itself signals delight, not disaster.'[16] As result of this human disobedience, cherubim guard the closed entrance to the garden. In contrast, the garden

11. This interpretation, too, is motivated by Keel, *Das Hohelied*, pp. 156-73.

12. Keel, *Das Hohelied*, pp. 158-62, where there are also pictures of contemporary gardens.

13. These plants, in Israel, are imported articles. For readers of that time they had exotic connotations too.

14. Keel, *Das Hohelied*, pp. 169-73.

15. P. Trible, *God and the Rhetoric of Sexuality* (Minneapolis: Fortress Press, 1978).

16. Trible, *God and the Rhetoric of Sexuality*, p. 152.

poem of the Song of Songs invites entrance (SoS 4.16). In this garden
there is no forbidden tree among all the plants; instead, everyone is
encouraged to eat and drink (cf. SoS 5.1). Cherubim keep outside the
garden 'those who lust, moralize, legislate, or exploit. They also turn
away. But at all time they welcome lovers to romp and roam in the
joys of eroticism.'[17]

3. The Participants

The Diocese's Women's Spiritual Welfare offered a one-day event
with the title, '"You are Beautiful, My Love": Love Lyrics from the
Bible'. That would, so we thought, appeal to women between the ages
of 30 and 60, who wish to 'do something', beyond everyday life, for
themselves. This assumes that the women have brought the different
aspects of their lives (purchasing, partnership, family responsibilities,
honorary engagements) into relative harmony. Admittedly, this does
not preclude that some individuals were conscious of disquiet or
faced change.[18]

Our offer consciously sought to convey the positive impulse 'to do
something for one's self'. The day was not intended as a source of
information or education for any special aspect of life.[19.] Instead, it
focused on the individual identity of the women attending.

The texts of the Song of Songs are considered suitable for initiating
a discussion with one's own self. Arising from the experience of
mutual love, the songs speak of seeing and being seen, of beauty and
passion, of joy and desire.

From the multiple aspects of the songs and from the likewise multiple possibilities to discuss individual identity and personhood, we
selected several main points, bearing in mind the life situation of
women and aspects of unveiling feminine identity.

Gender-specific socialization determines not only role behaviour
but also self awareness. Consequently, socializing authorities exert a
powerful influence over the feminine body through the power of
definition. As a result, girls and women may have great difficulty in
becoming aware of their own bodies and their potential, of feeling

17. Trible, *God and the Rhetoric of Sexuality*, p. 162.
18. Cf. T. Faltermaier et al., *Entwicklungspsychologie des Erwachsenenalters*
(Grundrisse der Psychologie, 14; Stuttgart: Kohlhammer, 1992), pp. 58-71, 116-37.
19. The day was not planned as professional education nor as reflexion about
love relations or experiences of partnership.

comfortable in their own bodies and free to communicate with and through them.[20] The social ideals of feminine beauty are unattainable; therefore every woman thinks she is not beautiful (enough) by comparison to the perfection of women's bodies as seen on posters and television: These conjure up unavoidable images of the self as too fat, too wrinkled and so on. If one were to believe the headlines of the cosmetic industry, the feminine body consists, from head to toe, of 'problem areas' only.

The goal of this Bible Day was to stimulate self-awareness. Working together, in the protective environment of a small group, the women were encouraged to risk observing themselves. Accordingly, the discussion about the Song of Description (4.1-7) aimed at the experience of body language. The Garden Song (4.12-15) was shown to create awareness of one's own capacities and to strengthen joy in them. Personal experiences of lust and love in partnership, which the participants possibly brought with them, were not the central issue. The day with the Song of Songs sought to provide an open forum for everyone present.

In any case, the women who come to such an event are strongly motivated. For most, it is not easy to find a Saturday free of the responsibilities of work and family. These women came with the expectation of a day for themselves, a day in which they could experience something different, in which they could join other women and just enjoy their lives. This indicates, on the one hand, strong motivations; on the other hand, it limits the participants' readiness to engage in difficult, uncomfortable or strenuous tasks. It should be noted that the group— the women who join in this single day—offers the protection of relative anonymity, thus enabling the participants to speak, react and explore with more openness and freedom. At the same time, a frank exchange about personal experiences of body and desire demands delicacy and consideration.

20. Cf. Helga Bilden, 'Geschlechtspezifische Sozialisation', in K. Hurrelmann and D. Ulrich (eds.), *Neues Handbuch der Sozialforschung* (Weinheim/Basel: Beltz, 1991), pp. 279-301; Karin Flaake, ' "zuerst, toll! Jetzt bin ich endlich 'ne Frau. Aber jetzt geht's mir auf die Nerven!": Weibliche Adoleszenz, Körperlichkeit und Entwicklungsmöglichkeiten von Mädchen', in S. Becker and I. Nord (eds.), *Religiöse Sozialisation von Mädchen und Frauen* (Stuttgart: Kohlhammer, 1995), pp. 23-34.

5. *The Procedure*

The following is intended to sketch our day with the Song of Songs. The goals identified above—to discover a text from the Hebrew Bible and, through this medium, to discover aspects of our own identities—provide a methodological guideline. First, the text orientation demands that the biblical verses must be understood as independent, without being used or twisted to accommodate other purposes, and interpreted in accordance to their original meaning. Second, the participant orientation also requires respect for the experiences, needs and even the resistance of the women, integration of all aspects in the process and the creation of a space for new experiences. The *Threestep* method, developed by the *Deutsches Katholisches Bibelwerk* for group work on biblical texts, serves as a methodological-didactic model.[21] The *Threestep* consists of:

1.   A projective phase—an approach to the biblical text;
2.   an analytical phase—understanding the biblical text; and
3.   an appropriation phase—going forward from the text.

The morning and afternoon of the conference were shaped in accordance with this *Threestep* program.

The Morning: Song of Songs 4.1-7
The Introduction round immediately thrusts the women into the middle of Song of Songs landscape: the participants are directed to select one picture from an array of garden pictures. The selected picture should have a special appeal to the participant who selects it, and she describes this picture and herself in the Introduction round.

Then, by a meditative Body Exercise, the participants are directed to the theme of the Description Song: They are to imagine their own faces: not as seen in a mirror, but from inward—as if they were wearing it like a mask.

After a brief introduction to the Song of Songs as part of the Hebrew Bible, the group leader reads the text (4.1-7) aloud. As an example, the leader explains the kind of metaphors in the first image (see above).

In work groups, the participants can develop the other images of the text and understand their meaning. To this end, they receive cards that are prepared in four colours. Four different colours belong together in a set. These colours represent:

21.   Cf. Katholisches Bibelwerk (eds.), *Grundkurs Bibel Altes Testament: Werkbuch für die Bibelarbeit mit Erwachsenen* (Stuttgart: Verlag Katholisches Bibelwerk, 1993).

1. parts of the human body;
2. images from nature;
3. human capacities; and
4. meaning of nature.

The participants are asked to attempt and create an order in the cards. Human body parts and images of nature are provided in the text; the deeper dimensions are exposed when the intended meanings and human capacities are introduced. If the original images are then taken away, a new level of poetry is revealed, reflecting the characteristics, fascinations and powers of the beloved person. Focusing on this, the analysis is concerned with the dialogical aspects of identity. From these concepts, the participants are requested to write a new poem.[22]

As a conclusion of the unit, the participants are invited to return once more to the Body Exercise. The original biblical text of the Song of Description is read aloud. The participants try to be conscious of the feelings that are now awakened by hearing the text. They can note these experiences for themselves and, if wished, present them to the group.

The Afternoon: Song of Songs 4.12–5.1

The entrance into the new work unit is accompanied by afternoon fatigue. The participants are stimulated into wakefulness of mind and body with a 'tree dance'. The participants are challenged with the idea that they imagine themselves as trees, move as trees, experience winter and summer, grow and die as trees. This exercise leads to a later exercise in identification with the garden.

After reading the text of 4.12–5.1, the women try to perceive its meaning in work groups. The participants consider jointly questions such as the following: Who is speaking in this song? To whom is the speech addressed? Is there an alternation of speaking voices?

The participants underline all the nouns in the text with a coloured pen: What does the garden consist of? With a second pen of a different colour, they identify all the activities and movements (especially in the second half of the song): What happens in the garden? Who acts? The results are exchanged among the group.

After this textual exploration, the participants have time (at least 45 minutes) and space to pursue for themselves the symbol of the garden in order to paint a garden picture. A variety of art and craft materials

---

22. See Appendix.

are available to them. After the general introduction to the individual self-work, each participant receives a page with 'impulse' questions. These questions are intended to stimulate the participants' personal images and impressions. If I am a garden, what grows in me? Which situations or places do I know where I can really have pleasure? When and where is life a festivity? What gives colour to my life? In which situations do I feel that I offer something beautiful and valuable? What gives me the sensation that I radiate something special? When and where do I feel that I am something special? What are the sources of my life? Is there something in my life that is so valuable and holy that I do not allow everybody to see it?

The work that is done separately, individually, follows a conversational and exchange period, either with a partner or in a small group. In the group as a whole, the pictures the participants have painted are exhibited along with the original presentation of garden pictures, without commentary.

In the conclusion to the day we return to the dance with which the afternoon session began, and read a meditative text.

6. *In Conclusion: Some Reflections*

The women experienced great joy in writing and painting, despite their initial fears over their limited capacities. Their astonishment over what they had hidden in themselves, and what they can do was, perhaps, amplified by their initial doubts. They became ready to elaborate on themes about their own self-awareness and to talk about them. The course of the day showed the adequacy of the concepts and methods we had used.

The garden as a metaphor for the individual, for an individual life, revealed itself as very fruitful. Many women approached the images spontaneously, almost all had (mostly positive) experiences with their own gardens at home. We thus learnt that gardens offer a very intimate, positive and open image.

Hence, the day came to a close with the realization of the goals we had in mind. The participants could discover a bit of the Bible and a bit about themselves, and they enjoyed the day! We, the leaders of the day, were touched by amazement and joy at this experience.

APPENDIX:
TWO POEMS BY THE PARTICIPANTS

1

You are for me the most beautiful one!
I love you.
If I look into your eyes, I see,
That you love me as well.
Your boundless temper is contagious—
You give me new power to live.
When you laugh, the sun rises.
Your lips invite me to kiss,
What you say, tells of love.
When you kiss me, the world around me disappears.
You incline to me, and I feel only happiness.
I admire your sincereness.
I feel secure with you,
Near to you I gain power.
You are super.

2

You are beautiful, my beloved
I like you.
When you look at me,
I burn.
Your joy of life is contagious.
It makes me strong.
When I look at you and your beauty,
I feel bewitched.
When you talk to me,
My desire for you increases—
And I feel that you return my love.
Your intimacy is mysterious for me
And gives me wings.
I am fascinated by your bearing.
It shows me, how proud and self-aware you are.
I feel secure with you.

BIBLIOGRAPHY

Adler, Rachel, 'The Jew who Wasn't There: Halakhah and the Jewish Woman', in
   Heschel (ed.), *On Being a Jewish Feminist*, pp. 12-18.
—'The Virgin in the Brothel and Other Anomalies: Character and Context in the
   Legend of Beruriah', *Tikkun* 3.6 (1992), pp. 28-32, 115-21.
Afshar H., 'Muslim Women in West Yorkshire, Growing up with Real and Imagi-
   nary Values amidst Conflicting Views of Self and Society', in H. Afshar and
   M. Maynard, *The Dynamics of 'Race' and Gender: Some Feminist Interventions*
   (London: Taylor & Francis, 1994), pp. 127-47.
Ahmed L., 'Women and the Rise of Islam', in *Women and Gender in Islam: Historical
   Roots of a Modern Debate* (New Haven: Yale University Press, 1992), pp. 41-63.
Alter, Robert, 'The Garden of Metaphors', in *idem*, *The Art of Biblical Poetry* (New
   York: Basic Books, 1985), pp. 185-203.
Alter, Robert, and Frank Kermode (eds.), *The Literary Guide to the Bible* (Cambridge,
   MA: Harvard University Press, 1987), pp. 4-13.
Anderson, G., 'The Garden of Eden and Sexuality in Early Judaism', in H. Eilberg-
   Schwartz (ed.), *People of the Body, Jews and Judaism from an Embodied Perspective*
   (New York: SUNY Press, 1992), pp. 47-68.
Anderson, J.C., J.L. Stadley and R.A. Culpepper (eds.), *Taking it Personally: Autobio-
   graphical Biblical Criticism* (Semeia, 72; 1995).
Bach, Alice, *Women, Seduction, and Betrayal in Biblical Narrative* (Cambridge: Cam-
   bridge University Press, 1997).
Bakhtin, M., *Rabelais and His World* (trans. M. Iswolsky; Bloomington: Indiana Uni-
   versity Press, 1984).
Barr, Jane, 'The Influence of St Jerome on Medieval Attitudes to Women', in J.M.
   Soskice (ed.), *After Eve* (London: Collins Marshall Pickering, 1990), pp. 89-102.
Bauckham, Richard, 'The Book of Ruth and the Possibility of a Feminist Canonical
   Hermeneutic', *BibInt* 5 (1997), pp. 29-45.
Beal, Timothy K., 'Tracing Esther's Beginnings', in Athalya Brenner (ed.), A *Femi-
   nist Companion to Esther, Judith and Susanna* (Sheffield: Sheffield Academic,
   1995).
Bekkenkamp, Jonneke, *Canon en keuze: Het bijbelse Hooglied en de Twenty-One Love
   Poems van Adrienne Rich als bronnen van theologie* (Kampen: Kok 1993).
—'Het Hooglied: Een vrouwenlied in een mannentraditie', in Ria Lemaire (ed.), *Ik
   zing mijn lied voor al wie met mij gaat: vrouwen in de volksliteratuur* (Utrecht:
   HES, 1986).
—*Want ziek van liefde ben ik* (Amsterdam: University of Amsterdam Press, 1984).

Bekkenkamp, Jonneke, and Fokkelien van Dijk-Hemmes, 'The Canon of the Old Testament and Women's Cultural Traditions', in M. Meijer and J. Schaap (eds.), *Historiography of Women's Cultural Traditions* (Dordrecht: Forest Publications, 1987), pp. 91-108, reprinted in Brenner (ed.), *A Feminist Companion to the Song of Songs*, pp. 67-85.

Bell, A.F., *Luis de Leon: A Study of the Spanish Renaissance* (Oxford: Clarendon Press, 1925).

Belsey, Catherine, *Desire: Love Stories in Western Culture* (Oxford: Basil Blackwell, 1994).

Berg, Sandra B., *The Book of Esther: Motifs, Themes and Structure* (Missoula, MT: Scholars Press, 1979).

Biale, R., *Women and the Jewish Law* (New York: Schocken Books, 1984).

Bilden, Helga, 'Geschlechtspezifische Sozialisation', in K. Hurrelmann and D. Ulrich (eds.), *Neues Handbuch der Sozialforschung* (Weinheim: Beltz, 1991), pp. 279-301.

Black, Fiona C., 'The Grotesque Body in the Song of Songs' (PhD dissertation University of Sheffield, 1999).

Black, Fiona C., and Exum, J. Cheryl, 'Semiotics in Stained Glass: Edward Burne-Jones's Song of Songs', in J. Cheryl Exum and Stephen D. Moore (eds.), *Biblical Studies/Cultural Studies: The Third Sheffield Colloquium* (JSOTSup, 366; GCT, 7; Sheffield: Sheffield Academic Press, 1998), pp. 315-42.

Bloch, Ariel, and Chana Bloch, *The Song of Songs: A New Translation* (New York: Random House, 1995).

Bloom, Harold, *A Map of Misreading* (New York: Oxford University Press, 1975).

—*The Book of J* (trans. by David Rosenberg; interpreted by Harold Bloom; New York: Grove Weidenfeld, 1990).

Boyarin, Daniel, *Carnal Israel: Reading Sex in Talmudic Culture* (The New Historicism: Studies in Cultural Politics, 25; Berkeley: University of California Press, 1993).

Brenner, Athalya, 'An Afterword', in Brenner (ed.), *A Feminist Companion to the Song of Songs*, pp. 279-80.

—' "Come Back, Come Back, the Shulammite" (Song of Songs 7.1-10): A Parody of the *wasf* Genre', in Athalya Brenner and Y.T. Radday (eds.), *On Humour and Comic in the Hebrew Bible* (Sheffield: Almond Press, 1990), pp. 251-76; reprinted in Brenner (ed.), *A Feminist Companion to the Song of Songs*, pp. 234-57.

—*The Intercourse of Knowledge: On Gendering Desire and 'Sexuality' in the Hebrew Bible* (Leiden: E.J. Brill, 1997).

—*The Israelite Woman: Social Role and Literary Type in Biblical Narrative* (Sheffield: JSOT Press, 1985).

—' "My" Song of Songs', in Brenner and Fontaine (eds.), *A Feminist Companion to Reading the Bible*, pp. 567-79.

—'On Feminist Criticism of the Song of Songs', in Brenner (ed.), *A Feminist Companion to the Song of Songs*, pp. 28-37.

—'Pornoprophetics Revisited: Some Additional Reflections', *JSOT* 70 (1996), pp. 63-86.

—'To See Is to Assume: Whose Love Is Celebrated in the Song of Songs?', *BibInt* 3 (1993), pp. 1-20.

—*The Song of Songs* (OTG; Sheffield: JSOT Press, 1989).

— 'Women Poets and Authors' in Brenner (ed.), *A Feminist Companion to the Song of Songs*, pp. 86-97.

Brenner, Athalya (ed.), *A Feminist Companion to the Song of Songs* (Feminist Companion to the Bible, 1; Sheffield: Sheffield Academic Press, 1993).

Brenner Athalya, and Carole R. Fontaine (eds.), *A Feminist Companion to Reading the Bible: Approaches, Methods and Strategies* (Sheffield: Sheffield Academic Press, 1997).

Brenner, Athalya, and Fokkelien van Dijk-Hemmes, *On Gendering Texts: Female and Male Voices in the Hebrew Bible* (Leiden: E.J. Brill, 1993).

Breukelmann, F., *Bijbelse theologie: Het eerstlingschap van Israel* (Kampen: Kok, 1992).

Brooks, Peter, *Body Work: Objects of Desire in Modern Narrative* (Cambridge, MA: Harvard University Press, 1993).

Butting, Klara, *Die Buchstaben werden sich noch wundern: Innerbiblische Kritik als Wegweisung feministischer Hermeneutik* (Berlin: Alektor, 1994).

Buzy, Denis, 'Un chef-d'œuvre de poésie pure: Le Cantique des Cantiques', in *Mémorial Lagrange* (Paris: J. Gabalda, 1940), pp. 147-62.

Cano, Rogelio Reyes, ' "Retrato de Fray Luis de Leon" por Francisco Pacheo', *Insula* 539 (1991), p. 1.

Carroll, Robert P., 'Desire under the Terebinths: On Pornographic Representation in the Prophets—A Response', in Athalya Brenner (ed.), *A Feminist Companion to the Latter Prophets* (The Feminist Companion to the Bible, 8; Sheffield: Sheffield Academic Press, 1995), pp. 275-307.

Cassuto, U., *A Commentary on the Book of Genesis. Part II. From Noah to Abraham* (Jerusalem: Magnes Press, 1984).

Choho E., 'De eer', in M. Alkan *et al.* (eds.), *Islam in een ontzuilde samenleving* (Amsterdam: KIT, 1996), pp. 15-25.

Christ, Carol P., 'Feminist Studies in Religion and Literature: A Methodological Reflection', in Rita M. Gross (ed.), *Beyond Androcentrism: New Essays on Women and Religion* (Missoula, MT: Scholars Press, 1977), pp. 35-51.

—*Diving Deep and Surfacing: Women Writers on Spiritual Quest* (Boston: Beacon Press, 2nd edn, 1986).

Clines, David J.A., 'Why is There a Song of Songs and What Does It Do to You if You Read It?', in *idem*, *Interested Parties: The Ideology of Writers and Readers of the Hebrew Bible* (JSOTSup, 205; GCT, 1; Sheffield: Sheffield Academic Press, 1995), pp. 94-121.

Cohen, Jeremy, 'Scholarship and Intolerance in the Medieval Academy: The Study and Evaluation of Judaism in European Christendom', *American Historical Review* 91 (1986), pp. 592-613.

Culler, Jonathan, *On Deconstruction: Theory and Criticism after Structuralism* (London: Melbourne & Henley, 1983).

Deckers, D., 'The Structure of the Song of Songs and the Centrality of *nepeš*', in Brenner (ed.), *A Feminist Companion to the Song of Songs*, pp. 172-96.

Deckers-Dijs, Mimi, *Begeerte in bijbels liefdespoësie: Een semiotische analyse van het Hooglied* (Kampen: Kok, 1991).

Dijk-Hemmes, F. van, 'The Imagination of Power', in Brenner (ed.), *A Feminist Companion to the Song of Songs*, pp. 156-70.

—*Sporen van vrouwenteksten in de Hebreeuwse Bijbel* (Utrecht: Faculteit der Godgeleerdheid, Universiteit Utrecht, 1992).

—'The Imagination of Power and the Power of Imagination: An Intertextual Analysis of Two Biblical Love Songs: The Song of Songs and Hosea 2', *JSOT* 44 (1989), pp. 75-88 (reprinted in Brenner [ed.], *A Feminist Companion to the Song of Songs*, pp. 156-70).

Eco, Umberto, *Foucault's Pendulum*.

Eilberg-Schwartz, Howard, *God's Phallus: And Other Problems for Men and Monotheism* (Boston: Beacon Press, 1994).

—'The Problem of the Body for the People of the Book', in H. Eilberg-Schwartz (ed.), *People of the Body: Jews and Judaism from an Embodied Perspective* (New York: SUNY Press, 1992), pp. 17-46.

Exum, J. Cheryl, *Plotted, Shot, and Painted: Cultural Representations of Biblical Women* (JSOTSup, 215; GCT, 3; Sheffield: Sheffield Academic Press, 1996), pp. 19-53.

—'Developing Strategies of Feminist Criticism/Developing Strategies for Commentating the Song of Songs', in David J.A. Clines and Stephen D. Moore (eds.), *Auguries: The Jubilee Volume of the Sheffield Department of Biblical Studies* (JSOTSup, 269; GCT, 7; Sheffield: Sheffield Academic Press, 1998), pp. 206-49.

—*Fragmented Women: Feminist (Sub)versions of Biblical Narratives* (JSOTSup, 163; Sheffield: JSOT Press, 1993; Valley Forge, PA: Trinity Press International, 1993).

—'How Does the Song of Songs Mean? On Reading the Poetry of Desire', *SEÅ* 64 (1999), pp. 47-63.

—'A Literary and Structural Analysis of the Song of Songs', *ZAW* 85 (1973), pp. 47-79.

—*Was sagt das Richterbuch den Frauen?* (SBS, 169; Stuttgart: Katholisches Bibelwerk, 1997).

F. Merniss, *Women and Islam: An Historical and Theological Enquiry*, 'The Hijab, the Veil' (Oxford: Basil Blackwell, 1991), pp. 85-101, .

Falk, Marcia, *Love Lyrics from the Hebrew Bible: A Translation and Literary Study of the Song of Songs* (Sheffield: Almond Press, 1982).

—*The Song of Songs: A New Translation and Interpretation* (illustrated by Barry Moser: San Francisco: HarperSanFrancisco, 1990).

—'The Song of Songs', in James L. Mays (ed.), *Harper's Bible Commentary* (San Francisco: Harper & Row, 1988), pp. 525-28.

—'The *wasf*', in Brenner (ed.), *A Feminist Companion to the Songs of Songs*, pp. 225-33.

Faltermaier, Toni (*et al.*), *Entwicklungspsychologie des Erwachsenenalters* (Grundrisse der Psychologie, 14; Stuttgart: Kohlhammer, 1992).

Fisch, H., *Poetry with a Purpose: Biblical Poetics and Interpretation* (Bloomington: Indiana University Press, 1988).

Fitzmaurice-Kelly, J., *Fray Luis de Leon: A Biographical Fragment* (Oxford: Oxford University Press, 1921).

Flaake, Karin, ' "zuerst, toll! Jetzt bin ich endlich 'ne Frau. Aber jetzt geht's mir auf die Nerven!" Weibliche Adoleszenz, Körperlichkeit und Entwicklungsmöglichkeiten von Mädchen', in S. Becker and I. Nord (eds.), *Religiöse Sozialisation von Mädchen und Frauen* (Stuttgart: Kohlhammer, 1995), pp. 23-34.

Fontaine, Carole R., ' "A Heifer from thy Stable": On Goddesses and the Status of Women in the Ancient Near East', in Alice Bach (ed.), *The Pleasure of her Text: Feminist Readings of Biblical and Historical Texts* (Philadelphia, PA: Trinity Press International, 1990), pp. 69-95.

—' "Many Devices" (Qoheleth 7.23–8.1): Qoheleth, Misogyny, and the *Malleus Maleficarum'*, in Athalya Brenner and Carole Fontaine (eds.), *A Feminist Companion to Wisdom and Psalms* (FCB, Second Series; Sheffield, Sheffield Academic Press, 1998), pp. 137-68.

—'More Queenly Proverb Performance: The Queen of Sheba in Targum Esther Sheni', in Michael L. Barr S.S. (ed.), *'Wisdom, You are my Sister': Studies in Honor of Roland E. Murphy, O.Carm., on the Occasion of his Eightieth Birthday* (CBQMS, 29; Washington, D.C.: Catholic Biblical Association, 1997), pp. 216-33.

Foucault, Michel, *L'ordre du discours* (Paris: Editions Gallimard, 1971).

Fox, Michael V., *The Song of Songs and the Ancient Egyptian Love Songs* (Madison: University of Wisconsin Press, 1985).

Frymer-Kensky, Tikva, *In the Wake of the Goddesses* (New York: Fawcett Columbine, 1992).

Garcia, Felix (ed.) *Obras completas castellanos de Fray Luis de Léon* (Madrid: Biblioteca de antores Cristianos, 1959).

Gelles, Benjamin, *Peshat and Derash in the Exegesis of Rashi* (Leiden: E.J. Brill, 1971).

Goitein, S.D., 'Women as Creators of Biblical Genres', *Prooftexts* 8 (1988), pp. 1-33.

—The Song of Songs: A Female Composition', in Brenner (ed.), *A Feminist Companion to the Song of Songs*, pp. 58-66.

Gordis, R., *The Song of Songs and Lamentations: A Study, Modern Translation and Commentary* (New York: Ktav, 1974).

Goulder, Michael, *The Song of Fourteen Songs* (JSOTSup, 36; Sheffield: Sheffield Academic Press, 1986).

Graham, E., *Making the Difference: Gender, Priesthood and Theology* (London: Mowbrays, 1995).

Green, Arthur, 'Bride, Spouse, Daughter: Images of the Feminine in Classical Jewish Sources', in Susannah Heschel (ed.), *On Being a Jewish Feminist* (New York: Schocken Books, 1983).

Grosz, E., *Volatile Bodies: Towards a Corporeal Feminism* (Bloomington: Indiana University Press, 1994).

Heinevetter, H.-J., *'Komm nun, mein Liebster, dein Garten ruft dich!' Das Hohelied als programmatische Komposition* (Athenäum Monographien-Theologie, 69; Frankfurt a.M: Athenäum, 1988).

Heschel, Susannah (ed.), *On Being a Jewish Feminist* (New York: Schocken Books, 1983).

Hölz, K., 'Fray Luis de Léon y la Inquisición, *Insula* 539 (1991).

Joyce, Paul, *Hockney on Photography: Conversations with Paul Joyce* (London: Jonathan Cape, 1988).

Kaplan, E. Anne, 'Is the Gaze Male?', in her, *Women and Film: Both Sides of the Camera* (London: Routledge, 1983).

Katholisches Bibelwerk (eds.), *Grundkurs Bibel Altes Testament: Werkbuch für die Bibelarbeit mit Erwachsenen* (Stuttgart: Verlag Katholisches Bibelwerk, 1993).

Kayser, W., *The Grotesque in Art and Literature* (trans. U. Weisstein; Bloomington: Indiana University Press, 1963).

Keel, Othmar, *Das Hohelied* (Zürcher Bibelkommentare, 18; Zürich: Theologischer Verlag, 1986).

Kelly, J.N.D., *Jerome: His Life, Writings and Controversies* (London: Gerald Duck-worth, 1975).

Kolodny, Annette, 'Dancing through the Minefield: Some Observations on the Theory, Practice and Politics of a Feminist Literary Criticism', in Elaine Showalter (ed.), *The New Feminist Criticism: Essays on Women, Literature and Theory* (London: Virago, 1985), pp. 144-67.

Kristeva, Julia, 'A Holy Madness: She and He', in her *Tales of Love* (trans. L.S. Roudiez; New York: Columbia University Press, 1987), pp. 83-100.

—*Powers of Horror: An Essay on Abjection* (trans. Leon S. Roudiez; New York: Columbia University Press, 1982).

—*Tales of Love* (trans. Leon S. Roudiez; New York: Columbia University Press, 1987).

Lacan, J., *Ecrits: A Selection* (trans. A. Sheridan; New York: PAJ Publication, 1977).

LaCocque, A., *Romance She Wrote: Hermenueutical Essay on the Song of Songs* (Harrisburg, PA: Trinity Press International, 1998).

Landy, Francis, *Paradoxes of Paradise: Identity and Difference in the Song of Songs* (Sheffield: Almond Press, 1983).

—'The Song of Songs', in R. Alter and F. Kermode (eds.), *The Literary Guide to the Bible* (Cambridge: Harvard University Press, 1987).

Layton, Anson, *Arguing with God: A Jewish Tradition* (Northvale, NJ: J. Aronson, 1990).

Lemaire, Ria, 'Vroegmiddeleeuwse vrouwenlyriek en hoofse mannenpoëzie', in *Sprekend: Teksten Lezingencyclus 'Vrouwen en letteren'* (Nijmegen: de Feeks, 1981).

—'Vrouwen in de volksliteratuur', in Ria Lemaire (ed.), *Ik zing mijn lied voor al wie met mij gaat: Vrouwen in de volksliteratuur* (Utrecht: HES, 1986), pp. 11-42.

Leon, Fray Luis de, 'Les Nombres de Christo', in Felix Garcia (ed.), *Obras completa castellanos de Fray Luis de Léon* (Madrid: Biblioteca de Autores Cristianos, 1959).

Lerner, G., *The Creation of Patriarchy* (New York: Oxford University Press, 1986).

Luxemburg, Jan van, Mieke Bal and Willem Weststeijn, *Inleiding in de literatuur-wetenschap* (Muiderberg: Coutinho, 1982).

Magonet, Jonathan, 'The Liberal and the Lady: Esther Revisited', *Judaism 1980/29*.

Mariaselvam, A., *The Song of Songs and Ancient Tamil Love Poems: Poetry and Symbol-ism* (AnBib, 118; Rome: Pontifical Biblical Institute, 1988).

Marks, E., and Isabelle de Courtivron, *New French Feminisms: An Anthology* (New York: Schocken Books, 1981).

Matter, E. Ann, *The Voice of my Beloved* (Philadelphia: University of Philadelphia Press, 1990).

McFague, Sallie, *Models of God: Theology for an Ecological, Nuclear Age* (Philadelphia: Fortress Press, 1987).

Meinhold, Arndt, *Die Gattung der Josephsgeschichte und des Estherbuches: Diaspora-novelle I* (ZAW, 87; 1975).

—*Die Gattung der Josephsgeschichte und des Estherbuches: Diasporanovelle II* (ZAW, 88; 1976).

Merkin, Daphne, 'The Women in the Balcony: On Rereading the Song of Songs', in Christina Buchmann and Celina Spiegel (eds.), *Out of the Garden: Women Writers on the Bible* (New York: Fawcett Columbine, 1994), pp. 238-51.

Merrill, Eugene, 'Rashi, Nicholas de Lyra and Christian Exegesis', *WTJ* 38 (1978), pp. 66-79.

Meyers, Carol, *Discovering Eve: Ancient Israelite Women in Context* (Oxford: Oxford University Press, 1988).

—'Gender Imagery in the Song of Songs', *HAR* 10 (1986), pp. 209-23; reprinted in Brenner (ed.), *A Feminist Companion to the Song of Songs*, pp. 197-212.

—'Returning Home: Ruth 1.8 and the Gendering of the Book of Ruth', in Athalya Brenner (ed.), *A Feminist Companion to Ruth* (Sheffield: Sheffield Academic Press, 1993), pp. 85-114.

Michel, D., *Untersuchungen zur Eigenart des Buches Qohelet* (BZAW, 183; Berlin: W. de Gruyter, 1989).

Miles, Margaret, *Carnal Knowing: Female Nakedness and Religious Meaning in the Christian West* (New York: Vintage Books, 1991).

Moore, Stephen D., 'The Song of Songs in the History of Sexuality', *Church History* (forthcoming).

Morton, Nelle, *The Journey Is Home* (Boston: Beacon Press, 1985).

Moye, J., 'Song of Songs—Back to Allegory? Some Hermeneutical Considerations', *Asia Journal of Theology* 4 (1990), pp. 120-25.

Murphy, Roland E., *The Song of Songs: A Commentary on the Book of Canticles or the Song of Songs* (Hermeneia; Minneapolis: Fortress Press, 1990).

Ozick, Cynthia, 'Notes toward Finding the Right Question', in Heschel (ed.), *On Being a Jewish Jeminist*, pp. 133-38.

Pardes, Ilona, *Countertraditions in the Bible: A Feminist Approach* (London: Harvard University Press, 1992).

—' "I am a Wall, and my Breasts like Towers": The Song of Songs and the Question of Canonization', in *idem*, *Countertradition in the Bible*, pp. 118-43.

Patai, Raphael, *The Hebrew Goddess* (New York: Avon, 1978).

Patterson, Orlando, *Slavery and Social Death: A Comparative Study* (Cambridge, MA: Harvard University Press, 1982).

Peers, E.A., *Studies of Spanish Mystics* (London: SPCK; New York: Macmillan, 1951).

Plaskow, Judith, *Sex, Sin and Grace: Woman's Experience and the Theology of Reinhold Niebuhr and Paul Tillich* (Lanham, MD: University Press of America, 1980).

—*Standing Again at Sinai* (San Francisco: Harper & Row, 1990).

Polaski, Donald C., ' "What Will Ye See in the Shulammite?" Women, Power and Panopticism in the Song of Songs', *BibInt* 5 (1997), pp. 64-81.

— 'Spirituality and Politics: Lessons fromB' not Esh', *Tikkun* 10.3 (May–June 1995), p. 32.

Pope, Marvin H., *Song of Songs* (AB; Garden City, New York, Doubleday, 1977), pp. 67, 142-44.

Pope, M.V, 'Metastases in Canonical Shapes of the Super Song', in G.M. Tucker, D.L. Peterson and R.R. Wilson (eds.), *Canon, Theology and Old Testament Interpretation: Essays in Honor of Brevard S. Childs* (Philadelphia: Fortress Press, 1988), pp. 312-28.

Rabin, C., 'The Song of Songs and Tamil Love Poetry', *JBL* 89 (1973), pp. 27-37.

—'The Song of Songs and Tamil Poetry', *SR* 3 (1973), pp. 205-19.

Rashi, *The Megiloth and Rashi's Commentary with Linear Translation* (trans. Avraham Schwartz and Yisroel Schwartz; New York: Hebrew Linear Classics, 1983).

Rich, Adrienne, *Sources* (California: The Heyeck Press, 1983).

—*The Dream of a Common Language: Poems 1974–1977* (New York: W.W. Norton, 1978).

—*On Lies, Secrets, and Silences: Selected Prose 1966–1978* (New York: W.W. Norton, 1978).

—'When We Dead Awaken: Writing as Re-Vision', in *idem*, *On Lies, Secrets and Silences: Selected Prose 1966–1978* (New York: W.W. Norton, 1978).

—*Twenty-One Love Poems* (California: Effie's Press, 1976).

—'Reforming the Chrystal', in *Poems: Selected and New, 1950–1974* (New York: W.W. Norton, 1975).

—*The Will to Change: Poems 1968–1970* (New York: W.W. Norton, 1971).

Robertson, D.W., *Augustine: On Christian Doctrine* (New York: Liberal Arts Press, 1958).

Rosenberg, David (ed.), *Congregation: Contemporary Writers Read the Jewish Bible* (New York: Harcourt Brace Javonovich, 1987).

Rosenthal, L.A., 'Die Josephsgeschichte mit den Büchern Esther und Daniel verglichen', *ZAW* 15 (1895).

Ruether, Rosemary Radford, *Womanguides: Readings toward a Feminist Theology* (Boston: Beacon Press, 1985).

Russo, Mary, *The Female Grotesque: Risk, Excess and Modernity* (London: Routledge, 1994).

Schnur, Susan, and Sarah Blustain, 'Paradoxes and Mysteries of Sacred Space: Sacred Wall?', *Lilith* (Spring–Summer 1996), p. 14.

Schoer N., and E. Weed (eds.), *The Essential Difference* (Bloomington: Indiana University Press, 1994).

Schulman, Grace, 'The Song of Songs: Love is Strong as Death', in David Rosenberg (ed.), *Congregation: Contemporary Writers Read the Jewish Bible* (New York: Harcourt Brace Javonovich, 1987).

Setel, T.D., 'Prophets and Pornography: Female Sexual Imagery in Hosea', in Brenner (ed.), *A Feminist Companion to the Song of Songs*, pp. 143-55.

Smit, J., 'Er is een land waar vrouwen willen wonen', in *Teksten 1967–1981* (Amsterdam: Sara, 1984).

Smith, Barbara Herrnstein, 'Contingencies of Value', in Robert von Hallberg (ed.), *Canons* (Chicago: The University of Chicago Press, 1983).

Sölle, Dorothie, Joe H. Kirchberger, and Herbert Haag, *Great Women of the Bible in Art and Literature* (Macon, GA: Mercer University Press and Eerdmanns Publishing, 1994).

Sontag, Susan, *Against Interpretation* (London: André Deutsch, 1987).

Soulen, Richard N., 'The *waṣfs* of the Song of Songs and Hermeneutic', *JBL* 86 (1967), pp. 183-90.

Stanton, Elisabeth Cady, *The Woman's Bible*, part II (repr. Polygon Books: Edinburgh, 1985 [1895]).

Streete, Gail Corrington, *The Strange Woman: Power and Sex in the Bible* (Louisville, KY: John Knox Press, 1997).

Swidler, Leonard, 'Beruriah: Her Word Became Law', *Lilith* 1.3 (Spring–Summer 1977).

Thompson, C.P., *The Strife of Tongues* (Cambridge: Cambridge University Press, 1989).

Thompson, Philip, *The Grotesque* (The Critical Idiom; London: Methuen and Co., 1972).

Trible, Phyllis, *God and the Rhetoric of Sexuality* (Minneapolis: Fortress Press, 1987).

—'Love's Lyrics Redeemed', in Brenner (ed.), *A Feminist Companion to the Song of Songs*, pp. 100-20.

Turner, D., *Eros and Allegory: Medieval Exegesis of the Song of Songs* (Cistercian Studies Series, 156; Kalamazoo: Cistercian Publications, 1950).

Turner, Denys, *Eros and Allegory: Medieval Exegesis of the Song of Songs* (trans. D. Turner; Cistercian Studies Series, 156; Kalamazoo, Cistercian Publications, 1995).

Veen S., 'Being Present, Being Represented: Some Dilemma's of Muslim Women in the Netherlands' (Unpublished paper for the conference 'Corporeality, Religion and Gender', 1997).

Waskow, Arthur, *Godwrestling* (New York: Schocken Books, 1978).

Weems, Renita J., *Battered Love: Marriage, Sex, and Violence in the Hebrew Prophets* (OBT; Minneapolis: Fortress Press, 1995).

—'Song of Songs', in Carol A. Newsom and Sharon H. Ringe (eds.), *The Women's Bible Commentary* (Louisville, KY: Westminster/John Knox Press, 1992), pp. 156-60.

—'Song of Songs', in *The New Interpreter's Bible* (Nashville: Abingdon Press, 1997), pp. 363-434.

Westermann, Claus, *God's Angels Need No Wings* (trans. David L. Scheidt; Philadelphia: Fortress Press, 1979).

Whedbee, J.W., 'Paradox and Parody in the Song of Solomon: Towards a Comic Reading of the Most Sublime Song', in Brenner (ed.), *A Feminist Companion to the Song of Songs*, pp. 252-62.

Winkler, John J., 'Double Consciousness in Sappho's Lyrics', in *idem*, *The Constraints of Desire: The Anthropology of Sex and Gender in Ancient Greece* (New York: Routledge, 1990), pp. 162-87.

Wyler, Bea Esther, 'The Incomplete Emancipation of a Queen', in Athalya Brenner (ed.), *A Feminist Companion to Esther, Judith and Susanna* (The Feminist Companion to the Bible, 7; Sheffield: Sheffield Academic Press, 1995).

Yuval-Davis N., and F. Anthias (eds.), 'Introduction', in *Woman—Nation—State* (London: Macmillan, 1989), pp. 1-15.

INDEXES

INDEX OF REFERENCES

OLD TESTAMENT

OTHER ANCIENT REFERENCES

Mishnah		*t. Sanh.*		Josephus	
Yad.		12.10	142, 161	*War*	
3.5	142			7.8.2–9.2	158
		Midrash			
Talmuds		*Kalla*		Jerome,	
b. Sanh.		1.4	161	*Ep.* 106	135
101a	161	1.6	161		

Made in the USA
Lexington, KY
21 January 2013